CW00384457

NOR DID THEY FIGHT ANYMORE

Nor Did They Fight Anymore by David A. Maurer

Front and back cover images courtesy of David A. Maurer

Cover and interior design: Jacqueline Cook

Hardcover ISBN: 978-1-61179-402-1

eBook ISBN: 978-1-61179-403-8

10 9 8 7 6 5 4 3 2 1

BISAC Subject Headings:
BIO008000 BIOGRAPHY & AUTOBIOGRAPHY / Military
BIO026000 BIOGRAPHY & AUTOBIOGRAPHY / Personal Memoirs
HIS036050 HISTORY / United States / Civil War Period (1850-1877)
HIS027180 HISTORY / Military / Special Forces
HIS027070 HISTORY / Wars & Conflicts / Vietnam War

Address all correspondence to:
Fireship Press, LLC
P.O. Box 68412
Tucson, AZ 85737

Visit our website at:
www.fireshippress.com

To my wonderful wife Connie,
who has patiently listened to all my war stories,
sometimes more than once.

Acknowledgments

Although this is a work of nonfiction, I don't profess to be a historian and I apologize for any errors within. My deepest thanks and gratitude go out to all Civil War historians and writers who have guided me through the war and brought it alive. I especially owe a debt of gratitude and thanks to the late, Robert S. Westbrook, who provided me with a day-by-day account of the war in his book, "History of the 49th Pennsylvania Volunteers." I'm also grateful to my friend Art Beltrone who started me on the long journey that culminated with the completion of this book.

Introduction

My family had long believed that my great-granduncle, Jacob Shriver, had made it through the American Civil War unscathed. Family lore held that after his service as an infantryman in the Union Army, he migrated from Pennsylvania to central Minnesota, where he lived out his life as a farmer. A point of remembrance is that he was nearly blind.

The significant thing, as it related to me, was that Jake had survived the conflict, thereby affirming that Maurers didn't die in wars. This ascribed Achillean power came to me via my great-great grandmother, Ursula Rosilia Shriver Maurer. Ursula was Jake's sister, and she married my great-great grandfather, Frederich John Maurer.

I heard about all this when I learned that my uncle, Al Maurer, had brought it up during a visit with my folks. I was serving my first tour of duty in Vietnam at the time, and he was assuring my mother that I would make it back home safely,

"Maurers don't die in wars," declared Al, who, as a U.S. Marine during World War II, participated in some of the bloodiest fighting in the Pacific Theater. "That goes all the way back to the Civil War and old Jake."

This assumption of wartime invincibility might have remained intact if I hadn't become interested in the Civil War during the mid-1970s. I was attending Monterey Peninsula College in California, and during an American History class the professor rattled off the number of dead and wounded resulting from the Battle of Antietam on Sept. 17, 1862, the war's bloodiest day. When fighting ended late that afternoon near Sharpsburg, Maryland, some 23,000 men had been killed, wounded, or gone missing. Having spent 900 days in combat units in Vietnam, I knew how unsettling it can be to see far fewer crumpled corpses on contested ground.

I tried to imagine what a slaughter of that magnitude would have looked like. There are photographs, of course, showing windrows of tattered, bloated bodies awaiting burial. More human wreckage is seen around a whitewashed church, and along a sunken road that became known as Bloody Lane. Hundreds of dead, perhaps, but thousands?

Thinking I had misheard the body count, I asked the teacher to repeat himself. I was assured that the tally was the accepted, historic figure. Taken aback, I glanced around the room to gauge the reactions of my classmates. Not one of them had recoiled in the least. What registered in their minds were inert, faceless figures. I saw shattered lives and immeasurable grief. My time in Vietnam saw to that.

That revelation sparked my interest in the Civil War, and I began my education with Shelby Foote's three-volume masterpiece, "The Civil War: A Narrative." My wartime experience with the 1st Cavalry Division (Airmobile), and later with U.S. Army Special Forces, augmented the prose. I was familiar with the nuances of combat, such as how the distinct odor of a scared man's sweat is sharply different from perspiration resulting from work or exercise. Such bits of insight gave me the ability to picture particular settings and events with deeper clarity.

I also became aware of commonalities that I shared with these men of the blue and gray. I was drawn closer to them when I learned that the last confirmed living veteran of the Civil War, Union drummer boy, Albert Woolson, didn't die until Aug. 2, 1956. Not only had our lives overlapped by 10 years, but the old veteran also made his home in

Duluth, Minnesota, about 150 miles north of my hometown.

In June 1987 I moved to Charlottesville, Virginia, to start work as the feature story writer for the city's newspaper of record, The Daily Progress. Largely because Virginia was the northernmost state to have seceded from the Union, more major battles were fought there than any other state. My kinship with Jake made me particularly interested in his regiment, the 49th Pennsylvania Volunteers, which was part of the Army of the Potomac, headquartered in Virginia.

My search for material related to the 49th PV put me in touch with Art Beltrone, an expert in military artifacts and memorabilia. We became friends, and in the early 1990s, he mentioned a day trip he was planning to the National Archives in Washington, D.C., to do research. I asked him if he would look for information relevant to my great granduncle. Among the things he discovered was evidence that Jake hadn't survived the war. The person we thought was Jake was actually his father, John.

A few hours of educated sleuthing at the National Archives had turned a long-held family truth into a myth. Included in the mimeographed documents that Art gave me was Jake's death certificate. He died at 4 a.m. June 18, 1864, in Carver Army Hospital in Washington. The cause of death was a gunshot wound to his left hip. Friends claimed his body, and my guess was that he had been buried in nearby Arlington National Cemetery. After an official at the cemetery told me they had no record of his interment there, I gave up hope of finding his grave.

Months later, my mother told me about meeting an amateur genealogist named George Martin Lahr. George had done extensive research on a branch of his family tree with ties to the Maurers and Shrivers of Pennsylvania. I got in touch with George, and he told me that Jake was buried in the old section of Saint Severin Catholic Cemetery in Drifting, Pennsylvania.

I went in search of the cemetery in 1999. Initially, I drove by it, missing it in the unfamiliar countryside and an early morning fog. I continued down the road for a mile or so until I came to Moshannon Creek. It was July, and the shallow-running tributary that flows into the west branch of the Susquehanna River had been turned the color of gold by the rising sun. I parked my truck and walked onto a rusty girder-and-rivet bridge. As I admired the tranquil scene, I reflected on the two remarkable discoveries that brought me to that quiet stretch of road in Clearfield County, Pennsylvania. Learning of Jake's death, and later where he was buried, seemed more than coincidental.

I remembered what professor James I. Robertson Jr. had told me. I had met the Virginia Tech professor a year earlier when I interviewed him for a story I was writing about his just-released book, "Stonewall Jackson: The Man, The Soldier, The Legend." I later attended a talk he gave at the University of Virginia Bookstore. As the widely acclaimed Civil War historian was closing his remarks, he suggested to the audience that the next time they visited a national cemetery or Civil War battlefield, they take a moment to pause in silent reflection. He felt that during such times of quietude, listeners might hear whispers from the past. Later, I told him of my plan to visit Jake's grave and assured him that I would do what he suggested. He clasped my shoulders firmly in his hands and said, "You, you will get a message."

While memories of Jake remained alive in loved ones, his plot would have been cared for. But as time stilled those caring hands, neglect and weather toppled the gravestone. With each passing year, the marble slab settled deeper into the gray soil. By the time I arrived at the cemetery, the marker had nearly disappeared. I might have missed it completely if not for the small American flag secured in a bronze holder that read, "GAR 1861-1865." The letters stand for Grand Army of the Republic, which was a political group made up of Civil War veterans. A small, circular opening in the soil revealed a flat piece of stone a few inches below the grass. I knelt and started pulling away the covering sod. When I saw the name Jacob, I knew I had located the grave of the Civil War soldier who had inexplicably come into my life. After clearing dirt and washing the tombstone with water, I read the inscription.

JACOB SHRIVER, SGT., CO.D 49TH PA. INF.

Standing by the grave, I waited for the pronouncement Professor

Robertson seemed so certain I would receive. All I heard was the soft trill of songbirds in nearby trees.

A few years later I visited the Spotsylvania Court House battlefield where Jake was wounded. I paused for a few seconds before stepping out of the wood line bordering the open field he had charged across. As though on cue, birds began to sing. It was the identical, hushed sound I had heard at Jake's grave. For years, I had vaguely thought about writing a book that would entwine and compare Jake's war experiences with my own. The uncanny revelations that opened Jake's life to me, and the spiritual moment I experienced on that Virginia battlefield, inspired me to write this book.

I had experienced two completely different wars. My first tour with the 1st Cavalry Division, 1965-66, had shown me war as fought on a large scale with historic battles and few comforts. During that year I had gotten two days off and ate most of my meals from cans of C-rations.

When I returned to Vietnam in August 1968 as a recently graduated Special Forces soldier the changes were remarkable. I volunteered for a top-secret unit called Military Assistance Command, Vietnam – Studies and Observations Group (MACV-SOG). Our job was to conduct reconnaissance and direct-action missions in Laos, Cambodia, and North Vietnam. The North Vietnamese were using the supposedly neutral countries of Laos and Cambodia as sanctuaries for stockpiling supplies and massing troops. Our job was to monitor their activities and do as much damage as we could to their supply dumps and armed forces.

I was assigned to Command and Control North, just outside Da Nang. Instead of a pup tent, I lived in a plywood hooch with a tin roof. There were blankets, clean sheets, fresh food, and even flush toilets if I bothered to walk up to the headquarters area. I spent 18 months there, most of it in Recon Company. Our areas of operations were in Laos and North Vietnam, and our high casualty rate reflected how dangerous the missions were.

The recon teams consisted of two or three Americans and either Vietnamese, Montagnard or Chinese Nung mercenaries. The two recon teams I was on, RT Louisiana and RT Hawaii, had Nung and Vietnamese. The relationship I had with my little people was one of respect and in time love.

I learned a lot about myself during my tour with the 1st Cav., and it helps me to understand what Jake endured. My time in Recon Company showed me what war is like as a leader and having to make split-second, life and death decisions.

I wrote my first book, "The Dying Place," because I felt compelled to tell the true story about what I experienced during my time in Recon Company. Most of all I wanted to let the world know about a bunch of guys who courageously served their country with no expectations of being honored or recognized for what they did.

I'm quite certain Jake never imagined anyone would write a book with him as the main character. But this is the book that I now feel compelled to write.

NOR DID THEY FIGHT ANYMORE

DAVID A. MAURER

FIRESHIP
PRESS

Chapter One

During the winter of 1860-61, my great-granduncle, Jacob Shriver, could let his thoughts wander while bucking a two-man crosscut saw or swinging a single-bit ax in the forests of western Pennsylvania. A thick-shouldered lumberjack, his workplace was beneath cathedraled spires of white pine. With the cold air heavy with the scent of felled timber, he pondered the plight of a troubled land and his duty to it. His concern was not for a schoolbook nation of words, immortal men, and dates to remember. His country was of the heart, and now it seemed, perhaps, that it was about to die.

The Raftsman's Journal, its newsprint smudged and crumpled from days of rough handling, offered weekly updates on the escalating crisis. By the tallow light of a bunkhouse candle, Jake read words of impending war. Beyond the slab-brown shacks of Leonard Kyler's lumber camp, war fever had become a contagion. Clearfield County, Pennsylvania, didn't have a hope of avoiding it. Jake had consequential decisions to tangle with, and by early summer, time had run out.

I barreled headlong into war, a smile on my face. I imagined battles not unlike the re-enactments my buddies and I staged after watching movie matinees featuring bloodless combat. Better, of course, because of real machine gun fire in place of our vocalized *ratatat*. It wouldn't have mattered if I had been told about groaning corpses illuminated by night flares. Before my telling hour arrived, war was a painless thing.

War's preference for the young ensures that certain birth years will be favored. Jake was born October 17, 1838, on an 18-acre farm near, Kyler, Pennsylvania. I was born May 16, 1946, in St. Cloud, Minnesota. We were ideally positioned for the cull that swept us into events beyond imagining. And to think, neither of us had to go. I was absolved by having just completed a year-long hardship tour in South Korea and wouldn't have had to do another overseas tour during my three-year enlistment. Jake could have been honorably pardoned, too, as he was the primary provider for his family. An illness had left his father nearly blind, and two younger brothers, Joseph and Christian, were crippled. And there was Jake's mother, Ursula, and sisters, Josephine, Mary Ann, Catherine, and Ursula Rosilia. My great granduncle's importance to his family was unassailable. What likely weighed most heavily on his mind was whether duty to country should rank above ties of blood.

The bold-print headlines stacked on the front page of the April 17, 1861, edition of *The Raftsman's Journal* brought that vexing question to the fore. "War Commenced! Fire Opened on Sumter! Anderson Returned the Fire! Fort Sumter's Guns Silenced! Surrender of the Fort!" As dire as the words were, many Northerners predicted only a mild disruption of civil affairs before an amicable resolution would be reached. President Abraham Lincoln called for 75,000 volunteers to serve for three months. Enough time, it was widely supposed, for the crisis to be rectified.

Prophecies of a minor dust up were silenced by the butchery of July 21, 1861. The July 24th edition of *The Raftsman's Journal* was filled with accounts of what transpired near a murky creek in northern Virginia. Most troubling was that the South's victory at the Battle of First Bull Run brought the Rebels to within a day's march of the nation's capital.

"Total Rout of our Army," proclaimed the pulse-quickening headline. "Whole Regiments Cut Up. IMMENSE LOSS OF LIFE."

Union soldiers were said to have been mowed down, "like a scythe would cut down grass." After hours of blunt-force fighting, Federal troops were said to have gone into a "perfect panic." Until then, the battle could have gone either way. For most of the day, the fighting appeared to favor Union forces, and, by early afternoon, confident officers were declaring a Northern victory. Two events, occurring nearly simultaneously, ended such talk.

At this early stage of the war, many Rebel combatants hadn't been issued proper uniforms, and they streamed into battle wearing whatever clothing came to hand. About 3 p.m., an attacking Rebel unit wearing blue uniforms was misidentified as friendlies, and Federal troops holding important high ground held their fire. Many hapless defenders were gunned down as if by a firing squad. By the time the mistake was realized, the Rebels had overrun the position.

The second thing that favored the Confederates was the timely arrival of reinforcements by train. Prior to the Civil War, infantry moved at foot speed. The South was quick to realize the railroad's war fighting potential for rapidly moving troops and supplies to where they were needed. When thousands of Rebels were transported by train from the Shenandoah Valley to a railroad junction near the battlefield, it transformed how future engagements would be fought and strategized. The rush of reinforcements into Confederate lines around 4 p.m., was more than the Yankees could handle and they began to fall back. Withdrawing in the face of the enemy is difficult for seasoned veterans and proved beyond the ability of green troops to execute.

The retreat quickly turned into wild-eyed flight as panic swept through Federal ranks. Some brave men held their ground, but they were too few to make a difference. Neither curses or shaming could stop those fleeing the scene. Blinded by fear, sweat-drenched soldiers threw away their rifles, cartridge boxes, knapsacks and anything slowing their rush to safety. Adding to the chaos were terrified civilians who had ventured out from Washington in buggies and wagons to watch their boys in blue whip the upstart Southerners and end the rebellion.

Perhaps as many as 500 civilians had massed on high ground about five miles from the battlefield. From that vantage point they could hear the roar of fighting but could see little more than smoke on the horizon. When word reached them that Federal troops were carrying the day, some of the civilian celebrants uncorked bottles of Champagne to salute the Union victory.

Thinking the battle was nearing an end, some rubberneckers ventured nearer to the fighting. Their breath probably caught in their throats when they saw a tidal wave of Yankees stampeding toward them. Politicians, picnickers, and newspaper reporters were caught up in a maelstrom of whirling horses, careening caissons and fear-crazed soldiers punching and pushing their way to the rear.

The Warrenton Turnpike was the route to salvation, but the narrow dirt road quickly filled with traffic. Wounded, riderless horses added to the turmoil, bucking, and plunging without direction. Many of the retreating soldiers didn't begin to regain their composure until they had raced several miles to the small town of Centreville. From there, they faced a miserable, 25-mile slough back to Washington.

It was a costly defeat for the Union, and only luck spared retreating civilians from being among the dead and wounded. Not so fortunate was 85-year-old bedridden widow, Judith Carter Henry, who is widely believed to have been the first civilian casualty of the war. She was mortally wounded by shell fragments while abed in her farmhouse located on fiercely contested Henry House Hill. By the end of the war, it has been estimated as many as 50,000 civilians were killed. A study conducted in 1889 put the number of soldiers who perished during the conflict from all causes at 620,000. Modern accountings place the number as high as 850,000.

As unprepared for war as soldiers on both sides had been, this first major battle of the Civil War left no doubt of the savagery they were willing to inflict on each other. Hundreds of corpses, strewn about in differing attitudes of posture and disassembly, put the lie to notions of martial glory.

Compounding the horror were more than 2,500 wounded men, some of whom would be subjected to barbaric surgeries, or receive no medical care at all.

Many Southerners thought the war had been won and expected

to be allowed to go their separate way. In fact, the shocking defeat stiffened Northern resolve, and wakened the citizenry to the peril the nation was in. The United States of America was clearly in a struggle for its existence, and I don't think anything short of that would have compelled Jake to leave his family and join the Union Army for a three-year hitch.

It was likely early morning when Jake said his goodbyes. He was probably heartsick as he shook hands with his father and took the cloth-wrapped food his mother had prepared. What can be known of the parting except the certainty of tears and promises? Jake left too much behind to have done it on a lark or a quest for adventure. Only love of country, and its preservation, seem strong enough incentives.

How lonely the 30-mile journey to Milesburg must have been. Was Jake filled with a sense of foreboding as I had been on July 16, 1963, when I left home to enlist in the Army? I had turned 17 a few months earlier, the minimum age for joining up. I got no resistance from my parents who, because of my age, had to sign a waiver. They knew I had little interest in going back to high school in the fall, and the Army seemed like the best way to get me out on my own. What I had opened myself up to started sinking in as I waited for the Greyhound bus that carried me the 70 miles to Minneapolis.

The only advice pertaining to the military I received came from my maternal grandfather, Joe Sandkamp. Daddy Joe had been an Army ambulance driver in France during World War I. I knew he lost a lung to mustard gas, but I never heard him talk about his service. We were sitting on our living room couch when he told me, "No matter what happens, don't go over the hill." When I asked him what that meant, he told me it was an Army term for being absent without leave, in other words, running away. I promised I wouldn't do that, but during that final afternoon at home, I was thinking about calling the whole thing off.

I grew up in a house next to the east side of the St. Germain Bridge, which crossed the Mississippi River. A few blocks beyond the west side of the span was the Greyhound bus station. It had been a favorite haunt for me and my buddies, because of the pinball machines that lined a wall. When I arrived at the terminal on my final day as a civilian, I joined a small group of guys who were there for the same reason I was. I knew who they were, because of the brown, manila envelope each of us carried.

Inside was our bus ticket, instructions, and vouchers for meals and hotel room. Those who were there with parents, wives or girlfriends were all talked out. With little to say, we kept glancing at the white-faced wall clock. I didn't realize my childhood was slipping away tick by tick.

When it was time to board the bus, I filed with the others into the cavernous departure area. A bus driver wearing a gray, blue-trimmed uniform punched my ticket. I climbed the steps, the all-important envelope in one hand and a small travel bag in the other.

The bus rolled out of the shadows, turning left onto St. Germain Street. The pedestrians on the other side of the coach window were in a world I was no longer a part of. I had walked the sidewalk they were on, passed the same storefronts, but the sense of familiarity and belonging were gone. As the bus crossed the old bridge, I caught a glimpse of my bedroom window, framed in gray stucco.

Just beyond the bridge was the OK Shoe Shop, where an old cobbler had sharpened my ice skates for free. Then Mac's Drugstore, where I had purchased a two-dollar box of Valentine candy, its red, velvet bow found decades later among my mother's keepsakes. Carl's Supermarket, and memories of a dollar-a-day job filling jugs with vinegar during canning season. Tom's Lunch, where a 10-cent order of toast could buy a kid squatter's rights to listen to jukebox music on winter evenings. They had all become as lifeless and heart-tugging as mementos in a scrapbook. It wasn't until the bus reached the outskirts of town that I realized the first part of my life had ended. I held the manila envelope all the way to Minneapolis.

Chapter Two

Milesburg is a borough in Centre County, Pennsylvania, with a population of about 1,100. In Jake's time, it was an iron-producing village with a forge and furnace. On Monday, Aug. 19, 1861, the hamlet was being used as a turnout point for the purpose of transforming civilians into soldiers. Jake was one of 153 men who gathered there that day to be sworn into the ranks of the United States Army. They were subjected to a cursory physical and eye examination administered by an Army surgeon. The physician peered into Jake's mouth, listened to his heart with a stethoscope and thumped his chest and back. To demonstrate mobility, the men were told to jump, kick, bend, and twist.

Lameness, obvious health problems and missing front teeth were grounds for rejection. Opposing front teeth were needed to tear open gunpowder packets used in arming muzzle-loading rifles. Teeth also had to stand up to the rigors of eating hardtack biscuits. The thick cracker, consisting of flour, water and sometimes salt, had been a part of military fare for centuries, and came by its name honestly. If soldiers didn't have a cup of hot coffee to soften the biscuits in, they sometimes pounded them into chewable submission with rifle butts.

I took my physical examination on July 17, 1963, in the basement of the Federal Building in Minneapolis. My going-over was more thorough than Jake's and took most of the morning. Blood was taken, groins were checked for hernias, butt cheeks were spread, feet inspected, blood pressure taken and, lastly, an eye exam. That worried me. During my first vision check in grade school it was discovered I had a lazy eye, or amblyopia, in my left eye. I wore a patch over my good cyc for weeks in an attempt to strengthen the weak eye, to no avail. I was left with 20/200 vision in my left eye and 20/20 in my right. The Army eye exam picked up the shortcoming, but it wasn't serious enough to keep me out.

During my second enlistment I cheated on the eye exam by squeezing my face to the left side of the machine so I could read both charts with my good eye. This gave me 20/20 in both eyes, a requirement for Jump School and Special Forces.

What almost sent me home was my weight. The minimum weight for a recruit at the time was 130 pounds. I tipped the Toledo scale at 135 pounds, and was 5 feet, 7 inches tall. When Jake enlisted, he was an inch and a half taller than I was, and heavier. He had gray eyes, while mine are blue. His complexion was dark, mine fair. What we shared in common was our desire to serve.

The Marines were my first choice, but the recruiter said I had some growing to do before I would be ready to join their ranks. I stepped across the hall to the Army recruiting office and was received with open arms. It meant a lot to me then, and now, that despite my youth and size, the Army was willing to give me a shot at becoming a soldier. But on that Friday morning in July, as I shuffled from station to station in my underwear, I was a scrawny kid beset with fear and doubt. All the guys I was with were draftees and older than I was. They were facing two years' active duty, while I had signed up with the regular Army for three years. I learned that being in the regular Army and having an "RA" designation in front of my service number, rather than a "US" like the draftees, mattered to career soldiers.

As a volunteer I could walk away from the induction process at any time. This made the inner voice imploring me to quit all the more insistent. But as I followed the directional arrows from medic to medic, I began to hear another voice telling me to stay the course. It was a voice I became familiar with during the tough times ahead. Early that afternoon, those of us who passed the physical were escorted into a wood-paneled room with the Stars and Stripes prominently displayed next to the state flag of Minnesota. The nagging inner voice imploring me to quit became still when we were told to raise our right hand and recite the oath.

> "I, David A. Maurer, do solemnly swear that I will support and defend the Constitution of the United States against all enemies, foreign and domestic. That I will bear true faith and allegiance to the same; and that I will obey the orders of the President of the United States and the orders of the officers appointed over me according to regulations and the Uniform Code of Military Justice. So, help me God."

The words of the oath hadn't changed much since Jake spoke them.

> "I, Jacob Shriver, do solemnly swear that I will bear true allegiance to the United States of America, and that I will serve them honestly and faithfully against all their enemies and opposers whatsoever, and observe and obey the orders of the President of the United States, and the orders of the officers appointed over me according to the rules and articles for the government of the armies of the United States."

With these words, Jake and I entered the brotherhood of the U.S. Army for three-year hitches. This proud and venerable organization traces its birth back to June 14, 1775, when the Second Continental Congress, meeting in Philadelphia, unanimously authorized the formation of the American Continental Army. This action united the Minutemen, six new companies of riflemen and various other factions that had been battling the British in New England since the previous year. The new force was trained and led by Virginia politician-planter

George Washington.

The nation's father once said, "Discipline is the soul of the Army." This hardened will and strict obedience to orders is what sets soldiers apart from armed civilians. Basic training is where the stiffening agent of discipline is instilled, as well as the rudiments of war. The transition from civilian to soldier was one of the most traumatic experiences of my life. The changeover is particularly jarring, because the old self has to be stripped away before the soldier can emerge. It's a strange paradox, but in order to defend and preserve individual freedom, one must give it up.

Jake and I had time to think about our decision to join the Army as we traveled to our duty stations. After being sworn in, Jake and the others marched to the railroad depot in Milesburg. A train transported them 100 miles to Camp Curtain in Harrisburg, Pennsylvania. The camp was established as the state's military training center on April 18, 1861, three days after President Lincoln's call for 75,000 military volunteers. The camp was named for Republican Governor Andrew G. Curtain. His efforts during the conflict resulted in him being called, "the greatest of the Northern war governors." He was also referred to as, "the soldier's friend," because of his ardent support of soldiers and their families.

Minnesota was the first state to respond to Lincoln's urgent request for troops, and Pennsylvania quickly followed. According to John Milton Hay, the president's personal secretary, 523 men of, "unlicked patriotism poured ragged and unarmed out of Pennsylvania," and marched into the nation's vulnerable capital. The patriotic show of support resulted in Congress entering into the record its vote of thanks to the state. By war's end, 427,000 Pennsylvanians had enlisted, filling the ranks of the 270 Army regiments the state created.

Immediately after the swearing-in ceremony, we loaded onto a bus that carried us 585 miles south to Fort Leonard Wood, Missouri. The farther I got from home, the more alone I felt. When night came, the flash from my cigarette lighter would mirror my somber reflection on the bus window. My courage flared and faded as I listened to the tires humming beneath me. Deep into that sleepless night a distant farmyard light made me think of my empty bed back home.

It was dark when the bus pulled into the Reception Center at Fort Leonard Wood. My military career started with a sergeant bellowing out a stream of words that started with, "Welcome," and ended with an order to get our butts off the bus. The following minutes blurred into a chaotic melange of stumbling feet, bright floodlights, incomprehensible commands, and sensory overload. The humid air held the strong, unappetizing aroma of cheap bacon frying in a nearby mess hall.

After being shoved, pushed, and yanked into something resembling a formation, the berating members of the reception committee assured us that we represented the absolute low point in recruitment history. We held that burden of shame until the next busload of enlistees arrived. When the cadre figured we were suitably terrorized, they herded us into a wooden, World War II-era building to start in-processing.

We were too rattled to realize we had received our first lesson in how to think clearly during stressful situations. During the ensuing weeks of training, we were often put under time constraints in order to learn how to focus on what was essential at the moment. Four years later when I arrived at the reception center at Fort Campbell, Kentucky, the disorienting tactics had no effect on me. I had reenlisted after a nine-month break in service and arrived by bus in the middle of the night just as before. The rapid-fire orders threw the others into a tizzy, but I wasn't fazed. After the long, sleepless bus ride, I wandered off and found myself a place to sleep in a nearby barracks.

Army basic training efficiently turns civilians into rudimentary, yet functional, soldiers. An essential part of this eight-week transformation is stripping away individualism. This meant receiving a 20-second haircut that left my slick pompadour and ducktail on the barbershop floor. My shearing revealed a few head dents I didn't know I had. Worse yet, the buzz cut made me look five years younger.

Losing my hair was traumatic but getting issued military footwear and clothing was physically exhausting. What it took to create a properly turned-out American soldier in the 20th century was considerably more than in Jake's day. He was issued a coat, jacket, three trousers, three shirts, three pair of flannel underwear, two pair of shoes, two pair of woolen socks, a tie, kepi hat and cover. I was issued four pair of fatigue pants and shirts, two class A dress uniforms, four tan poplin dress shirts, four pair of khaki pants, two short-sleeve khaki shirts, two long-sleeve khaki shirts, several pair of white boxer shorts, T-shirts, cushion-soled socks, black dress socks, field jacket, two pair of boots, a pair of low quarter shoes, two black ties, two black web belts with brass buckles, an overcoat, a pair of black leather gloves with inserts, two baseball caps, two garrison caps and a saucer hat to be worn with our dress uniform. All this was crammed into a duffel bag that we hauled from station to station, warehouse to warehouse.

Soaked in sweat, I struggled with the increasing weight. This was an era when water was used as a disciplinary tool, and we wouldn't get any until we were back in the barracks. The march back became an ordeal, and the sound of a dropped duffel bag drew the immediate attention of the cadre. They savaged exhausted trainees with curses and insults until they were moving again. After dropping my duffel bag the first time, the frequency of drops increased as my exhaustion grew. It was a preamble for what was to come.

No sooner would we get back from one outing than we were being formed up to endure another. Our immunization shots were administered by needle-less, high pressure guns that fired serum through the skin. Before we walked between the lines of medics doing the shooting, we were cautioned not to flinch or pull away. Doing either of those things could result in serious injuries.

Topping all this off was the miserable awareness of being at the absolute bottom of the military pecking order. We seized on anything that could elevate our position a tick upward. Being at the reception center long enough to have had name tags sewn on your fatigue shirts was a status symbol. Getting dog tags was cause for another ascending click. As ridiculous as it was, guys leaving to start basic training were seen by the newbies as seasoned veterans. Of course, as soon as we arrived to start our training, we were at the bottom again.

My recruiter hadn't mentioned the reception center, and while struggling under the full weight of it, I felt betrayed. Another tough lesson I learned while there was that kitchen police, or KP as we called it, was a duty, not necessarily a punishment. I hadn't been in the Army three days when I was roused out of bed long before daylight and told to report to the mess hall. Scared stiff, I got there as quickly as I could. I unwittingly did the right thing, as I was one of the first to report to the mess sergeant. This landed me the cushy job of outside man. This basically consisted of crushing boxes and cans before throwing them in a dumpster and helping out in the kitchen when needed. The best job was dining room orderly, but I had yet to learn that. The worst job was washing pots and pans. That duty station went to the late arrivals. Ending up as a "pots and pans man," was so detested that some guys slept on the mess hall steps in order to be the first KPs in line when assignments were given out.

My first shift on KP lasted 18 hours. It was no fun, but I learned an invaluable lesson. When a cook told me to carry a large pan of hot water into the dining area, I picked it up on the kitchen side of the serving line and walked it all the way around to the dining room. The cook told me it would have been a lot easier if I had walked to the other side of the serving line before picking up the heavy pan. I felt foolish for not having figured this out myself, but it's a lesson I never forgot. It taught me that there is usually a hard way and an easier way to do something. Take a moment to think, and the best option will often come to mind.

Jake hadn't had to tolerate the indignation of having his nearly shoulder-length hair cut to stubble length, much less being in such a lowborn caste that a name tag could lift one's social status. He did have to wear shapeless, ill-fitting government-issued clothing. Like others in this frumpy predicament, he likely spent a few bucks to have the company tailor address his sartorial shortcomings. Neither did he have to put up with the harassment and subjugation that veterans in established units often heap on greenhorns. Jake had the good fortune of joining a new regiment made up of men from his own region. The 49th PV was officially mustered into existence on September 14, 1861, at Camp Curtain. Jake became a member of Company D and stayed with it for the duration of his service.

After several days at the Reception Center, we were bused to the training area. I was assigned to C Company, 4th Battalion, 3rd Training Regiment. We were some of the first trainees to be housed in new, air-conditioned brick barracks. This was a much-appreciated upgrade from the stifling hot wooden barracks we had been living in. I certainly had better accommodations than Jake could have dreamed of. He had to live in a tent or makeshift hut during his entire stint in the Army. Having lived in a pup tent or a poncho lean-to during most of my first tour in Vietnam, I learned how miserable an existence that can be.

The two-man tent was introduced to American GIs during the Civil War. There had been a few improvements made to the design by the time it was my turn to link up with a buddy and snap our shelter-halves together to form the tent. When the "A" or "Wedge" tent was introduced to Union soldiers in late 1861, it was quickly dubbed the "dog" or "pup" tent, because a canine would have found it satisfyingly roomy, but not two grown men. The average height of a Federal soldier was about 5 feet 8 inches, whereas the tent was 5 feet, 2 inches long and 4 feet, 8 inches wide. Long before I crawled into a pup tent for the first time, the size had been increased to 7 feet long and 5 feet wide. Snaps had replaced buttons as fasteners, and each of us was issued metal tent pegs and a tent pole that could be broken down into three sections. Front and back flaps had also been added.

After being issued two blankets, two sheets, pillow, and pillowcase, we were assigned a bunk in a squad bay. We also got a wall locker and footlocker to store our gear and clothing. Next stop was the supply room, where we were issued our field gear. This consisted of our tent items, backpack, canteen, gas mask, poncho, first aid pouch, steel helmet and liner, entrenching tool, ammo pouch, compass and carrying pouch, sleeping bag and cover, air mattress, mess kit, eating utensils, bayonet, and scabbard, as well as a cotton-canvas pistol belt and load-bearing suspenders. All this gear had to be kept in immaculate condition and made "clearing" supply an ordeal when it came time to turn it back in.

When Jake joined the Army, uniforms and field gear were being provided by the individual states. This resulted in a motley array of uniforms and equipment, much of it of poor quality. If Jake had picked up the May 29, 1861, issue of *The Raftsman's Journal*, he would have learned that just weeks into the conflict, wartime profiteering in Pennsylvania had reached shameful heights.

"It appears that much dissatisfaction exists at the miserable way in which the Pennsylvania troops have been supplied with clothing and food under our State authorities," the story read. "The blankets and clothing, according to accounts, have many of them being cheap, flimsy, rotten stuff: almost ready to fall to pieces. The shoes have, in some cases, been pasted together or the soles filled with pine shavings. In truth, it is said that the Pennsylvania troops are the most miserably clad of all volunteers called into the service."

I hadn't been in Vietnam two hours before my first exposure to shameless greed presented itself. I arrived with the 1st Cav's advance element in August 1965. After landing on the beach at Qui Nhon, we loaded onto 2 ½-ton trucks that transported us to our base camp at An Khe in the Central Highlands. The base was named after Maj. Donald Radcliff, the division's first combat death. As we broiled under a midday sun waiting for the convoy to assemble, an American GI from a nearby support unit came by with cans of cold Cokes. My first thought was that this kindhearted individual, having taken note of our suffering, was doing what he could to relieve our discomfort. A wonderful example, I thought, of the special brotherhood shared by Americans. This assumption was shattered when I learned he was selling drinks he had bought for 10 cents a can, for two and three dollars apiece. More than 50 years later I can still see that worthless bastard hawking his wares truck to truck.

Worse yet, one of our own guys took advantage of our situation. When we arrived at An Khe it wasn't much more than a large clearing cut out of the jungle. The open field was dubbed the Golf Course, and it was used as a parking lot and staging area for our 450-plus helicopters. We had nothing but our issued gear, and we quickly learned the value of simple items that could make our lives a little better. One of our sergeants was allowed to visit the nearby village, and purchase comfort items for us. He stocked up on things like small mirrors, candles, and wash basins. He then resold the merchandise to us at inflated prices. He was making a pile of money until an officer got wind of the scheme and put an end to it.

Although unscrupulous merchants sold shoddy equipment and foodstuff to Federal forces, Confederate soldiers rarely had the quality or quantity of equipment enjoyed by their opponents. Their supplies were often scrounged from the battlefield or taken from captured wagons and boxcars. The tin canteens issued Union troops were particularly prized by the Rebels. They were well made, and covered with cloth, which helped keep the water cool. The Union haversack was another item a Confederate soldier was keen to get his hands on. They were used to carry food and various small items, and the liner could be removed for washing.

Like modern-day infantry soldiers, Union troops carried an assortment of pouches fastened to their belts. Included was a cartridge box, another box for percussion caps, and a bayonet in a scabbard. They also carried a knapsack that they crammed with things like their shelter half, gum blanket, clothing, and personal items. A sleeping blanket and great coat were rolled up and secured to the top of the knapsack.

When I joined the Army in 1963, it was making the transition from the M-1 Garand rifle to the M-14 rifle. The M-1 had been the principal infantry rifle during World War II and the Korean War. The M-14 came into the Army's supply chain in 1959 and was first issued to infantry units. By 1963, there still weren't enough of them to issue to basic trainees, so we carried the M-1 and qualified with it on the firing range. Although we were given classroom instruction on the M-14, and learned how to field strip it, we never got to fire one. After basic training, I was never again issued an M-1.

Jake and the others in his regiment were issued Harpers Ferry muskets. These were likely exchanged for Springfield Model 1861 rifles when they became widely available. An important accessory was the bayonet. Although Jake would be a participant in one of the great bayonet charges in military history, the long, sharp blade was rarely used for its intended purpose. Civil War soldiers often used their bayonets to secure a tent, hold a candle or skewer a piece of meat for roasting.

Despite the unlikelihood of using the bayonet in combat, Jake and

I endured many hours of bayonet training. My training was conducted on hot, hardpan practice fields. During these torturous sessions, the instructors periodically yelled out, "What's the spirit of the bayonet fighter?" We obediently yelled back, "To kill." At the command, "Long thrust and hold," we'd lunge forward to impale our imaginary foe. Until we heard the order, "recover," we stayed in a crouched position. Often the order came to drop our left hand, which meant we were then holding the 9 ½-pound rifle and 1-pound bayonet with just our right. Invariably the rifle started nosing downward, which gave the prowling instructors the opportunity to get in our face. Occasionally we'd hear a thud as a hapless trainee passed out and toppled to the ground. The individual was then dragged to a shaded area and doused with water. If the soldier didn't come around quickly, he was taken to the hospital by an ambulance that was always parked nearby during these exercises.

Outdoor training exercises were never canceled, regardless of how hot it got. The cadre used the heat to toughen us up and instill discipline. One of their favorite training areas for close-order drill and bayonet practice was next to the post swimming pool. Hearing and seeing people splashing around in the water made the scorching heat, dust and dryness in our mouths that much worse. During those trying hours, I often thought about my buddies back home, swimming in the cool water of the granite quarries outside town.

When we returned to the barracks after a long march, or torturous hours on a practice field, we lined up at the water fountains. Because everyone was thirsty, each guy took several swallows and then went to the back of the line. I was amazed by how the water was immediately absorbed by the body.

After the initial half-dozen swallows or so, it was as if I hadn't had any water at all. Once, after a 10-mile force march back from a rifle range, I nearly passed out. We had arrived at the barracks but were still standing in formation. A loud ringing started in my ears, and I felt sick to my stomach. Just as my head started to spin, and I was in danger of going down, we were dismissed, and I managed to get inside the air-conditioned barracks.

I tried to be a good soldier, and my sergeants were never particularly tough on me. My platoon sergeant, Sergeant First Class Robert Brown, was actually kind at times. He was a veteran of World War II and was interested in creating good soldiers rather than making basic training more of a nightmare than it inherently is. We chipped in and bought him a watch as a going away present.

I wasn't feeling like much of a soldier when going on guard duty for the first time. An important part of it was preparing for the inspection that determined whether or not you were, "standing tall." This meant wearing a clean, pressed uniform, having your boots highly shined and your brass belt buckle gleaming. I also had to know my chain of command from my squad leader all the way up to the president. In addition, we all had to know a number of General Orders verbatim. The first one was, "I'll guard my post in a military manner, keeping always on the alert and observing everything within sight or hearing." Another was, "I'll quit my post only when properly relived."

Jake's General Orders were condensed into one statement. "I am required to take charge of this post and all public property in view; to salute all officers passing, according to rank; to give the alarm in case of fire, or the approach of an enemy, or any disturbance whatsoever; to report all violations of the Articles of War, Regulations of the Army, or camp or garrison orders; at night, to challenge all persons approaching my post, and to allow no one to pass without the countersign until they are examined by an officer or noncommissioned officer of the guard."

Prior to being marched to the guardhouse, Sergeant Brown inspected us. There is stiff competition to be the sharpest soldier because he gets selected as the supernumerary and doesn't have to pull guard. In basic training this distinction also earned the recipient a two-day pass. I wasn't aware of all this at the time, but I knew I had to look my best.

I hadn't shaved in my life, so I was surprised when Brown told me to return to the barracks and shave. I quickly did as I was told, but then he sent me back to do a better job. I cut myself during my second attempt but managed to pass the noncom's close scrutiny. The incident got me flustered, and I was dreading the real inspection at the guardhouse.

Standing in formation outside the guardhouse, Sergeant Rock told us he was the sergeant of the guard. He then started the inspection, going from man to man. After looking me up and down, he asked me who the sergeant of the guard was. I thought it was a trick question, but I answered, "Sergeant Rock is the sergeant of the guard." He moved to the next man. After the inspection was completed, Sergeant Rock announced that I had been selected as the supernumerary. I didn't know what the word meant, and as the others filed into the guardhouse, I asked Sergeant Rock what I was supposed to do. He told me to go back to the barracks and tell the sergeant in charge that I had been selected supernumerary. For a horrifying moment, I thought that meant I had been kicked off guard. He must have seen the stricken look on my face, because he assured me that supernumerary was a good thing and sent me on my way. I pulled guard duty countless times after that and was never again selected supernumerary. I sincerely doubt that I was the sharpest soldier on guard mount that day. What is certain is that I desperately needed something to lift my spirits, and Sergeant Rock gave me that.

Basic training is where you make mistakes and learn from them. My most embarrassing mistake occurred when we were being trained in how to conduct a reconnaissance patrol. My partner and I were sent out to scout an enemy encampment and gather what pertinent intelligence we could. We had been instructed on what to look for, such as indications of the enemy's morale, their numbers, and emplacements. When we returned from our mission, and with classmates looking on, I reported our findings to the sergeant in charge. After reporting how many enemy soldiers we had counted I added, "And they have low morals." Everybody started laughing, and the sergeant asked me, "What were they doing, jacking off?"

Years later, when I was a Special Forces recon team leader in Vietnam, I told my buddies the story. We all got a good laugh out of it. No one missed the irony that the peach-fuzz kid ended up leading a small band of Vietnamese and Chinese Nung mercenaries on recon missions into Laos and North Vietnam.

During my nine years in the Army, I attended a number of military schools. It's no surprise that Special Forces training was far more rigorous, mentally, and physically, than basic training. Jump School was no picnic, either. But basic training had an overarching element the other schools couldn't assume. During those seemingly endless weeks in Missouri, when activities started before first light and often continued well into the night, I was dealing with the psychological upheaval of being changed from one person into another.

Our training cycle started July 29, 1963, and was completed September 19th. During that time, we were subjected to real dangers, such as when we donned our gas masks and had to spend time in a chamber filled with lethal mustard gas. If any of us doubted the seriousness of this exercise, the burning sensation we felt on the back of our unprotected necks clued us in. We also had to remove our gas masks in a chamber filled with tear gas, in order to experience what that feels like. The purpose of this was to give us confidence in our gas masks. On another scary occasion we crawled through an obstacle course while machine gun bullets zipped by a few feet above our heads. This exercise was conducted at night, and as I crawled out of the trench to start low crawling through the course, it looked like the red tracers were just inches above us. Explosive charges detonating nearby added another layer of realism to the event.

Arming and throwing a fragmentation hand grenade for the first time required another gut check. I didn't miss the fact that there was deep sand behind the protective, concrete wall over which we threw the grenade. The sand was there to keep the grenade from rolling around if a trainee inadvertently dropped it. An instructor stayed close to us as he talked us through the procedure. Later, during actual combat, I would let hand grenades, "cook off," for a few seconds prior to throwing them to ensure the enemy wouldn't have time to throw them back. That's not to say I became complacent, or lost respect, for these hand-held bombs. Quite the contrary. I always added additional safety measures to grenades I carried into combat. After making sure the safety pin was properly crimped, I taped it over with black electrical tape fashioned with a quick-release tab. As an additional precaution, I taped the safety level as well. And I never hung grenades from my web gear. A guy I knew made the mistake of taping a white phosphorous grenade to his web gear. As he moved through thick brush a twig snagged in the safety pin ring and pulled it out. Before he could free the grenade, it went off. That tragedy taught me a hard lesson about grenades, but basic training taught me the fundamentals.

On August 20, 1861, a day after Jake joined the Army, William F. Ketchum of Buffalo, New York, received a patent for his Ketchum hand grenade. The dart-like device came in 1-, 3- and 5-pound sizes. Their effectiveness was limited because they had to land on their nose to detonate. One account tells of Confederate soldiers catching the devices in spread-out blankets and throwing them back. Jake's basic training wouldn't have included this innovation, nor did he get much of the same training I received in basic. His initial training largely consisted of drills, marching, military facing movements and how to maneuver on the battlefield. And a lot of time and attention was given to practicing the procedures for loading and firing weapons.

My Special Forces training stands alone in my life experiences. When I reported to Training Group, I was expecting to be greeted by the same in-your-face yelling and harassment as I had been subjected to in Basic Training and Jump School, only worse. When the cab dropped me off outside the brick, two-story building, I tried to prepare myself for whatever calamity was to come.

The only sign of life I saw after entering the building was light shining through an open doorway onto the floor that had been buffed to a mirror finish. Inside the small office was an honest-to-God Green Beret sergeant sitting behind a gray, metal desk. I had seen four Green Berets during my first three years in the army, and never one this close. Although he outranked me by four grades, he smiled, extended his hand, and welcomed me to Training Group.

All the while suspecting trickery, I was led down the deserted hall to a linen closet and issued bedding. I was then taken to a squad bay and assigned a bunk as well as a foot and wall locker. The sergeant offhandedly mentioned that the lockers weren't secured by locks as a point of honor. Back in the office he typed me out a pass, told me which bars in Fayetteville Special Forces guys frequented, then asked me how I was fixed for money. When I said I was OK on that score, he gave me a meal card and told me where the mess hall was located. Lastly, he said my class would start the following Monday morning, and until then I was off.

My introduction to Special Forces left me in a state of wonderment. In the months that followed we were never yelled at, except when necessary, such as during POW training. The method of instruction was much like a father teaching his son. The instructors were never rude, aloof, or condescending. The worst punishment they'd levy would be a disappointed shake of their head, which hurt worse than a blow.

Many times, I heard them say, "We're going to train you the best we can, because we might be serving together down the road."

These glow-in-the-dark guys, as we called them, knew exactly what they wanted, even if they couldn't always articulate exactly what that was. They were unforgiving when it came to standards, and yet would make exceptions. This dichotomy kept my best friend, Eldon Bargewell, and myself from being washed out early in the training. When we flunked the written test for land navigation, we were crestfallen, because any failure on a test meant automatic termination.

When an instructor took us aside, we were expecting the worst. To our great relief he told us that they knew we had flunked because we didn't have the necessary math skills. He offered to tutor us in the evening for a week, after which they would test us again. If we passed, we could go on, if not we were out. We passed, and Eldon went on to reach the rank of major general and became one of the finest military leaders this country has ever produced.

On the other hand, one of the best students in our class was suddenly dismissed. The instructors had learned that when he was a civilian, he had been convicted of stealing a car. They told us he wasn't let go because he stole a car, but because he tried to hide it from them. "Hell," one of the instructors said, "knowing how to hot wire a car is a great skill set."

Every day we were tested in subtle and clever ways, reminiscent of the biblical story of how Gideon chose his 300-man army to defeat the Midianites. Taken to a river to drink, those who lapped water, "like a dog," were let go. Those who cupped water in their hands and brought it up to their mouths to drink were retained.

One evening I was changing a light bulb in the hallway when our first sergeant happened by. He took the burned-out bulb from my hand, broke it on the floor, picked up a large shard of glass and handed it to me. "Eat it," he said. Obediently, I put it in my mouth and bit down. To my surprise it broke into harmless grains of sand. He walked away without a word.

Periodically, without warning, we were put through some hell-on-earth experience that kept us wondering what could possibly be next. One wintry evening after classes had finished for the day, we were told our supper was on a truck we had to successfully ambush. With rucksack, web gear and weapons we were forced marched about 15 miles to the ambush site next to a dirt, logging road. The instructors carefully positioned us in a row along the bottom of a ditch that had several inches of water in it.

Flat on our stomachs, we remained motionless, half submerged in water. I know there was a bright moon that night because it reflected off the skim ice that eventually formed around me. When the deuce and a half finally came rumbling down the road, a shot was fired to initiate the ambush, and we jumped to our feet and immediately fell back down. Unable to stand, we crawled up the side of the ditch firing harmless blanks at the truck. By the time we got to the road we were able to get to our knees, and then push ourselves up on shaky legs.

The truck had stopped, and the instructors decided we had done well enough to deserve the food. We were each rewarded with a box of frozen C-rations. We expected to ride back in the truck, but no. The sun was just rising above the pine trees when we got back to the barracks. An hour or so later we were in class, starting another day.

I received much better training than Jake. But ultimately the real training comes on the battlefield where the learning curve can be so steep it bends back on itself. Early volunteers like Jake wanted to start fighting immediately. They didn't understand the importance of practicing things until they could be performed by rote. Neither did they understand the need for discipline and following orders without hesitation. During those first days at Camp Curtain, many of the new troops felt they could do whatever they wanted. They learned otherwise. And soon it was the brain-numbing chaos of combat that made them realize how unprepared for battle they were.

Chapter Three

On the evening of Sept. 6, 1861, a heavy downpour fell on Camp Curtain. The drenching brought with it a melancholy that quieted the men of the 49th PV. Nearly three weeks had passed since Jake entered the Army. He probably hadn't anticipated all the things he had to learn about military culture and its inherent rigors. As drumming raindrops made their inevitable inroads onto gear and bedding, he began to know precipitation anew. No longer was it solely a benevolent friend, settling dust and perking up row crops. Now, it had become a hated thing, too, with its insistent elbowing at corner and crease until everything in one's world rested in a puddle.

Sodden lesson delivered; the lowering clouds continued on their indifferent way. Robert S. Westbrook, the regiment's diarist, declared the new day, "pleasant and cool." He arrived at this opinion after he and his mates had their spirits lifted by strong coffee and a hot breakfast. While the sun dried their gear and clothing, the men, with full bellies, assembled on the parade field for morning drill. As officers and sergeants barked commands, the wet ground was stomped into a slurry of mud.

At this early stage of training, the recruits lacked precision, but not enthusiasm. It would take many hours of practice for them to obtain proficiency in the art of moving en masse during battle. But the elan and pride that would propel them into combat was already alive in them, and it would distinguish their unit throughout the war.

After several hours of drill, the men were given the rest of the day off. The nearby Susquehanna River was a popular destination for those wanting to get away from camp for a few hours. Jake knew the river well, as it was a main thoroughfare used for floating large rafts of white pine to the hundreds of sawmills along its banks. If he had fond memories of the Susquehanna, as I have of the Mississippi, it would have given him a sense of connection to home. Wherever I've seen the river of my youth, even at the terminus of its 2,320-mile journey, it's like seeing a dear friend.

Except for the usual morning inspection, Sunday was a day of rest for Jake. One of the first orders issued by Maj. Gen. George B. McClellan, commander of the Army of the Potomac, was General Order No. 7, dated Sept. 6, 1861. It addressed his soldiers' spiritual wellbeing.

It reads; "The Major General Commanding desires and requests that in future there may be a more perfect respect for the Sabbath on the part of his command. We are fighting in a holy cause and should endeavor to deserve the benign favor of the Creator. Unless in the case of an attack by the enemy, or some other extreme military necessity, it is commended to commanding officers that all work shall be suspended on the Sabbath; that no unnecessary movements shall be made on that day; that the men shall, as far as possible, be permitted to rest from their labors; that they shall attend divine service after the customary Sunday morning inspection, and that officers and men shall alike use their influence to insure [sic] the utmost decorum and quiet on that day.

"The General Commanding regards this as no idle form; one day's rest in seven is necessary to men and animals; more than this, the observance of the holy day of the God of Mercy and of Battles is our sacred duty. George B. McClellan, Major General Commanding."

The Army doesn't require soldiers to attend church, but war and impending danger certainly has an impact on attendance. When I was going through Jump School in the summer of 1967, there was a chapel near our barracks. On the Sunday before Jump Week, when we made our five qualifying parachute jumps, the church was packed. An instructor remarked that it was probably the most frequented house of worship in the Army.

Jake and the others certainly weren't praying for rain during devotionals at Camp Curtain. Showers and constant activity turned the east end of the 80-acre compound where the 49th PV was bivouacked into a stinking, slurry of mud. On the morning of September 11th, the regiment packed up and moved to the west end. By the time it started raining that afternoon, the men were sheltered in tents pitched on more favorable ground.

On Friday, September 20, Governor Curtain visited the camp and presented the 49th PV with their colors. He had paid for the flag with his own money, and the men thanked him with thunderous cheers. The regiment's commander, Col. William H. Irwin, assured Curtain that, "While I have an arm to wield a sword or a man to fire a gun, the colors will never drop in the face of an enemy, nor be desecrated by the touch of Rebel hands." Through some of the fiercest fighting of the war, the men of the 49th PV kept that promise.

At dawn the following morning, the men were roused from bed with the call, "Pennsylvania infantry, wake up." This was the day they headed off to war, and they broke camp with a heightened sense of purpose. The men were in high spirits as they marched through Harrisburg to the Northern Central Railroad terminal. It required two trains to move the regiment to its destination - Washington, D.C.

I had been carried to war by a troop train as well, but one traveling in the opposite direction Jake's had taken. My train ride took place in July 1965, and carried me from Fort Sill, Oklahoma, to Oakland, California. Once in California, we heard reports that war protesters were planning to stop the train by lying on the tracks. The threat didn't materialize, but this was our first indication that we didn't have the full support of the American public.

We arrived at the bleak Oakland docks without incident. I was surprised to see members of a familiar humanitarian organization selling coffee and doughnuts to us as we waited to board ship. I had assumed such fare would be free to GIs going off to war, many of whom would soon be dead. I didn't have any money, having lost it all in about five minutes via a poker game on the troop train. But even if I had had 15 cents for a doughnut, I wouldn't have gone near that canteen wagon. I left the country with hurt feelings, but before the men of the 49th PV reached their destination, their journey was marred by catastrophe.

Around 9 p.m., September 21, 1861, the lead train transporting Jake's regiment was approaching Baltimore, Maryland. Several soldiers had opted for seating on the rear bumper guard of the last railroad car rather than in the cramped interior. The train, made up of 18 cars, slowed to less than 12 mph as it rounded a curve. Close behind was the second transport train, with Charles Johnson at the throttle. It had 11 cars, and was traveling at about 20 mph. The engineer was watching for the glimmer of a red warning light attached to the rear of the train ahead. What he didn't know was that the red light was being blocked from view by the dangling legs of a seated soldier. Without warning, the locomotive plowed into the rear of the railroad car, careened off the tracks, and toppled onto its side like a wounded beast.

Sergeant John W. Stephens performed the regiment's first heroic act by rushing into the battered engine compartment. He then located a lever that allowed him to stop scalding steam from escaping. Johnson was alive, but one of his legs was terribly mangled. The lower extremities of Pvt. John Fulton and Pvt. Daniel S. Parker were pulverized by the impact, and they quickly succumbed to shock and loss of blood. Cries of pain and distress came from several seriously injured soldiers lying broken and bleeding in the dirt and scattered debris. A half-moon just above the horizon, and lanterns, provided what little light there was.

The lead train, having sustained only damage to the rear car, transported the dead and injured to nearby Bolton Depot. An undertaker identified in a newspaper account as Mr. Weaver took charge of the two fatalities and arranged for them to be buried in Loudoun Park

Cemetery. They were among the first Union soldiers to be interred in Baltimore's largest graveyard. By war's end, more than 2,300 Federal troops would be laid to rest there, as well as 600 Confederates. The injured soldiers were treated at a government hospital, and Johnson was taken to his residence on Grundy Street in Baltimore. A professor named Smith assessed the damaged leg, which was amputated.

The second train arrived in Baltimore the following morning, and the regiment regrouped. With two men dead, and several others seriously hurt, the gaiety that had marked the journey was gone. Tired and somber, the soldiers marched from the city's Northern Central Depot to the Baltimore and Ohio Station, where they loaded onto railroad cars for the 40-mile trip to the nation's capital.

The regiment arrived at its destination about 2 p.m. without incident. It was Sunday, September 22, 1861, and the troops entered a city teeming with war-related activities. For the first time, Jake was able to see something of the size and scope of the war effort. Washington's prewar population of about 41,000 was growing by the day and would top out at more than 160,000 by war's end. This was the city that embodied the beliefs and principles that Jake felt were worth defending with his life. Its grandeur, as yet unrealized, was nonetheless emerging. It was becoming evident in the dome-less Capitol building under construction, and the uncompleted Washington Monument, which wouldn't be finished until 1884.

Jake and the others in his outfit pitched their tents about a mile north of the Capitol building. They named the area Camp Juniata after the Pennsylvania county some of the men were from. For the next several days the volunteers enjoyed a peaceful preamble to war. In the run-up to battle, officers and noncoms are distracted by a torrent of preparatory chores. As logistics are arranged and maps pored over, those in the lower ranks are largely left alone. Jake and his buddies didn't have to trouble themselves with cooking chores, as they were taking their meals at the nearby Soldiers' Relief mess hall. After performing daily duties such as policing the campgrounds, they had time to wander about, and some of them chose to hike two miles to a bathing area.

I would have gladly walked the few miles from our area to the 1st

Cav's shower point, but I had the benefit of riding there in a truck. The facility was located on the western perimeter of our base camp and drew water from nearby Song Ba River. Most of my tour of duty from August 1965 to June 1966 was spent in the field, so a hot shower was a rarity. The shower point rumbled with the sound of generators powering heaters and pumping water through tentacles of pipes and hoses. Wood slats salvaged from artillery shell boxes formed a walkway through the inevitable puddling and were also used to make the benches lining the walls of large, olive-green tents. Shower heads were spaced like cattle stanchions along the center of the tents, where we luxuriated in the spray of hot water. Never did I hear anyone tell us to hurry up or stop wasting water. The only command I ever heard was, "Get the soap out of your eyes," and that came one evening in response to the rattle of nearby gunfire.

As sparse and mud-drab as the shower point was, it offered a comfort bordering on a spiritual rebirth. Once out of the filthy fatigues we had worn for weeks, we gratefully bowed into its cleansing grace. The cascade of steaming hot water washed away grim and dark moods. We reveled in the soothing benediction of clean clothes on freshly scrubbed skin. No cigarette was more enjoyed than those smoked as we waited for the others to finish. We knew our luster would last only until a fresh powdering of red dust settled on us during the ride back. That awareness didn't lessen the contentment of having momentarily regained a measure of humanity. From that time forward, I have tried never to forget to thank God whenever I shower. Our transformation in the heated water of the Song Ba River taught me never to take civilized comforts for granted.

The idle days Jake enjoyed in the relative ease of the capital were short-lived. On Friday, September 27, 1861, the regiment got its marching orders. The rainy morning was spent breaking down tents and loading them and haversacks onto wagons. When the thoroughly soaked men marched out of Camp Juniata around 3 p.m., the movement marked their passage from preparation for combat to war itself. This transition doesn't necessarily occur with the first exchange of gunfire. Mine came a few days after arriving in Vietnam. It was daytime, and I was on guard duty at the base of Hon Cong Mountain, which was actually a large, heavily forested hill. I was standing on top of a Conex container, looking across the perimeter road at a green wall of vegetation. Realizing how easily I could be shot off my perch, I climbed down, crossed the road and for the first time stepped into the jungle of Southeast Asia.

As the greenery closed in behind me, it felt as if I was being embraced and welcomed back to a place where I belonged. In that moment, closed off from distracting sights and sounds, I entered war and something of the jungle entered me. Never during the months that followed was I ever frightened or angered by it. Though it cut me with its thorns and left me exhausted and dripping sweat, it never ceased being my benevolent friend.

Jake and the others learned during the trying hours following the shouted command, "Forward march," that the pains of war aren't reserved for battle alone. Bending into a cold, wind-driven rain, they headed out to meet a future that would change each of them. After sloughing through Georgetown, they followed the Potomac River until they reached Chain Bridge, where they crossed into Virginia. It was well after dark when the order to make camp was passed along the line of march.

Wet, tired, and hungry, they searched for the baggage wagons carrying the few comfort items that existed in their lives. Shoulders slumped and curses rang out when they learned the wagons had slid off the road and toppled into a ditch. Some unfortunates were detailed to march back and help right the upset wagons. At the accident site, grimacing men gripping wheel spokes spit and slipped as they wrestled wagons back onto the road. By the time this was accomplished, mud-splattered officers and men had had enough. Desperate for warmth, they tore an old, abandoned house apart board by board.

Soon the bivouac area was blazoned with campfires, around which men huddled and shivered as steam rose off their soaked uniforms.

At first light the following morning, a clearing sky helped lift the mood of the men. The arrival of wagons transporting tents and haversacks was another welcome sight. Rows of tents quickly blossomed across a field dubbed Camp Advance. As it was being established, high-ranking officers were finalizing unit structure. That day, Saturday, September 28, 1861, was memorable in that Major Gen. Winfield S. Hancock's 3rd Brigade came into existence. It consisted of the 49th PV, 5th Wisconsin, 6th Maine and 43rd New York. The new brigade was part of the Second Division of the VI Army Corps.

The previous night of mud and suffering opened the green troops' eyes to the fickle nature of life in the field. A lesson in the mysterious ways of the military soon followed. Late that afternoon each man was issued four rounds of ammo and ordered to sleep with equipment on so as to be prepared to move out at a moment's notice. At 11 p.m., marching orders were given, and they tramped out of camp for about a mile. Several men were assigned picket duty, and as they took up guard positions in advance of the columns, the rest of the men milled about. At 4 a.m., they were told to return to camp. Just as they were bedding down, they were roused yet again. This time they were marched to a hill a short distance east of camp. After four hours of holding down that position, they marched back to camp. The willy-nilly maneuvering cost the men a night's sleep and accomplished nothing. The morale-sapping waste of energy set a pattern to be repeated time and again during the war.

Jake and his peers, not being privy to the intelligence available to commanders, were blind to the big picture. The hasty to-and-fro movements suggest a response to some perceived aggressive action by the enemy. In fact, the Confederates were retreating, not advancing. After the Battle of First Bull Run, the Rebels held Munson's Hill, Upton's Hill, and Mason's Hill. From these heights they had a clear view of the flatland area of Bailey's Crossroads and, with the help of telescopes, could see the nation's capital.

Considerable consternation was created for the citizens of Washington when a large Confederate flag started flying on Munson's Hill. More troubling than the Stars and Bars were the black cannons positioned nearly hub to hub along its crest. The cannons turned out to be logs, splash-painted black to resemble cannons. Rebel sharpshooters firing from elevated positions were plenty real. On September 28, the Confederates quietly withdrew from the hills and fell back to Centreville. For weeks the Federals had been held at bay by batteries of timbers. The blush of embarrassment surely deepened as newspapers piled on with ridiculing accounts of the deception.

On September 30, 1861, the men of the 49th PV packed up again and marched a few miles south. There they established Camp Griffin, about five miles from Chain Bridge. In the following days, the regiment slipped back into routine camp life. After police calls and drills were finished, many soldiers ventured into nearby woods to harvest chestnuts. Roasting the nuts became an evening pastime. Before being tossed into skillets to roast, an X was cut on each rounded nut to allow steam to escape. Yelps and laughs often followed as eager hands plucked hot chestnuts from the pan, juggling them until they cooled.

The next couple of weeks were relatively uneventful, except for the capture of a Confederate surgeon by Federal cavalry near Fairfax. The physician was found hiding under hay in a stable. Westbrook noted in his diary that it was presumed the doctor would, "abandon his profession awhile."

Things heated up on October 21, when the antagonists clashed on a high bank along the Potomac River called Ball's Bluff. The battle took place about 30 miles upriver from the capital and resulted in another humiliating defeat for the Union. Washingtonians were presented with evidence of this latest debacle when corpses of Federal soldiers started being pulled from the river as far south as Mount Vernon.

Although the sides were evenly matched in terms of numbers of combatants, ineptitude, and miscalculations on the part of Union commanders led to the resounding defeat. The lopsided tally of casualties was around 1,000 for the men in blue, and less than 200 for the Confederates.

Jake's commander, Col. W.H. Irwin, was proving himself dangerously unfit for command. The veteran of the Mexican War was a heavy drinker and given to rash behavior when under the influence. This was disturbingly showcased November 20, 1861, during the largest review of military power ever presented on the continent. It took place on an undulating plain between Munson's Hill and Bailey's Crossroads. The affair was something of a coming-out-party for the Army of the Potomac, which, since August 20, 1861, had been under McClellan's command. Although he proved lacking as a battlefield commander, he was a brilliant organizer. He is widely credited with transforming a higgledy-piggledy assortment of military units into a genuine army. Westbrook notes in his diary that the 49th PV spent considerable time practicing, "McClellan's light infantry drills." During the days prior to the big show smaller practice reviews were held. On October 26, Jake's regiment took part in one of the dry runs, which involved about 12,000 infantrymen, 600 cavalry troops and some 18 pieces of artillery.

With the Federals being shamed and bloodied at every turn, the president wanted to bolster morale and show the citizenry that the Union had an army worthy of the name. On the day of the Grand Review, he waived the requirement of having a military pass in order to venture into Virginia via the Long Bridge. The large number of carriages and pedestrians funneling onto the span resulted in an epic traffic jam. The number of civilians who successfully maneuvered through the bottleneck and saw the review is estimated to have ranged between 20,000 and 30,000. Military guards along the access routes made sure the throngs of travelers making the 8-mile trek didn't stray off the Leesburg Pike.

The soldiers who participated in the review were already on Virginia soil and avoided the crush of humanity at the bridge. On that brisk November morning those stationed the farthest from the parade grounds were on the march before 3 a.m. The 49th PV decamped at daybreak and arrived at Bailey's Crossroads around 10 a.m. The sky was clear, but a chilling wind buffeted the troops during the long wait for the dignitaries to arrive. Westbrook writes that McClellan and President Lincoln arrived at noon, escorted by 1,800 cavalrymen. When the assemblage was complete, seven divisions and more than 100 pieces of artillery were arranged in what a reporter for the New York Times termed, "a semicircle of about 4 miles." A historical marker on the site puts the number of military participants at about 50,000. McClellan claimed 65,000 marchers, and others put the count as high as 70,000.

Riding on horseback, it took Lincoln and McClellan more than an hour to inspect the troops before taking up positions in the reviewing stands to watch them march by in formation. The 49th PV marched with the third division past the reviewing stand. Irwin had been warding off the cold with nips of booze, and by early afternoon he was swaying in the saddle. For reasons known but to himself, as soon as the 49th PV passed the stands, he started drilling his men. The facing and flanking movements effectively stalled the following units, and abruptly brought the parade to a halt.

Hancock became incensed when he saw the cause of the disruption and spurred his horse into a gallop toward the inebriated colonel. Westbrook said the outraged general, "in very forcible language," had Irwin put under arrest. He was later court martialed for being, "so intoxicated as to be unable to perform the duties of a commander." He was sentenced to a loss of rank and pay for two months and confined to camp. It was a singular blemish on an otherwise splendid performance.

McClellan overlooked the matter in a letter to his wife, claiming the whole affair went off without a hitch and that he was, "completely satisfied and delighted beyond expression."

One of the civilians who witnessed the massive exhibition of power and pageantry was poet and social activist Julia Ward Howe. Either the anticipation of the display, or the actual event itself, inspired her to write, "The Battle Hymn of the Republic." Accounts vary as to exactly when she put her stirring words to the music of, "John Brown's Body." Some have her penning the words two days before the Grand Review, and others the morning after. What is generally agreed on is that she was in her room at the Willard Hotel in Washington when the verses came to her in a rush, and she hastily scribbled them down with a nub of pencil.

The men of the 49th PV, didn't come away from the affair either inspired or impressed. They were mortified by the disorder caused by their drunken commander. Westbrook wrote that after the incident the men, "turned and straggled back to camp." Embarrassment doesn't draw blood, but Irwin's irrational conduct forespoke of worse things to come. Not long after the review he roused the entire regiment in the middle of the night to ask their permission to take a leave of absence. That harebrained stunt cost the men sleep. Irwin's impetuous conduct during the Battle of Antietam the following September cost lives.

Chapter Four

By the first week in December 1861, Jake could roughly measure morning temperatures by the density of his breath clouds. With the cold came the instinctive urge to burrow in. Canvas tents, fortified with logs and found lumber, transformed the Union encampment into an orderly shantytown. Wooden signs at entrances to rude huts were inscribed with names such as, "Quaker Bridal Chamber," "Git up and Git," "Bower of Love," and "The Rose Cottage." On Christmas Day some of the men in G Company 49th PV distracted themselves from thoughts of home by planting cedar trees along pathways in their area.

Four days into the new year the hiss of sleet on cloth roofs had by evening given way to the silence of falling snow. When Jake left his hut the following morning to attend reveille the snow was 5 inches deep. For the rest of the month ice, sleet and snow alternated with periods of rain that turned the red soil into a quagmire. According to Westbrook's diary, much of the talk around campfires, centered on the number of officers resigning their commission and leaving for the comforts of home. Drilling and target practice kept the stalwart troops from going stir-crazy, and the issuance of new rifles and cold-weather items such as caps, mittens and overcoats helped lift flagging spirits.

During my Special Forces training I got a dose of what Jake and his buddies had to deal with during their first winter afield. My ordeal occurred in January 1968 during a two-week field training exercise in Pisgah National Forest in North Carolina. The FTX was the culmination of 15 weeks of communications training. Our class was divided into four-man teams, each of them tasked with communicating via Morse code with Fort Bragg nearly 300 miles away. It was an around-the-clock effort requiring hand cranking a portable generator that supplied the power needed to transmit and receive encrypted messages.

The most trying aspect of the exercise was descending and climbing out of the Linville Gorge. Dubbed the "Grand Canyon of Eastern USA," the deep ravine was carved by the Linville River. Steep, heavily forested walls present a difficult challenge for climbers, especially when shouldering heavy rucksacks. The day we hiked into the mountains we were bucking strong headwinds that turned a snowstorm into a blizzard. Our rucksacks were crammed with radio and camping equipment, as well as two-weeks rations. With snow falling as fast as the temperature I overheard a forest ranger comment to one of our instructors that we were the only people crazy enough to venture into the mountains in those conditions. The instructor said it would be better training if the conditions were worse.

The only concession made during the near whiteout conditions was not having to traverse the gorge. We were given map coordinates for where we were to set up individual camp sites, and away we went. Enough snow fell during the storm to effectively shut down the state of North Carolina. But the freezing cold was what made those two weeks memorable. We made a hut with our ponchos, shelter halves and tree branches. We also dug a fire pit, but despite our best efforts we couldn't keep a fire going.

The worst part was having to crawl out of our sleeping bags several times during the night to make scheduled commo checks with Fort Bragg. We knew we probably wouldn't be able to get through, because making commo in the mountains at night was dicey at best. We had to make the effort, because this was a graded exercise and if we flunked there were no second chances. The image that comes to mind when I think of that ordeal is being balled up in my sleeping bag, fully clothed, hands tucked between my legs, and shivering. I didn't suffer frostbite, but whenever I'm outside on a cold day my hands start to hurt within minutes.

When we trudged out of the mountains after a fortnight of suffering, we passed a Marine bivouac site filled with white, arctic tents. Gray smoke was rising from stovepipes sticking out of the tents' peaked roofs. The leathernecks milling about were wearing parkas, cold-weather mittens, and Mickey Mouse boots. We were wearing regular-issue field jackets with liners, gloves, boots, and bomber hats. The Marines were waiting for weather conditions to improve before commencing their cold weather training. Normally, such an encounter would be cause for good-natured catcalls and wry comments. This time the over-the-beach boys simply watched us pass, and never said a word. Neither did we.

The Pisgah exercise taught me how difficult and painful winter survival can be. I'm grateful for having had that experience because it gives me an idea of what Jake had to endure for months, rather than a few weeks. The wretched conditions he endured during that trying winter cost lives. On Sunday, February 2, 1862, some of the men in the regiment visited the camp graveyard. A cold wind was blowing as they walked between snow-sprinkled graves, pausing here and there to remember a lost friend.

Westbrook estimated the number of graves to be about 130. It's likely all the dead perished without firing a shot at the enemy.

After months of drills, dress parades and bayonet and target practice the Federal troops were eager to get on with the job of preserving the Union. During the time spent in winter camp, McClellan and his staff had come up with a battle plan they felt would win the war. The undertaking involved shipping the Army of the Potomac down the Potomac River, out into Chesapeake Bay and southward to the Virginia Peninsula. The troops would then march in a northwesterly direction with the goal of capturing the Confederate capital of Richmond and bringing the war to a victorious conclusion.

The plan avoided throwing inexperienced troops against strong Confederate defenses outside Washington. However, the end run around Rebel forces required a massive logistical effort. Nearly 400 vessels of various types and seaworthiness were used to transport 121,500 Federal troops from Alexandria, Virginia, to Fort Monroe, a distance of 200 miles. Several weeks were needed for the motley flotilla to transport men, 74 ambulances, 44 artillery batteries, more than 1,100 supply wagons and nearly 15,000 animals to their destination.

On March 23, 1862, Jake and his mates left their winter camp and marched to Alexandria where they boarded the steamer North America. The entire regiment, as well as elements of the 43rd New York, were shoehorned onto the ship. The boys in blue were so eager to fight that a brawl involving the two outfits erupted in the engine room the first night. Hard feelings didn't last long. When the New Yorkers disembarked the following morning, they marched away to the song, "Bully for You," performed by the 49th PV Regimental Band.

That morning the steamer's engine room was bustling with a different kind of activity than the night before. Sweating men, stripped to the waist, shovel-fed coal to the boiler fire. When the steamer left the dock around 10 a.m., Jake likely found a place along the crowded deck rail to watch Fort Washington, Mount Vernon and other shoreline sights appear and fade in the distance. By early evening the ship had successfully navigated the Potomac River and was cutting through the waves of Chesapeake Bay. As a full moon rose into the dark sky a man in Jake's company, A. P. Decker, mistook it for a distant lighthouse. He was made aware of his mistake by an officer who overheard the comment. After that, whenever a full moon appeared, the young soldier was sure to hear someone exclaim, "Decker, there's your lighthouse."

Decker and the others saw a real lighthouse when they reached Fort Monroe around dawn on March 25. The Old Point Comfort Light has been in service from at least 1775 and continues to *serve* as a navigational aid. The men were eager to disembark and were trooping down the gangplank by 7:30 a.m. and assembling by companies on the wharf. I had been transported to war in July-August 1965 on the troopship USS Geiger. It was loaded to the gunwales with men, equipment and even a couple of carefully wrapped Huey helicopters. We were looking forward to sampling the great Navy chow we had often heard about.

Sadly, the cooks aboard the Geiger weren't interested in upholding their end of the Navy's culinary reputation. We were fed in shifts, ate standing up, and rested our trays on long, rimmed tables. The rims were there to keep trays from sliding off when the ship was pitching and rolling in rough seas. What salad greens we got were wilted and nearly spoiled. It seemed like every other meal during the 17-day voyage consisted of beans and frankfurters. The food was so bad that it was actually a relief to eat cold C-rations after we got ashore.

The morning we were preparing to make our landing at Qui Nhon, South Vietnam, we observed an airstrike in the distance. Flashes of red from exploding bombs were followed by gray smoke rising above the green jungle. As I watched my first act of war, I loaded bullets into magazines for my M-14 rifle. It wasn't lost on me that those bullets would be directed at humans, rather than cardboard targets on a rifle range. Later, as I clambered down the rope netting to the landing craft, I thought about Uncle Al, who had done the same numerous times while serving with the 2nd Marine Division during World War II.

Instead of being greeted by enemy fire during our beach landing, we were met by children hawking soft drinks. That should have tipped me off that this was going to be a war like no other. A few years later when I was home from Vietnam on extension leave, Al and I enjoyed three days together aboard his plain-as-paste houseboat. We spent most of the time inside the cracker-box shanty he had cobbled together, drinking beer, whiskey and filling an old, sand-filled hubcap with cigar and cigarette butts. With the faint sound of the Mississippi River lapping against the aluminum pontoons, we talked of war.

Al had never spoke about the war before, and at a young age I was told not to ask him about it. All we knew about his exploits came to us from people he had served with. That's how we knew he had been put in for the Congressional Medal of Honor, but all the witnesses to what he had done were killed before they could be officially interviewed. Al said he could talk about the war with me because I would understand.

I told Al about my beach landing. Deep into the second day he got around to telling me about his experiences on a small atoll in the central Pacific called Tarawa. He said by the afternoon of the first day of battle the water was blood red from the beach to the coral reef several hundred yards offshore. I said, "You mean there was blood in the water."

"No," he answered. "The water was blood red." Years later I was watching the Johnny Carson Show when his guest, Eddie Albert, said almost the exact thing. He had been there with the Navy, serving as a coxswain of a landing craft. During the battle the Marines fought nonstop for 76 hours until nearly all the Japanese defenders had been killed. The beach I crossed into war had been as peaceful as a summertime visit to the lake.

As the 49th PV marched to Hampton, Virginia, they also waltzed into war without a shot being fired. The small port town, once as lovely as any in the South, had been reduced to charred ruins by Confederate soldiers. It had been put to the torch on the night of August 7, 1861, to keep it from being any use to the hated Yankees. The arsonists did a thorough job of it, leaving only blackened chimneys and the scorched brick walls of St. John's Church standing. The needless act was fueled by emotions as wild and uncontrolled as the conflagration that consumed hundreds of homes and businesses.

Westbrook used two words to describe the aged, colonial town he and the others marched through. "Totally wrecked."

Later that afternoon, with the grim ruins behind them, the regiment moved into a field near the mouth of a small river. As they started setting up camp for the night a soldier flushed a rabbit from its nest and the chase was on. Westbrook noted that the sight of 1,000 men in joyous pursuit of the hare was something few who witnessed the event would forget. The lighthearted romp proved to be a final whirl before the reality of hard war set in. As the vast Army of the Potomac flooded onto the peninsula like an unstoppable sea of blue, the men felt certain of victory. Pvt. Warren Lee Goss spoke of it to a Southern woman watching the legions of Union soldiers invading her homeland. He told her he was certain they would have little trouble marching into

Richmond. Years later, while writing his memoirs, he remembered her prophetic words.

> "No," the woman said with stern assurance. "You all will drink hot blood before you all get thar."

For two days the men rested before resuming their westward march toward Newport News. In the early afternoon the point element clashed with the advance guard of a Rebel cavalry unit. Gunfire was exchanged and as the skirmishers retreated, the regiment formed battle lines and began advancing across an open field. On the far side of the clearing, they came to a swampy area about 70 yards wide. Members of the 43rd New York enthusiastically charged into the bog, immediately sinking to their waists in mud and green pond scum. Soldiers in the 49th found this hilarious, but Hancock failed to see the humor. From horseback he addressed the floundering soldiers. "What the hell are you doing?" he questioned. One of the New Yorkers replied, "Hunting my boots, General."

Things remained quiet until the last day in March when a Rebel gunboat in waters off Newport News fired several shells into the area where the 49th was camped. Westbrook was amused by the various postures the inexperienced soldiers assumed when fired upon. "Some would fall flat, others on their hands and feet and others on their heads with their feet in the air," Westbrook wrote. "The boys are very green as was demonstrated today when the boys ran back into the woods and picked up cannonballs, not aware whether they were shells or solid shot."

After our arrival at An Khe in August 1965, mortar and rocket attacks became a nightly occurrence. Initially, a mortar round exploding on the far side of the sprawling camp could make us run for cover. It didn't take long for us to learn when incoming rounds were too distant to do any harm.

These harassing attacks usually occurred at night, but there were exceptions. One afternoon three of us were in an open area when we were startled by the nearby flash and boom of an exploding mortar shell. Anticipating more on the way we squirmed into a drainage pipe beneath the road we were on. A few days later I returned to the culvert to demonstrate how we had wormed our way into the narrow tube. It took considerable effort for me to squeeze my shoulders into the opening, much less my entire body.

That event taught me that humans are capable of extraordinary feats and contortions when trying to save their hides. Individuals engaged in close combat have an intensity of manner and movement that's unmistakable. After the Vietnam War ended and documentaries began appearing on television, I noticed that quite a bit of the so-called combat footage had obviously been staged. I guess I was surprised, but I shouldn't have been considering I had seen a staged firefight one afternoon at An Khe. Our PX [post exchange] at the time was a metal shipping container next to the 7th Cav's area. A bunch of us were standing in line to buy candy bars and cigarettes when we were approached by a camera crew working for a major television network. A member of the crew asked us if we wanted to be on the evening news back home. We were all up for that, expecting to be filmed then and there. But what they wanted to do was take some of us to the nearby perimeter and get footage of us pretending to be in a firefight. Most of us scoffed at the idea of faking something like that, but a few of the guys went along with it. A little later we heard firing from the area they had headed toward.

Civil War photographers posed corpses on the battlefield in order to produce more dramatic pictures. When one knows what to look for it's easy to discern fake combat imagery from the real thing.

Thinking about where the cameraman is positioned when filming is probably the best way to discern what is real. I've seen footage where the cameraman was in front of an infantry platoon supposedly on a combat patrol. There's no way he would have been allowed to be ahead of the point man if there had been any chance of encountering the enemy.

There certainly weren't any photographers in front of Jake's outfit when brief, sporadic gunfights and shell explosions started occurring with increasing frequency. Minutes, perhaps hours, of quiet would suddenly be shattered by a thunderous airburst or volley of musket fire. When a Confederate shell exploding at treetop level killed a soldier from Maine, his mangled corpse provided a stark image of horrors to come.

From the outset, the ambitious military campaign to end the war was slowed by rain, hail, snow, and swampy terrain. Flanked on the south by the James River and on the north by the York, the Virginia Peninsula is 50-miles-long and 15 miles across at its widest point. Much of it consisted of dense swampland swarming with fleas, mosquitoes, and venomous snakes. During my Special Forces training I learned that swamps offer unique challenges. Moving through dark, brackish water is slow and treacherous. One can be slogging through waist-deep water one moment and swimming the next.

At this early juncture of the war the Army of the Potomac was hamstrung by incompetent, inexperienced officers. Union soldiers doing the fighting never lacked courage or toughness but suffered terribly because of men unfit for command. This was certainly true for the men of the 49th PV, whose commander, by any measure, was inept. A case in point took place on April 7, when the regiment was directed to set up camp in a marshy area. Irwin had been on the wrong side of his commander, Brig. Gen. Hancock since his drunken behavior during the Grand Review the previous autumn. When Hancock saw the flustered and increasingly angry men sloshing about while trying to set up a semblance of a camp he rode up to Irwin.

"Colonel, what the hell's the matter?" Hancock bellowed. "Oh, it's the bad state of the ground," Irwin replied.

"Bad hell," Hancock snorted. "It's the bad luck of the regiment. Will I have to be general, colonel, captain, sergeant, and corporal?"

T. A. McFarland with Company D offered a sharp retort. "We don't care a damn, only so you let us camp." The men then gave the popular general three cheers, which likely served to reduce the tension. McFarland's outburst, at least in part, was probably brought on by hunger pangs. The campaign was just getting under way and already the Federal troops were going without food. The culprit was mud. Long lines of grim-splattered wagons, tilting this way and that, stood still as statues in the mire. Westbrook reported that some of the men were paying a nickel for a single, "hard as a stone," hardtack biscuit. He added that the hunger-plagued men were shooting any hapless animal wandering into their gun sights.

Mud has caused armies to flounder throughout history, and the accursed sludge has grown increasingly problematic with the advance of technology. Ancient foot soldiers might have lost a sandal in the goo, but heavy artillery pieces, trucks and armored vehicles have been held hostage by it. During recon missions in Laos and North Vietnam we were instructed to bring back soil samples. When I asked why, I was told the samples were used to develop chemicals that would create a slippery form of mud that would render roads impassable along the Ho Chi Minh Trail. I've since learned about Operation Popeye, which was a cloud seeding operation conducted during the Vietnam War. The aim was to induce greater mud-creating rainfall over the extensive network of roads into South Vietnam we called the root structure. According to accounts it met with some success.

The food situation for Jake and the others improved markedly on April 9th, when the famished Yankees commandeered 70 head of cattle left behind by retreating Rebels. The meat provided the men with needed energy for the exhausting work of building corduroy roads through the muddy expanses. This required felling trees and placing the logs sideways on the roads for wagons to travel on. Food was precious to the soldiers, but many of them were wasteful and undisciplined when it came to clothing and equipment.

While marching toward Yorktown on a particularly hot day many of the men cast aside what they considered nonessentials. By midday the route of march had taken on the appearance of an outdoor rummage sale with coats, pants, shirts, and blankets littering the ground and draped over bushes and tree limbs. If a soldier spotted an article of discarded clothing in better condition than what he was wearing he made an exchange. Such disregard for issued clothing was unthinkable in the Army units I served with. That said, many of the guys didn't bother to bring their field jackets with them when we shipped out in the summer of 1965. The thinking was that they wouldn't be necessary in the tropics of Southeast Asia. How wrong they were was driven home during the rainy season when it sometimes felt cold enough to snow.

I packed my field jacket but made an error of omission that caused me no small amount of discomfort during my first year of war. While still in the States I discovered that my air mattress had a slow leak and would lose its firmness during the night. Laziness kept me from making a trip to supply to trade it in for a new one. I stupidly didn't factor in the certainty that the minor leak would get worse.

Once in country I was never able to get another air mattress. Consequently, after an hour or so of comfort I would spend the rest of the night sleeping on ground as hard as the lesson that mistake taught me.

Jake didn't have the luxury of an air mattress, but that was a minor inconvenience compared to some of the things he and the other enlistment men had to deal with. Despite being in the field, working on improving roads and pursuing the enemy, at every opportunity their officers were ordering them out for dress parades. During the first few months after arriving at An Khe we spent our days standing guard, filling sandbags, building bunkers, digging foxholes, and clearing the huge field, dubbed the Golf Course, where our helicopters were stabled. We worked from sunup to sundown, but thankfully never had a parade.

No one enjoyed a parade more than McClellan. The men loved, "Little Mac," but he was a logistician, not a hard-driving battlefield commander like Gen. Ulysses S. Grant was proving himself to be. The peninsula quickly revealed two of McClellan's most pronounced shortcomings: a cautious nature and tendency to grossly overestimate the strength of the enemy. This latter fault led him to estimate Confederate strength on the peninsula as 100,000 men when, in reality, there were less than half that number. President Lincoln urged McClellan to, "Break the enemy's line from Yorktown to Warwick River at once," but the strong suggestion was ignored. Instead of smashing through the Rebel stronghold at Yorktown and maintaining forward momentum, McClellan placed it under siege. This brought the formidable Army of the Potomac to a standstill.

The *New York Herald* newspaper termed McClellan the "Napoleon of the present war," but the comparison was far off the mark. One of the few things McClellan shared with the Corsican was devoted soldiers. McClellan largely won the affection of his men by seeing to their wellbeing. Before the Peninsula Campaign was launched, he stated that he wasn't about to, "throw these raw men of mine into the teeth of artillery and entrenchments if it is possible to avoid it." He won additional favor from his troops when he told them, "I am to watch over you as a parent over his children," and he meant it. Such a promise is commendable, but it often led to hesitation and inactivity, which in war can be as deadly as a bullet.

By mid-April the Federal troops were within a few miles of Yorktown. It appeared to be the very picture of bristling artillery and entrenchments that McClellan said he wouldn't charge his men into. He ordered artillery to commence hammering the enemy works, and after dark on April 16 every enlisted man in the 49th carried a sandbag weighing about 100 pounds to within 300 yards of the Rebel lines. The sandbags were used to create a protective barrier, behind which men could work with picks and shovels in relative safety as they created their own fortress.

McClellan's belief that he was facing a much larger force than actually existed was partly due to a clever ruse orchestrated by Maj. Gen. John Bankhead "Prince John" Magruder. The imaginative general had only about 10,000 men manning the fortifications around Yorktown. Nonetheless, he had to stall the Yankees long enough for Gen. Joseph E. Johnston and his army to bolster the defenses around Richmond. Magruder's creative jugglery in deceiving the Yankees at Yorktown ranks high in the annals of Civil War chicanery.

Magruder's plan involved an opening in a grove of trees bordering a road he knew was kept under constant observation. From early morning until late afternoon, he had the same file of men continuously march through the clearing, creating the illusion that thousands of soldiers were moving into position. He also had his cannoneers aggressively blazing away at anything resembling a target.

McClellan was completely taken in by Magruder's deception, which convinced him that placing the town under siege was the right thing to do. When the hard-working Union troops finished building earthworks, they lined them with sharpened wooden spikes facing the enemy. The Rebels sat back and watched their foes laboring needlessly on defenses they knew would never be tested.

The Southern boys had something else to watch and shoot at - observation balloons. Soon after the outbreak of war in the spring of 1861, manned, gas-filled balloons started appearing in the skies in and around the nation's capital. Thaddeus S. C. Lowe, one of the most skilled balloonists of the day, convinced President Lincoln of their wartime potential by giving him a demonstration on June 16, 1861. The balloons were an ideal way to scout enemy positions, monitor troop movements, direct artillery, and accurately map unfamiliar areas. A number of balloonists vied for the position of Chief Aeronaut of the Army of the Potomac. Lowe got the job and went to work claiming control of the skies.

Born in Jefferson Mills, New Hampshire, Aug. 20, 1832, the enterprising aeronaut had to overcome a number of challenges in order to transform the new unit into a viable force. Humans had been traveling aloft in balloons since the late 18th century, but with few exceptions they hadn't been used for military purposes. Lowe realized that war balloons needed to be stronger than civilian models and easily transportable. This was also true for the equipment needed to produce the hydrogen gas that provided the necessary lift for the balloons. Lowe met the first challenge by using India silk and cotton cording in the construction of seven military-grade balloons in his Philadelphia workshop. He also concocted a varnish that when applied to the skin of the balloons made them virtually leak proof. But it was his brilliant design for a transportable hydrogen gas generator that was perhaps his greatest contribution in getting the new air force off the ground.

The generators were constructed at the Washington Navy Yard by skilled joiners working with tanks and copper tubing. Two generators were built for each balloon, and because of their complexity it was months before they were ready for use. Three of the seven balloons were small so they could be quickly inflated and were ideally suited for windy conditions. The four larger balloons could carry heavier payloads such as telegraph equipment, and as many as five men. They also had the ability to soar to heights of 1,000 feet while tethered to the ground by ropes and cables.

Lowe favored the tethered method, called captive flight, rather than free flight where the balloon travels at the whims of the wind. During a free flight early in the war he had come down behind enemy lines. As he awaited rescue, he had plenty of time to ponder the advantages of being quickly reeled back down to a friendly liftoff point. His future wartime balloon ascents were of the tethered variety.

McClellan recognized the wartime potential balloons offered and included them in his battle plan for the Peninsula Campaign. Transporting balloons and generators to the war zone necessitated the creation of the first aircraft carrier. This honor was bestowed on the USS *George Washington Parke Custis*, which served as a lowly coal barge before being converted into the country's first flattop. On March 28, 1862, it docked at Hampton with Lowe, his handpicked assistants, three balloons and the necessary inflation wagons. Two small balloons, the *Constitution*, and the *Washington*, were offloaded as well as a large balloon named the Intrepid. The latter was Lowe's flagship and the balloon he most liked to operate.

The balloons, baskets and sundry equipment were loaded onto four army wagons, and with two inflations wagons in tow, the caravan headed north toward Yorktown. On April 5, having been guarded by soldiers with the 13th New York, the balloonists and their equipment arrived safely a few miles outside Yorktown. The next day the first balloon ascent was made, followed by many others. A platoon consisting of about 30 men was quickly trained to assist the aeronauts. There was no difficulty in finding men eager to experience lighter-than-air flight. The initial enthusiasm dropped off considerably after Brig. Gen. Fitz John Porter went on an unscheduled free flight the morning of April 11, 1862.

Porter was the commander of III Corps. He made several trips aloft with Lowe, and that morning he decided to take the Intrepid up on his own. The balloon staging area was about 50 yards from the 49th PV's campgrounds, giving Jake a front row seat for the drama that followed.

Accounts vary widely as to Porter's actions and demeanor during the unplanned flight, but the gist of it is somewhat consistent.

Arriving at the balloon staging area around 5 a.m., Porter woke the ground crew and ordered them to unfasten all but one tether line secured to a large tree. The sky was beginning to lighten in the east as he climbed into the wicker basket and instructed the groggy crew to send him skyward. During the ascent the tether rope snapped, and the general was on his way. It was later determined that the rope broke because acid used to make hydrogen gas had been spilled on it. Whether this was an accident, or an intentional act of sabotage was never resolved.

Robert Knox Sneden, a Union private with the 40th New York, provided an account in his diary for why the rope separated. He wrote that a disgruntled sergeant from the 50th New York Engineer Regiment had a run-in with a captain who usually took the balloon up first thing in the morning. The two had exchanged words the previous evening, after which the fuming noncom decided to give the officer unfettered freedom of flight the following day. To ensure the rope broke when the balloon reached its usual altitude of a few hundred feet he doused it with acid he procured from the inflation wagon.

Porter's immediate concern wasn't why the balloon was suddenly on a wayward flight path, but that it was rapidly gaining altitude and heading toward Rebel lines. Jake was used to seeing balloons reach a predictable height and staying there. When the rope snapped, "like the explosion of a shell," as one witness described it, eyes were directed skyward. Some observers pointed out the obvious with shouts of, "the balloon is loose," while others scrambled to find the best location from which to watch the unfolding spectacle.

The moment Lowe learned of the mishap he mounted the nearest cavalry horse and took off after the floating orb. The balloonist enunciated each word as he shouted advice to the general.

"Open the valve," Lowe yelled repeatedly. "Climb to the netting and reach the valve rope." Either Porter didn't hear the shouted instructions or deemed them too risky. Whatever the reason, he didn't act upon the expert advice and continued to drift toward disaster. Lowe wisely curtailed his headlong pursuit when the balloon entered air space over no-man's land.

I can sympathize with Porter. While attending Jump School during the summer of 1967, I was in the second phase of training called Tower Week. It included descending by parachute from the top of a 250-foot tower. The first guy in our class to make the trip up had a gust of wind blow the open canopy of the T-10 parachute back into the tower's steel framing where it became entangled. For nearly an hour we watched heroic instructors high above the ground successfully rescue the hapless trainee.

Soon after the shaken trooper was safely on the ground it was my turn to go up. When the metal hoop the chute is fastened to reached the 240-foot level it jerked to a stop causing me to swing back and forth. An instructor far below instructed me by megaphone to pull down on the parachute's two front risers to ensure I drifted away from the tower. Fine.

The next thing I heard was the terrifying whirl of the cable drawing me up the final 10 feet, followed by the metallic click of the chute releasing from the holding hoop. I swear, from that moment on I didn't hear another word, so I continued to hold the front slip. I didn't let up on it as I drifted over the soft-landing area, then a wide grassy field and finally a paved street. I was still holding the front slip when I landed next to a dipsty dumpster outside the brick barracks housing students attending Officer Candidate School. Before I could get to my feet the instructor was screaming in my face.

"I kept telling you to let up, let up," he yelled. He then said something about having never seen a student travel that distance. I don't remember rigger rolling the chute or running back to the tower. All I cared about was being on the ground and not hanging from a steel girder.

Porter was doing some traveling of his own that April morning. By the time the balloon drifted within rifle range of the Yorktown defenders it was losing altitude. With Rebel bullets whistling through the air and thwacking into the gondola, Porter started jettisoning sandbags attached to the balloon for ballast. His frantic effort resulted in the balloon quickly ascending to about 2,000 feet where it entered an air current that began pushing it back toward friendly lines. The general's relief was short-lived when he realized the balloon's drift and descent would likely put him down in the middle of the James River. This watery possibility motivated him to follow Lowe's earlier suggestions.

Thousands of Union and Confederate soldiers, transfixed by the exciting air show, watched Porter climb out of the basket and make a grab for the valve line. He secured the draw cord but yanked it so forcefully that he lost his balance, toppling back into the basket. The valve was now wide open. Lowe penned the following observations.

> "The general in his eagerness to come to the ground had opened the valve until all the gas escaped," Lowe explained. "The balloon was constantly falling but the silk was kept extended and presented so large a surface to the atmosphere that it served the purpose of a parachute, and consequently the descent was not rapid enough to be dangerous."

Porter likely had a different view of the situation. He certainly had had enough of free flight and being once again over friendly territory he looked for a way out. His exit strategy is an indication of his desperation. When the basket neared the upper boughs of a large tree the full-bearded officer took a leap of faith. After crashing through spindly branches at the top of the tree, he managed to secure a weight-bearing limb. Rescuers reportedly found Porter, "in an exhausted condition," with only a damaged ego. After the incident Lowe noticed a reduction in the number of officers jostling for a place in the basket.

While serving with SOG I was forced to perform some aerobatics of my own high above the Laotian jungle. Oftentimes, because of mountainous terrain and triple-canopy jungle, extraction helicopters weren't able to get near enough to the ground for us to jump aboard. Initially, the answer was the McGuire Rig, invented by Special Forces Sgt. Maj., Charles McGuire.

This no-frill solution was a lightly padded canvas sling you sat in, and a wrist strap located toward the top of the rig through which the rider placed the left hand. The purpose of the lone safety feature was to keep the person from falling from the sling. One end of a 120-foot-long nylon rope was tied to the top of the rig, and the other end fastened through metal floor rings of a Huey helicopter.

Attached to the bottom of the sling was a heavy sandbag that broke through small branches and foliage on the way to the ground. The bags usually split open on impact with the ground, but if not, they were cut free.

Speeding through the air at the end of a rope thousands of feet above the ground made even practice flights unnerving. Get pulled out on strings, as we called it, while under fire, and being lifted up through a latticework of branches was memorable. Such madness was acceptable because the alternative was near certain death or capture.

My assistant team leader, Jerry Plank, and I once came out of a target via Swiss Seats we fashioned with rope we carried for that purpose. Normally Swiss Seats are used as a makeshift harness for rappelling. In this case a large number of NVA were assaulting our position, and the four of us remaining on the ground had to get pulled out by one helicopter. Problem was, there were four of us and two McGuire Rigs. We put the two remaining little people in the McGuire Rigs, and using snap links secured our Swiss Seats to the extraction ropes. The duration of the flight, coupled with heavy rucksacks, web gear and powerful slipstream made the trip torturous. I didn't suffer as much as Jerry. When we set down at the launch site, he wasn't able to get to his feet for several minutes. Later, back in our hooch, he showed me the puffy red welts on his inner thighs that were oozing blood.

Bill Brown was my assistant team leader on the mission that nearly ended with me falling to my death. We had been in heavy contact with NVA until an airstrike bought us time for an extraction. I sent four of my little people out on McGuire Rigs with the first Huey. Bill, I and two remaining Nungs were extracted by a second Huey. We hadn't cleared the trees when I saw NVA overrunning our position. It had been a close call, but the chills and thrills weren't done.

As the chopper gained altitude and speed, we trailed out behind it like the tail of a kite. Our sweat-soaked fatigues snapped and popped in the rushing air that got colder as we gained altitude. To keep from slamming into each other in the swirling airflow we'd link arms. Three of us had done that, but Brownie was swinging free in his own orbit. Every minute or so he'd smack into us before spinning away. I yelled at him to grab one of our rigs the next time around. When he attempted to do that, he grabbed my right arm and yanked me backward out of the canvas loop. The wrist strap saved my life, but the sling ended up under the backside of my knees. The heavy rucksack on my back, as well as the weight of my web gear, kept me from being able to reposition myself in the sling. For the rest of the flight back to the launch site I dangled, trapeze-style, from the sling.

Shortly after that incident we were issued the recently invented STABO rig. Thankfully, the McGuire Rig was retired to its place in history. It had saved lives, but the STABO rig was vastly superior. Special Forces soldier, Clifford L. Roberts, is said to have drawn out on a paper napkin a rough sketch of the design for the STABO rig after learning of the death of a wounded S. F. trooper who had fallen from a McGuire Rig during an extraction. Maj. Robert Stevens and Capt. John Knabb are also credited for contributing to the design, testing, and implementation of the system.

The STABO rig we were issued in 1969 was basically a parachute harness worn in place of our regular web gear harness. The leg straps were fastened up in the back until it was time for extraction. Ropes would be dropped from the helicopter just as before, but an inverted "Y" rope design allowed us to snap into metal D rings sewn into the top of the shoulder webbing. The new rig would have made my aerial predicament impossible. And it allowed us to have both hands free to push away branches and fire our weapon simultaneously. The basic concept is used today.

War's incessant call for innovations naturally produces countermeasures to combat them. On April 13, 1862, the Confederates sent up an observation balloon of its own at Yorktown. Capt. John Bryan had directed the building of a hot-air balloon out of dress silk painted with varnish. It was inflated by placing the opening of the envelop over a fire fueled by turpentine and pine wood. The hot-air technique was used because the Confederates lacked the ability to make hydrogen gas in the field. This meant their hot-air balloon couldn't stay aloft for much more than 30 minutes. Although a second balloon was made, the program fizzled largely because they couldn't be moved quickly from place to place. The Union's Balloon Corps didn't survive the war either. Military leaders, for the most part, viewed the daring balloonists as carnival showmen. And because the aeronauts were civilians they could be executed as spies if captured. By the late summer of 1863 Federal balloonists had ceased operations.

On April 16, 1862, Union soldiers fortifying positions outside Yorktown observed another rousing sight in the sky. A bald eagle appeared out of the blue and began describing "elegant circles" above their heads. The Yankees cheered and waved their hats, largely ignoring the harassing gunfire that had been plaguing them for days. Many felt the impromptu visit by the national symbol was an affirmation of their righteous cause. After the eagle departed, they returned to their difficult work with a renewed vigor and purpose.

Uplifted spirits notwithstanding, Jake and his fellow soldiers chafed at having been transformed from soldiers into common laborers. They were also forced to contend with their commander's bizarre behavior. During the night of April 18, the sound of "heavy musketry" rose above the hiss of rain on tent canvas. The shooting was along the Rebel's defensive Warwick Line stretching 12 miles across the peninsula from Yorktown to the Warwick River.

Irwin didn't give a moment's thought to the unlikelihood of the Rebels launching a night attack during a rainstorm. He scrambled the entire regiment from their tents and ran them some distance along a road in the general direction of the shooting. When the shadow-shooting sputtered out, the needlessly soaked and winded men were marched back to the bivouac area.

No sooner had Jake gotten settling back in, then Irwin again turned out the regiment. This time he ran them to Gen. Hancock's headquarters. As Irwin approached the general's tent the entrance flap was thrown back and Hancock steps into the downpour. Irwin spoke first.

"General, I have run the Forty-ninth out left in front, so that you will have the regiment handy," he said.

"Damn you, Colonel," Westbrook reported Hancock shouting. "Run the Forty-ninth back right in front and stay there until you receive orders to come." The diarist added that he and the others were, "delighted at the set-back the colonel received, considering it as some little recompense for our trip." Although tickled, they had to "laugh in our sleeves" when out of earshot of officers.

Up to that point the 49th PV hadn't suffered any combat deaths, but that ended the morning of April 28. During the night Confederate sharpshooters crept through a wooded area to a position near where the 49th PV was on picket duty. Around 8 a.m., Cpl. William Walker of Company A was killed instantly by a Rebel bullet striking him in the head. A brief exchange of gunfire followed, slightly wounding a few more Federals.

Union troops were slow to react, and it wasn't until 10 a.m., that men with the 6th Maine headed into the trees where the fatal shot came from. This triggered an immediate response from the concealed Rebels, and the woods exploded with the roar of heavy gunfire. For an hour the combatants mostly shot bark from trees and sent twigs and leaves fluttering to the ground. It was only when a soldier with the 43" New York was fatally shot in the head that the stalemate ended. Outraged by the death of their friend, a number of men spontaneously rose to their feet and charged the Rebels. Within minutes the Rebels were driven back to their rifle pits where vicious hand-to-hand fighting ensued. When the melee ended, upward of 20 Confederates laid dead or wounded.

The killing of Cpl. Walker might have been a retaliatory act. A few days before, an elite unit of Union marksmen wearing distinctive green coats and hats moved into the front lines with the 49th PV. Soon after, Confederate troops, especially artillerymen thinking themselves out of range of Federal rifles, started being toppled by well-aimed bullets. Col. Hiram Berdan's riflemen were making their arrival known with bloody efficiency. As the war progressed, the men of the 1st and 2nd United

States Sharpshooters regiments became legendary for their shooting accuracy at unprecedented distances.

They routinely killed men at 400 to 800 yards. Their longest confirmed kill was 1,200 yards. Southern soldiers who fancied themselves superior to Yankees, grudgingly admitted that Berdan's men were their equals.

Years before the start of the war, Berdan was widely considered "the best marksman in America." A mechanical engineer and inventor, the native New Yorker had made his mark, and fortune, by inventing among other things a repeating rifle and an improved method with which to separate gold from ore.

At the outbreak of the Civil War, Berdan came up with the idea to create a unit made up exclusively of the best crack shots in the Union. Their business would be shooting high-value targets such as officers and artillerymen. Berdan used his influence in Washington to wrangle an audience with Lincoln in order to present his idea. The president, a superb shot himself, quickly grasped the potential of such a unit. He gave Berdan the OK to create companies of 100 men from each of the loyal states.

The recruitment drive began in the spring of 1861. Posters announcing the formation of the unit, qualifications and incentives were tacked to fence posts, trees, and wooden buildings throughout the north. "RIFLEMEN, ATTENTION!" topped the placards. Below the bold lettering was printed information such as a $22 bounty when mustered into the unit and $100 bonus at the end of the war. The dollar signs caught the eye, but the requirements made average shooters shrug and walk away knowing they didn't have a prayer of pocketing the money.

A poster circulated in Maine during the summer of 1861 stated the following. "No man will be accepted or mustered into service who is not an active and able-bodied man, and who cannot when firing at a rest at a distance of two hundred yards, put ten consecutive shots into a target the average distance not to exceed five inches from the centre of the bullseye to the centre of the ball. All candidates will have to pass such an examination as to satisfy the recruiting officer of their fitness for enlistment in this corps."

Not all the states could find enough marksmen to meet the 100-man benchmark. States such as Michigan and New York had more than enough, and ultimately 18 companies were formed. During the fall and winter of 1861-62 throngs of civilians visited Camp of Instruction in Washington D.C. where the marksmen honed their military and shooting skills. Nearly every day the men put on shooting demonstrations for visitors who marveled at their ability to hit distant targets with apparent ease. Lincoln took a personal interest in the regiments and was often spotted among the spectators.

Berdan had no military experience, but he wisely filled the regiments with competent officers. And he strived to make his men better shots as well as exemplary soldiers. While serving with the 1st Special Forces Group on Okinawa the A-team I was on practiced what we called "point and shoot." We started with coffee can lids being thrown into the air 15 or 20 feet away. When we could consistently hit the lid, we tossed smaller targets until we ended up shooting poker chips. We missed more than we hit, but we did hit them.

Berdan's sharpshooters were taught how to take advantage of existing cover, and how not to expose themselves needlessly. Their flock coats and kepi caps were colored green, "to blend in with the foliage and trees during the leafy season." Their buttons were made from Goodyear rubber so as not to reflect sunlight. It's widely believed that this was the first time in American military history that a uniform was designed for the purpose of concealment.

Also drilled into the men was the importance of fire discipline, and to shoot only when a target presented itself. Jake could likely load and fire his single-shot musket a few times a minute. The M-16 rifle I was issued when serving with the 1st Cav. could fire semi and full automatic. Automatic fire is generally inaccurate and wastes ammo. Members of my recon team were taught to fire their first magazine on full automatic during initial contact with the enemy in order to momentarily gain fire superiority. After that we fired only single, aimed shots at NVA we could see or muzzle flashes.

Conserving ammo by making every shot count was important

because it often took an hour or more to get air support and extraction ships out to us. I carried 35, 20-round magazines for my CAR-15, but loaded each with 18 rounds to help prevent jamming. Because we were often assaulted by large numbers of NVA, we did a lot of shooting. I came out of one target with two rounds left in my last magazine.

Elite units need something that will identify them as such. In addition to their green uniforms, Berdan's men took to wearing a black ostrich feather in their forage caps. Special Forces have the green beret. Those of us authorized to wear the Special Forces shoulder tab and green beret with full flash—the shield-shaped embroidered cloth insignia signifying by color the group one is serving with and identifies the wearer as a qualified SF soldier—knows of its symbolic power. In October 1961 President John F. Kennedy agreed with Special Warfare Center commander, Brig. Gen. William P. Yarborough, that qualified members of the U.S. Army Special Forces should be allowed to wear the green beret as an official part of their uniform.

Years prior to the president's endorsement of the distinctive headgear, men with the 10th Special Forces Group in Germany had taken to wearing green berets when in the field. This practice was adopted among SF men stationed at Fort Bragg, the home of SF. Because the president interceded on our behalf the Army reluctantly approved our wearing of the rifle green, army shade 297, headpiece. In a message to SF personnel Kennedy entreated us to, "Wear the beret proudly, it will be a mark of distinction and a badge of courage in the difficult days ahead."

The green beret's strength is in its' symbolism. It takes a lot to earn one, and much more to deserve it. As headgear, it's basically worthless. It can be uncomfortably hot, doesn't shield one's eyes from the sun, soaks up water like a sponge and takes forever to dry. And yet, I was willing to endure anything, including death, for the privilege of wearing one. The proudest day of my life was Feb. 26, 1968, when I graduated from Special Forces Training Group and was authorized to have a "full flash" sewn onto my green beret.

The official graduation ceremony took place in the John F. Kennedy Center for Special Warfare auditorium. The real graduation occurred earlier during a private ritual held in a wooded area behind the John F. Kennedy Memorial Chapel. The grove of pine trees is now gone, but at the time it surrounded a small clearing and a set of bleachers. I had passed that way many times on my way to and from the PX. I figured it was a class site, but I never saw it used for that.

That morning we were marching from our barracks to the auditorium, but instead of taking a right turn toward the center we continued straight ahead into the copse of trees. With our berets in hand, we were instructed to file into the bleachers and take a seat. A few moments later a craggy-faced sergeant major wearing a green beret appeared before us. I had never seen him before and would never see him again. He was obviously one of the old timers we reverently referred to as "glow in the dark" guys. Dressed in an impeccable khaki uniform and wearing glistening jump boots he was the very image of a warrior god. He stood near enough that I was able to see three bronze stars on his jump wings, each denoting a combat jump.

The World War II veteran started by saying we were about to enter a family like no other. For the rest of our lives, whether we stayed in the military or not, we would be Special Forces soldiers first and foremost. Only excommunication for bringing shame upon the family could sever the bond of brotherhood. Then he revealed what set us apart and made us different. Our loyalty, he said, wasn't to the U.S. Army or the federal government. Our eternal allegiance was to the Constitution of the United States and our fellow Americans. And, unlike all other U.S. military personnel, we would never surrender "though we be the last." He then gave the order to stand and, "Don berets."

The oration lasted less than a minute, but each word spoken resonated in our souls. We marched out of that now vanished stand of trees as something more than the young men who entered it. In the months that followed, classmate after classmate was killed in combat. None of them broke the covenant made that day.

It wasn't Yorktown where Jake first experienced epic war. Although it tops the 49th PV's list of battles, it was hardly that. McClellan's "bad case of the slows," as Lincoln put it, caused the spring campaign to stall outside the colonial port. The cautious commander, always hesitant to act until every biscuit was baked, put off unleashing his army until all the heavy guns were manhandled into place. It took until May 3rd, for that to be accomplished. By then the Yankee's front bristled with cannons and massive coastal mortars capable of hurdling tons of ordnance a day into the Confederate stronghold.

That night the ground shook beneath Jake's bedroll, and outside his tent the darkness pulsated with flashes of cannon fire. The bombardment was being delivered, not by Union artillerists, but Confederate gunners. The following morning prior to sabbath worship services, Jake and the others worked at tidying up the camp. Their chores were interrupted by shouting and barked commands. The men figured the uproar foreshadowed a ground attack, and they quickly replaced huckleberry brooms with rifles. They were wrong. The commotion was ignited by a civilian balloonist some 300 feet in the air yelling groundward that Yorktown appeared deserted.

The revelation needn't have come as a surprise. The previous day McClellan dismissed reports made by runaway slaves that the enemy was abandoning the town. When word reached him that, "the rebels had left," he remained so invested in his mistaken appraisal of enemy strength and purpose that he initially turned a blind eye to reality. The truth remains the truth whether one agrees with it or not, and the balloonist's perception was soon verified by Federal troops who entered the town unopposed.

The Confederates had stalled the Union as long as they could, and when they faced overwhelming firepower, they skedaddled. Before taking their leave, they planted shells rigged to explode with the slightest disturbance. The improvised explosive devices (IEDs) were seeded in roads, houses and near springs and abandoned guns. A Union soldier picking a jackknife off the ground was killed instantly when it triggered a planted charge. Cavalry horses touched off explosions by stepping on detonating caps. An unwitting soldier opened a door and was killed instantly when the movement set off an explosion.

Union troops were outraged, and some Confederates saw this departure from chivalry as "cruel murder." Fault or applause went to Brig. Gen. Gabriel J. Rains for providing the knowhow needed to rig "land torpedoes" throughout Yorktown. McClellan, incensed by the "infernal devices" he considered cowardly, ordered Southern prisoners be used to find and deactivate them.

The Vietnam War marked something of a high water mark when it came to ingenious booby traps. The Viet Cong and NVA employed everything from sharpened, excrement-smeared punji stakes to venomous snakes and jury-rigged explosives to kill and wound. They were good, but they didn't have a corner on the sinister art.

When I returned to Vietnam in August 1968 and was assigned to SOG I learned of our own dirty tricks. I was a willing participant in a sophisticated top secret "salting" program conducted under the code name Eldest Son, later changed to Italian Green and Pole Bean. On every mission I carried in doctored AK-47 bullets that would explode when fired. I put them where they were likely to be found and used. The goal was to make the enemy question the safety of their ammo. We were told that only a few people could identify "bad" bullets from good. In late 1969 or early 1970 someone at our camp got a few doctored rounds mixed in with our supply of AK-47 ammo. We ended up destroying thousands of rounds.

We also slipped explosive 82mm mortar shells into the NVA's ammo dumps along the Ho Chi Minh Trail. I saw evidence of the program's effectiveness in an aerial intelligence photograph showing several dead NVA scattered around a ruptured mortar tube. A less deadly part of the program was placing transistor radios where NVA would likely find them. Listeners had a choice of one station - our own, which broadcasted news, music, and propaganda. Counterfeit North Vietnamese money was also planted in an attempt to disrupt their economy. I never had a qualm about doing any of this. I'd seen the results of their booby traps.

While Confederate prisoners disarmed booby traps and dug up planted shells, some of the men of the 49th PV amused themselves by reading letters left behind by the town's former occupants. As they chuckled and hooted over tender lines never meant for prying eyes, cavalry scouts were determining the Rebel's route of retreat. It was soon clear they were slowly heading for their capital. Relentless rain had turned roads into lanes of mud, causing cannons and heavily laden wagons to sink hub-deep into the slurry. It wasn't long before Union bullets were reaching the hard-pressed Rebels.

Gen. Joseph E. Johnston was the overall commander of the Confederate forces opposing McClellan's march up the peninsula. He knew his pursuers had to be held up, if only for a day, to buy time for his men to prepare a viable defense outside Richmond. The bulwark he needed was found in an array of 14 earthen fortifications guarding the approaches to Williamsburg. These firewalls were laced together by interlocking trenches. The largest stronghold was Redoubt 6 standing astride the Williamsburg Road.

Williamsburg, with its spires and rooftops festooned with Confederate flags, was less than three miles to the rear of what was later dubbed Fort Magruder. The redoubt was as plain and utilitarian as the picks and shovels used by slaves to build it. Grim-faced men stood shoulder to shoulder behind 15-foot-high dirt walls that were nearly as thick as they were tall. A 9-foot-deep trench fronting the fortification made scaling the wall even more challenging.

Inexplicably, Johnston had the original defenders of the fort join the retreat. For their replacements he ordered a division of Rebels who had already marched beyond Williamsburg to return to the fort and defend it. The division's commander, Maj. Gen. James Longstreet, was unfamiliar with the layout of the forts or the surrounding terrain. This would prove costly during the fighting on May 5th.

The 49th PV was relieved by another regiment at 10 a.m. on May 4th and marched from Yorktown back to its bivouac area. An air of excited urgency gripped the men as they hurriedly readied their packs for the expected departure. Marching orders came at noon and energized with the fever of the chase they soon put Yorktown behind them. They sloughed along a muddy road lined with abandoned fighting positions constructed of brush and fence railings. Deserted enemy camps were littered with partially destroyed goods and tattered tent canvas. At 8 p.m. they halted a few hundred yards from the soon to be contested Fort Magruder.

Jake's company was immediately sent forward in a downpour to bolster the skirmish line. Blindly feeling their way in the dark through the trackless mire, they tripped and bashed their knees against felled trees strewn about like jackstraws. They had just reached the front line when orders came for them to fall back. Such unnecessary movements are the hallmark of war. So frequent are these futile walkabouts that they quickly fade from memory. This one, however, was remembered for a broadside of friendly fire unleashed on the Pennsylvanians by edgy Union troops mistaking them for the enemy. Logs and debris that had been cursed minutes before were now havens of refuge from whining Minie balls. Providence carried the company through the incident unharmed, but blood aplenty would be shed the following day.

A gray, funereal dawn greeted hundreds of waking men who wouldn't see the sun go down. The killing started at first light when Union troops under the command of Brig. Gen. Joseph Hooker assaulted the main fort in a headlong attack. The fighting was brutal and relentless as gains were made and lost. Sheets of rain, uneven ground, entanglements, and the constant roar of battle heightened confusion. Some of the heaviest fighting took place in a depression that became known as the "Bloody Ravine."

Jake's brigade wasn't sent into the raging struggle, largely because of a tip received from an escaped slave who told of an undefended route to the right of the fort. The brigade headed out in that direction, and after a three-mile march swung to the left. After taking a few minutes to catch their breath, the brigade hurried down a hill and crossed a dam that used the waters of Cub's Creek to form Jones' Mill Pond. As the others stood by, Jake's Company D was sent up a hill overlooking the fort.

Gen. Hancock had ridden forward with the company, and when they reached the military crest of the hill, just below the topographical crest, he halted the men. He ordered D Company's color bearer, Sgt. Dock Hoffman, to take his squad to a nearby unoccupied fortification to see whether Rebel or Federal troops occupied the fort below.

A short time later Hoffman yelled to his commander, "General, they are damned Rebels." Nearby troops had a laugh at the less than proper way the sergeant addressed his superior. Hancock took no offense and told his sergeant to make certain. When he again affirmed that the enemy held the fort, the general ordered up a battery of eight cannons. Company D advanced a short distance and formed a line of battle. The guns were quickly positioned and started firing explosive shells into the fort below.

Westbrook recalled that the Rebels' answering cannonade fell 200 yards short of its intended target. The fighting continued to rage at the front of the fort but remained relatively quiet in the sector behind it. Things started heating up around 2 p.m., when the 5th Wisconsin Regiment positioned in front of the 49th PV started toward the fort. As the regiment advanced, individual soldiers took potshots at Rebels scurrying along a wood line on the Union's right.

Confederate commanders, Maj. Gen. D. H. Hill and Brig. Gen. Jubal Early, had been holding their troops in reserve, but were aching to get into the brawl. When they heard Union cannons booming to the rear of the fort they started toward the sound of the guns. As the troops from Wisconsin neared the woods, two companies of Confederate cavalry rode out of the trees followed by a flood of infantry. After making a showing, the mounted troops spun their horses back into the woods, but the infantry continued pressing forward.

A background of green foliage made the motley mix of gray and butternut uniforms emerging from the trees, stand out like coal on snow. Realizing they were vastly outnumbered the 5th Wisconsin fell back to their original position and braced for the impact of two regiments of charging soldiers. The confident Rebels thought they were striking the Union flank, but in fact were hitting them head on. When they reached the top of the hill, they found themselves facing cannon muzzles not 30 yards away.

The last thing scores of assaulting Rebels saw were red flashes of fire and mushrooms of smoke from the belching cannons. Less than a heartbeat later marble-size lead grapeshot shattered bones and eviscerated flesh. Volley after volley of canister rounds tore through the ranks of charging men leaving the ground covered with mutilated bodies and grievously wounded soldiers.

Unaware of the slaughter taking place, Hill sent the 5th North

Carolina Regiment forward. By the time he realized his error it was too late to stop the assault. More than 300 men from the Tar Heel State fell before the merciless guns. At this point historical accounts have Hancock leading a countercharge, but Westbrook claims it never happened.

"Hancock made no charge, for the ample reason that there was nothing in our front to charge on but dead and wounded soldiers and a few prisoners," Westbrook claims. "Hardly had the firing ceased until Company D, Captain Campbell's company, stacked arms and went to work getting the Rebel's wounded into the little fort a few paces to the rear. The writer, being a member of Company D, helped carry them in and saw, "many of the boys cut buttons from their clothes, take rings from their fingers."

In his official report Hancock wrote, "For 600 yards in front of our lines the whole field was strewn with the enemy's dead." The fighting that day had been vicious, but with few exceptions, terribly orchestrated. Confusion ruled the rainy hours as friend and foe sought footholds in slippery mud. The most notable feature of the struggle was the remarkable bravery shown that day by both sides. The Army Medal of Honor, which wouldn't be approved by Congress and signed into law until July 12, 1862, was awarded to seven Union soldiers for their exceptional valor. The stalwart stand of Hancock and his men, and the decimation of the Confederate regiments, resulted in the capture of the first Rebel battle flag during the war.

The outnumbered Confederates fought with such tenacity that only after they abandoned the fort late that night, was it occupied by Union troops. They had done all that had been asked of them, buying with their blood the necessary time for their army to withdraw. An estimated 41,000 Union and 32,000 Confederates troops participated in the day-long battle. More than 2,200 Union soldiers died or were wounded. Something in the neighborhood of 1,600 Rebels also drank hot blood, prophesied days earlier.

Costlier clashes laid ahead, and because of that the Battle of Williamsburg earns little more than passing mention in most history books. But for Jake and the others, it was war unveiled. For the first time they had faced the enemy in numbers, and they hadn't faltered. But any presumed glitter of glory lost its glint in the corpse-littered mud hole that for a single day had taken on strategic importance.

And what about McClellan who didn't make a showing until the fighting was practically over? In a letter penned to his wife after the battle, a reader would believe he had saved the day and won a tremendous victory. As suffering men fought for their lives, he complained about missing supper, spending the night in his clothes and being unable to wash his hands and face. The love his men felt for him would have likely soured considerably if they had read this vanity-laced letter. His aversion to fighting, and astounding ability for overestimating the enemy, places him among the worse battlefield commanders in history. These traits also doomed the Peninsula Campaign, but only after thousands more would die.

Chapter Five

As daylight spread over the Williamsburg battlefield on May 6, 1862, the spillage of war emerged. A hard freeze overnight had tortured the living and glazed the dead with a sheen of frost. Disarranged bodies laid in front of Redoubt 6, and throughout the savagely contested ravine. During the night many Union corpses had been stripped of clothing by the Rebels, leaving bone-white torsos strewn about like seashells on a muddy beach. Northern soldiers trembled with rage at what they considered a clear desecration of their dead. Ragged Southern troops saw it differently, of course, but no matter. Even in the gray vagrancies of war, soldiers don't forget such affronts, and they inevitably lead to ever-worsening atrocities.

After days of rain and sullen skies, Union private Warren Lee Goss remembered it as a "beautiful morning." Birds chirped as he approached a dead Federal soldier whose outstretched hand appeared to be reaching for a prayer book. Two ambrotype pictures rested on his chest, one of his children and the other his wife. Another soldier, lifeless as marble, held his rifle in an aiming position. At the edge of the 49th's campground a barn had been transformed into a makeshift hospital.

Inside the stagnant structure the air would have smelt of chloroform, blood, whiskey, and the fish-gut odor of deep wounds.

This early in the war the opposing forces were ill equipped to handle even a smattering of casualties, much less hundreds. For three days Union wagons, creaking under the weight of wounded soldiers and prisoners, carried their human cargo to a nearby river for transport north. Liberated slaves flocked to the Yankee camps, some finding work digging shallow graves for Union dead. The retreating Confederates abandoned many of their dead and wounded, leaving their care and burials to local civilians.

It wasn't until May 9, that the 49th PV resumed its pursuit of the Rebels. Marching out from Williamsburg they encountered long lines of burned and disabled Confederate wagons. This was taken as further evidence that the war would soon be over. The following evening the regiment was about six miles west of Barhamsville, putting them just 35 miles from Richmond. Speculation bounced between how soon the Confederate capital would fall, and when the war would end.

After the Battle of the la Drang Valley in November 1965, I too mistakenly thought the war would soon be over. I shared my 19-year-old optimism with a Vietnamese interpreter. He assured me that the war would go on for years. Jake and I might be forgiven our ignorance, not knowing what we were up against. I didn't know the first thing about the politics surrounding the Vietnam War, and my great granduncle wouldn't have been aware of McClellan's shortcomings. In later years my stomach has turned when I've learned how our leaders in Washington had undermined our efforts in Vietnam. Jake died before learning the full extent of his field commander's bungling.

Confederate President Jefferson Davis wasn't fully aware of McClellan's shortcomings either. He sent his wife and their four children to North Carolina in anticipation of a bloody struggle in the streets of the capital. While Davis was seeing to the safety of his family, other government officials were hurriedly packing archives into boxes destined for Columbia, South Carolina. The city's entire gold supply was stacked on a flatbed railroad car coupled to a locomotive that was kept under steam to ensure a rapid departure. As panicky citizens fled to the west and south, the Virginia legislature agreed to burn Richmond to the ground rather than see it occupied by the Yankees.

For the next few days Jake was tormented by marching orders that would be countermanded just as they were about to get under way. When they finally set out on May 13, they marched until they reached the south bank of the Pamunkey River at Cumberland Landing. Barges, steamers, gunboats, and various other vessels dotted the waterway. After a leisurely day of fishing, swimming, and washing clothes, the troops marched to White House Landing. Once there they pitched their tents on the farm inherited by Col. William Henry Fitzhugh "Rooney" Lee, second son of Confederate general Robert E. Lee. The landing derived its name from a large white house on the property. The first Union soldiers to venture up the front steps of the dwelling found a note affixed to the door.

The note read, "Northern soldiers who profess to reverence Washington forbear to desecrate the home of his first married life, the property of his wife, now owned by her descendants." It was signed, "A Granddaughter of Mrs. Washington." The message was penned by R.E. Lee's wife, Mary Ann Randolph Custis Lee, who had moved in with her son after losing her stately Arlington home.

McClellan respected Mrs. Lee's wishes and posted guards around the house to ensure it wasn't picked clean by souvenir hunters. He also had a detail of soldiers under a flag of truce escort Mrs. Lee through the front lines so she could reunite with her husband. No special consideration was given the large wheat fields surrounding the house. On May 17, the men of the 49th tromped one field flat while cavalry troops did the same to adjoining acres. As this food source was being trampled beneath foot and hoof, 500 tons of supplies were being unloaded daily at landing docks to sustain the push to Richmond.

Rain continued to be an almost daily annoyance. On May 19, Jake and the regiment sloshed through six miles of mud as rain soaked them to the skin. When they stopped to make camp in a cornfield that would be ruined by their presence, they were 14 miles from Richmond. The next day's march brought them to within 10 miles of the city's outskirts. Along the route exuberant slaves believing their salvation was at hand cheered the advancing men. Others sold the hungry troops hoe cakes "the size of a man's hand" for 15 cents apiece. The soldiers also grubbed through every garden they came across like a plague of locust. Protests were useless and answered with surly suggestions to charge Uncle Sam. Owing to the clash at Williamsburg, civilities that previously marked exchanges between Southern civilians and Yankee soldiers were largely absent.

For several days the 49th PV edged closer to the Chickahominy River flowing between them and their prize. Normally, the 87-mile-long James River tributary is an easily forded slow-moving runnel. But days of rain enlarged it across a mile-wide plain of jungly swampland. The Rebels, as well as a large part of the Union Army, crossed the river before it jumped its banks. The flooding then created a watery wedge that effectively split the invading army in two. Johnston was quick to take advantage of nature's assistance and set out to destroy the isolated Union force on the south side of the swollen river.

The Battle of Seven Pines took place on May 31 and June 1, 1862. The Confederate attack was supposed to commence at 8 a.m. on May 31. For various reasons the fighting didn't get going until 1 p.m., and then things didn't go well for either side. The 49th wasn't engaged, and only heard heavy cannonading and volleys of musketry on the far side of the river.

When the battle ended midmorning on June 1, both sides claimed victory. Although the Confederates stopped the Union advance on Richmond, they were forced back to the defenses circling the capital. More than 10,000 men had been killed, wounded, captured, or listed as missing. The bloodshed was only eclipsed by the two-day Battle of Shiloh, fought in southwestern Tennessee in early April.

McClellan was shaken by the sight and stench of the mangled and moldering dead. Adding to the grotesquery were numerous bonfires incinerating piles of dead mules and horses. For more than a week, Federal troops were kept busy burying the dead. Confederates were buried in mass graves, while Union dead were laid with care in individual graves with their names printed on markers if they were identifiable.

The lasting impact of the Battle of Seven Pines was due to a single casualty among the thousands who fell. As fighting ebbed on the first day of the battle, Gen. Johnston was seriously wounded by a bullet striking his right shoulder, and a piece of shrapnel that hit him in the chest. He lived, but it took him six months to recover. Davis quickly called on Gen. Robert E. Lee to lead the Army of Northern Virginia. The man who had been mockingly titled the "King of Spades" by his soldiers for insisting they dig defensive entrenchments around Richmond, quickly won their love and devotion. The war lasted as long as it did largely because of Lee's battlefield genius.

The revered Southern leader orchestrated an aggressive strategy that drove the Union off the peninsula, but at a cost of thousands of irreplaceable men. As the Rebels prepared for the savage fighting ahead, Jake endured constant spring showers and the monotony of camp chores. Irwin's eccentricities and the occasional shell burst were their most maddening nuisances. When Irwin withheld their ration of crackers on June 11, deeming them unwholesome, Westbrook commented on their ire. "Some of the boys would sooner shoot him [Irwin] this evening than a Rebel." The 49th's commander wasn't shot by his own men, but others haven't been as fortunate.

The word "fragging" was coined during my war to describe the deliberate killing of an unpopular soldier. Its etymology derives from the use oftentimes of a fragmentation grenade to perform the act. This kind of murder has occurred throughout military history but appears to have hit something of a high water mark during the Vietnam War. Listed among the reasons for this were low morale, racial tensions, degrading of discipline and the unpopularity of the war, especially during the latter years. I would add incompetence, reckless disregard for lives, and dangerous aggression. I personally don't know of a case where a fellow soldier was intentionally killed by another for any reason. Occasionally, I heard idle talk that someone would do us a favor by seeing that a medal-hungry jerk had an untimely accident. But I don't know of an incident when it was actually carried out.

While serving as a recon team leader I had a codeword in place that if I said it to an American team member while on an operation, we would silently count to five and then kill all the indigenous team members. The word was "thunderclap," and thankfully I never had to use it. I was advised to implement such a plan by Capt. Dick Meadows who at the time was commander of Recon Company at CCN. Meadows is a legendary figure in Special Forces and one of two men I consider the finest soldiers I served with. The other is Maj. Gen. (ret) Eldon Bargewell.

Meadows knew I was especially close with my Chinese Nungs and Vietnamese mercenaries, but he cautioned that I shouldn't trust them completely. The little people on my first recon team, RT Louisiana, proved their loyalty time and again. It was a different story with my second team, RT Hawaii. They too proved to be loyal, but I wasn't with them long enough to build the rapport I had with members of my first team.

The relationship I had with the indig on RT Louisiana wasn't without its tense moments. Soon after becoming team leader, I experienced an example of petty animosity brought about by my replacing a popular One-Zero. When I walked into the team hooch one afternoon, Cuong, who was in charge of the indig on the team and carried the numerical designation, Zero-One, gave me a dirty sidelong look and mumbled, "Mother fucking American," in Vietnamese.

I instinctively knew I couldn't let him get away with that. I grabbed him by the throat and bum-rushed him out of the hooch. What I did next was as much a surprise to me as it was to everyone else. A few feet away was a security fence made up of two rows of concertina razor wire with a third row resting on top. I picked Cuong up by his neck and belt and pitched him into the wire. He landed on his back on the top coil, and his weight made it sag down into the two base rolls. I dragged him out by the ankles and yanked him to his feet. Without raising my voice, I told him that I'd kill him on the spot if he ever looked at me like that again or repeated what he said. A nod of his head told me he had gotten my drift.

I told his teammates to take him to the dispensary to get bandaged, then I left for an hour or so to give things time to simmer down. When

I returned, Pau, our tail gunner and team cook, was busy preparing a feast. Cuong came up to me and said he was sorry. I accepted his apology, we embraced, and I never brought it up again. Cuong, on the other hand, loved to tell the story.

Like every indig on the team, Cuong was a hardcore, cutthroat mercenary. Without their respect I would be, if not doomed, certainly ineffective. The feast Pau prepared that day was the team's way of saying they accepted me as their leader. After that incident I never had a discipline problem with them again, and they gave me their gift of loyalty without reserve.

As laudable as their all-in loyalty was, it did have drawbacks. When I was assigned to RT Louisiana, Pau took it upon himself to be my bodyguard. I realized how seriously he took the job during a brisk firefight. I was flat on the ground, firing my weapon, when he crawled on top of me. I shoved him off, but a moment later he was back. A few sharp words ended his efforts to shield me with his body. After we got home, I told him how much I appreciated his thoughtfulness, but I needed mobility in those situations. He grudgingly accepted my explanation, and never did it again.

Several months later another incident of that sort occurred during an extraction under enemy fire. We were in double-canopy jungle, fighting for our lives from behind a deadfall. Twigs and leaves shot off surrounding trees and blasted free by exploding grenades and claymores were raining down. All the while a Huey helicopter was hovering above us, and sandbags attached to McGuire Rigs were slamming into the ground just feet away. As the team leader I was on the radio with the helicopter pilot, directing the defense of our position, and putting four of the indig in the rigs.

I told the pilot to start the extraction and was turning my full attention back to the gunfight when I felt something against my left shoulder. It was Toan, one of the indig I had just put in a rig.

"I die with you Mau, I die with you," he said. I suppose he had to yell to be heard above the roar of the helicopter throttling up to full power. I know I heard each word distinctly and will never forget the sincerity in his voice or expression on his face. That moment stands in my memory as a monument to love and an unfailing virtue. I got Toan back into the rig before the slack came out of the rope. We all made it out, thanks to courageous helicopter crews who routinely risked their lives for people they didn't know.

A day after Col. Irwin angered his troops by withholding their ration of hardtack, seven men in Jake's company risked their lives recovering the body of a cavalryman they didn't know. On June 12th, a dispatch courier with the 8th Pennsylvania Cavalry was delivering a message to the commander of a brigade bivouacked near the 49th PV. The cavalryman, crouched over his saddle and riding hell-for-leather parallel to the Confederate lines, presented an irresistible target. For a few moments it appeared to onlookers that all the bullets directed at the rider would miss their mark. Then a blaze of red appeared as a bullet tore away part of his head, and another slug drove into his chest. Death was instantaneous, but the nearly headless horseman remained in the saddle.

The horse swerved toward the gun smoke and muzzle flashes, and with long strides charged across a grain field. About 20 paces from the enemy's line the horse felt his master's weight slip from the saddle. As the man toppled to the ground the horse abruptly changed course and raced back to the Union line. For two hours the opposing forces did nothing. The standoff ended when a colonel with the 43rd New York Regiment rode into the 49th's campground and after reining in his horse pointed across the field.

"Boys, there lies one of our men; must we leave him there?" the colonel questioned in a forceful tone. A moment later he answered his rhetorical query. "No. If we do the Rebel son of a bitch will get him. Who will volunteer to bring him in?"

Seven men stepped forward. Leaving their rifles and encumbering equipment behind, they lowered themselves to the ground and set out. A thatch of early-season grain served as concealment as they low crawled toward the dead rider. They remained undetected until reaching the cavalryman, whereupon the strenuous effort needed to move the body caused their straining arms and legs to rise above the amber cover. The Rebels spotted the movement in the field and were again hard on their triggers. The men yanked the corpse along the ground a foot or two at a time as rifles barked and slugs kicked up dirt and snipped off stalks of grain. Some of the Union men watching the drama unfold believed they were witnessing a miracle. Westbrook was sure of it.

"A higher Divinity preserved them from the bullets of the enemy, and they came safely out, bringing the ill-fated cavalryman with them," the diarist wrote. There were no medals for these brave men, but by my reckoning their names deserve to be recorded and remembered. They were Jerry Cromer, George Cromer, Hance Campbell, Isaac F. Beamer, Theodore H. McFarland, Arthur Rogers, and Wash McCall. They all served with Company D, 49th PV.

The following morning Jake and the regiment were awakened by heavy cannon fire. After rushing from their tents and forming a line of battle they stood at the ready until 10 a.m., when they were relieved by the 5th Wisconsin. That afternoon some of the men enjoyed the pleasant weather by walking to the supply depot at Savage Station, located on the Richmond and York River Railroad. They marveled at an immense mound of hardtack that one observer said would create a string of biscuits stretching from Pittsburgh to Philadelphia. They also saw many soldiers arriving by rail.

With little action occurring, the men sought various ways to stay busy. One distraction was building arbors of twigs and branches along pathways and over tents. The relative quiet was broken by a single gunshot on June 16, when Pvt. John Musser of G Company 49th PV, was shot in the neck while on picket duty. On February 13, 1969, I was seriously wounded in the neck while on a recon mission in North Vietnam, code named Nickel Steel.

On the final day of a five-day mission, we moved onto a ridgeline and were awaiting extraction by helicopter. The NVA had been trying to locate us from day one and were closing in. I was about 10 yards from the others, when I heard rustling in the foliage below me. Not wanting to give away our position I pulled the pin from a grenade and was about to toss it when I heard something hit the ground nearby. A second or two later the shockwave of an explosion slammed into me, and I felt a searing pain on the right side of my neck.

My first thought was getting rid of the grenade so I didn't blow myself up. I threw it where I thought the NVA was, and then touched the wound with my left hand. When I saw just a smudge of blood on my fingertips, I thought I wasn't hurt as seriously as the burning pain indicated. In the seconds it took to crawl back to the others a tremendous volume of gunfire erupted, powerfully punctuated by the blasts from detonating claymore mines. As I dragged myself up to the others the team leader glanced at me and yelled, "They blew half your neck off."

It wasn't true. There was a lot of blood, but the shrapnel wound itself was about an inch long. I had been leaning forward when the piece of metal hit me, and it traveled downward into the muscle of my neck. I later saw an x-ray that shows the shard is about the size of a dime. The problem was that I was bleeding out. When I placed my hand on the wound, a stream of blood coursed down my arm and off my elbow. One of the Americans stopped shooting long enough to hurriedly wrap a sweat-soaked cravat around my neck. He had been wearing the olive-drab cloth as a sweatband, and it had the absorbency of wax paper.

As I started going into shock my ability to continue fighting was diminishing by the second. I was sitting with my back propped against a tree when bullets started blowing splinters out of the wood just above my head. When I rolled onto my side a puddle of blood that had pooled in my lap poured onto the ground. Being that low to the ground enabled me to see the up-and-down running motion of the assaulting NVA's green, rubber-toed bata boots in the foot or so of open space between the jungle floor and first sprigs of foliage. As I shot at the ankle-high targets, darkness started reducing my periphery vision. It was as if I was in a blacked-out ship cabin looking at two portholes of light. As the circles grew smaller, I knew I was dying.

I tried to recite the Act of Contrition but couldn't think of the words and concentrate on living at the same time. Just before I slipped away, the team interpreter, Hung, pushed a thick field dressing against the wound. This simple act stopped the bleeding and saved my life. After gulping down some water I started to feel my strength returning.

With the help of several airstrikes, we managed to hold off the NVA, and were extracted later that day without losing anyone. When I got to the hospital the surgeon opted to leave the piece of shrapnel in my neck, where it remains.

Musser wasn't as fortunate as I and died within the hour. At twilight the following day his friends carried him to the lower end of a garden, about 100 yards from S. Courtney's farmhouse. Heads bowed, prayers were offered, and he was laid to rest beneath a wood marker bearing his name, rank and regiment. In the following days hundreds of Union soldiers would be buried in rough ground without a prayer being said.

During those relatively quiet days, Jake and the others probably weren't pondering their mortality, but guessing the number of days until the war would end. They were told the timetable for them to be in Richmond was June 20, 1862. When the date arrived, the Rebel capital wasn't in sight and Union forces were largely inactive. The regiment was kept busy drilling and conducting bayonet practice, and only the distant sound of musketry and booming cannons assured them the war was still ongoing. When McClellan learned that Lee had replaced Johnston, his assessment of the new commander sounded like he was evaluating himself.

"I prefer Lee over Johnston," McClellan opined. "[Lee is] too cautious and weak under grave responsibility, personally brave and energetic to a fault, he yet is wanting in moral firmness when pressed by heavy responsibility and is likely to be timid and irresolute in action."

Johnston knew better. As he recovered from his wounds he told a friend, "The shot that struck me down is the very best that has been fired for the Southern cause yet. For I possess in no degree the confidence of our government, and now there is in my place one who does possess it, and who can accomplish what I never could have done, the concentration of our armies for the defense of the capital of the Confederacy."

Lee wasted no time in proving Johnston right. McClellan was finally ready to fight, and "Bobby Lee" accommodated him. On June 25, Union forces moved on the capital and got near enough to hear the pealing of church bells. Fierce fighting during the Battle of Oak Grove brought the Yankees to within five miles of Richmond, but no closer. The high-water mark of the Peninsula Campaign had been reached, and what laid ahead was a ghastly week of slaughter. Historians have recorded the thrusts, parries, gains, and losses of the Seven Days Battles in exhaustive detail. But words and a handful of photographs can't bring form to the indescribable.

Combat soldiers, like Jake and myself, experience battle within the limited scope of our senses. Every action, every firefight, is completely individual, because no one sees, hears, tastes, feels, smells, and thinks alike. What each of us do see, sometimes painfully clear, is our true self. The egocentric, protective props I'd hidden behind since childhood were blown away in the air-cringeling shockwaves of war.

I, like countless others, had been eager to step onto the field of battle and learn whether I would be brave or cowardly. Since the age of 10 or 11 I had known a coward lurked within me. The discovery came one evening when I and my best friend, Mick, were invited by his older brother, Tom, to ride with him in his cherished car to Tech High School where he needed to pick something up from his shop class. While Tom was inside, Mick got behind the wheel and inadvertently shifted the car out of gear. Unable to reach the brake pedal, the car rolled forward, hitting a steel post.

The dented fender was a death sentence. Mick told me I could leave the scene; no point in us both being killed. I hurriedly agreed and lit out for home. I was a couple blocks away before I realized the right thing to do was stay with my friend. I ran back to the parking lot, but they were already gone. Our friendship faded after that, and I've never forgiven myself for leaving him.

My first field of battle was in the la Drang Valley where my baptism of fire came courtesy of a battalion of North Vietnamese regulars with the 33rd Regiment. It was the afternoon of November 18, 1965, and I decided it was a good time to clean my M-14 rifle. Instead of field stripping it down to the major components, I completely disassembled it, placing the parts, big and small, on my spread-out poncho. When gunfire erupted in front of my position I dove into my shallow foxhole, dragging the poncho in behind me. My breath came in dry, ragged gasps as I hunted for the next part in the assembly sequence. Because of my stupidity I never fired a shot during the attack. The only worthwhile thing I did was stomp out a fire started by a tracer round near a pile of artillery shells. I hadn't been a coward, but I spent most of my time fumbling about in the bottom of a foxhole.

During the war my coward was most insistent during the confessional hours of deep night, and in idle hours when imagination has free rein. I think the scariest I ever was in Vietnam was during a cigarette break outside the Tactical Operation Center at CCN. During the first few months I was there I worked in the TOC's comma room sending and receiving messages. For hours that night I had been receiving short messages having to do with accounts coming from a wounded American. Periodically when he'd regain consciousness, he'd provide a little more information about what had happened during a recon mission in Laos.

The messages read like an action-adventure novel. Around three in the morning I needed some fresh air and went outside. As I smoked a cigarette, I thought about other recon teams in Laos that night, and likely in as terrifying a predicament as the wounded guy had been. I felt the terror of being in that situation and told myself I'd stay safe and sound in my comma room job for the duration of my tour. Of course, in the light of day I changed my mind. Interestingly, I never felt the paralyzing fear while on a mission that I had felt that night outside the TOC.

When you're fighting for your life there's no time to entertain the coward's hysterical break-and-run nonsense. Necessity, not bravery, required me to be my best when things were the worst. If I did anything worthy of being called courageous it was getting on the helicopters that carried us into target areas. I managed to maintain an exterior of calm as hot exhaust fumes slapped me in the face. I'd give a cheery thumbs-up as fear raked the lining of my stomach. My bleating inner coward frantically suggested ways to abort the mission. I never did, so I suppose that says something.

On June 26, 1862, the men of the 49th PV dug rifle pits and likely struggled with their own fears as the Battle of Mechanicsville roared nearby. The epicenter of the fighting was occurring on the steep banks of a narrow, waist-deep ribbon of water called Beaver Dam Creek. Windrows of smoke from bellowing cannons and small arms fire hung low on the field, as shock waves rattled doors and windows in nearby Richmond. Fatigue, impatience, faulty timing, and piecemeal deployment of Southern troops against dozens of cannons and well entrenched Federal infantry resulted in a one-sided bloodbath. Courageous Rebels, yelling themselves hoarse, repeatedly charged over their dead and wounded. Gray-clad soldiers who, through luck or guile, got near the fighting line were often reduced to unrecognizable pulp by pointblank blasts from cannons.

The area around the creek became a slaughter pen where valor was squandered in pointless sacrifice. When the foolhardy charges ended, nearly 1,500 Confederates laid still or moaning on the blood-sopped ground leading up to the Federal defenses. Less than 300 Yankees were killed or wounded during the debacle. As twilight shrouded the raw details of butchery, a Union soldier thought the dark mounds of human wreckage looked like, "flies in a sugar bowl."

An outwardly jubilant McClellan reacted to the lopsided victory as if it was a defeat. Concerned that his army could be cut off from its supply line, and believing he was vastly outnumbered, he began to give ground needlessly. Subordinate officers pleading with him to push on toward Richmond were rebuked. Whispered accusations of treason and cowardice were bantered about in huddled groups of Union men. Had the "young Napoleon" lost his nerve?

McClellan certainly had brave words for his troops after the Battle of Seven Pines. He vowed to be with them in the fighting ahead and share the danger of shot and shell. Generals shouldn't lead charges, but during the Civil War they needed to be near the action to make appropriate tactical decisions. McClellan put so much distance between himself and the front lines that he lost situational clarity. Most rank-and-file troops were mercifully unaware of their beloved commander's lack of sand. His verbal bravado gave them the impression he was a superbly confident warrior.

In a dispatch to Washington after the Rebel's thrashing at Beaver

Dam Creek, McClellan finished by stating, "I almost think we are invincible." As Union bands struck up patriotic airs, victorious Yanks whooped with joy, fully expecting to continue the march on Richmond. Their elation changed to stunned bewilderment when they learned that instead of marching against the thinly defended capital, they would be doing an about face.

In predawn darkness on June 27th, Brig. Gen. Fritz John Porter received orders from McClellan to hold Lee's troops at bay while he prepared to move the bulk of the army southward to Harrison Landing on the James River. Porter, a West Point graduate, had a good eye for defensive positions. He situated about 34,000 men, supported by 80 pieces of artillery, on high ground with Boatswain's Swamp to his front. A nearby brick-and-timber grist mill named for its owner, Dr. William Gaines, stood by a placid pond fed by Powhite Creek. The peaceful setting belied the savagery that would occur nearby and give name to one of the most vicious confrontations of the war.

The Battle of Gaines's Mill, fought June 27, 1862, marked the largest Confederate charge of the war with an estimated 57,000 scruffy, yet determined sons of the South, booming across contested ground. Around 2 p.m. an ominous tramp and clatter of massing men caused the defenders to tighten their grip on sweat-stained rifles. A half hour passed before Confederate banners appeared above the crest of the uneven terrain. Forward movement caused the battle flags to flutter slightly in the limpid air. Then appeared thousands of slouch-hatted men advancing on the double-quick. From their throats came an unearthly wail only attainable from men awash in adrenaline.

The battle cry was answered by an earthshaking salvo from Union cannons and musketry that produced a flashing wall of fire and a fog bank of smoke. Front ranks of attackers were sent pinwheeling into eternity. Pride and courageous resolve drove the living over bloody bodies blackened by the soot of gun powder. The living raced by dying men starring with uncomprehending wonder at their shattered bodies. Charge after charge faltered and failed as death drained away the will to press forward.

Union defenders were also dying by the score as Confederate

artillery blew gaping holes in the defensive lines. Still, as each attack was repelled, the men in blue cheered their success. The clashes were so loud that men relied on the muzzle flash and recoil from their rifles to be certain they'd fired. All afternoon charges and counter charges added to the casualty lists. At 6 p.m. ears began ringing with silence as the Confederates prepared for an all-out coordinated attack by Lee's entire force of 56,000 men. The onslaught, unleashed a half hour later, proved too much for the beleaguered and outnumbered Federal troops.

The Rebel's paid a ghastly price in order to break the Union defenses, leaving nearly 1,500 dead on the field and more than 6,400 wounded. The Union lost 894 dead, 3,107 wounded and 2,836 captured or missing. Despite being pushed out of their defenses, the rear guard successfully retreated across the Chickahominy River, burning the bridges behind them. Darkness, fatigue, and the need to sort out units that had gotten jumbled during the advance precluded the Rebels from following up on their success.

As the Battle of Gaines Mill was being waged north of the Chickahominy River, Jake and his outfit was located on Garnett's Hill, south of the river. When the sun reached its noonday peak its brilliance was rivaled by blossoming air bursts that sent sizzling shards of metal downward into Union troops. The incoming Confederate shells were answered by cannon fire unleashed by the Second Connecticut Artillery. Jake could have been among the 36 men from the 49th PV detailed to protect the guns. For more than an hour, incoming and outgoing shells blistered the sky. The artillery duel ended when the Rebel cannons were disabled or forced to withdraw by the more powerful cannons of the North.

This sideshow to the main event being fought near Gaines Mill earned battle status later that afternoon when an artillery barrage heralded a coming Rebel ground attack. At 6 p.m., attacking waves of Confederates boiled up from a nearby ravine and raced toward the dug in Federals. The whooping aggressors met with what Westbrook described as, "a sheet of fire." The Rebels continued to attack valiantly but were repulsed each time. The struggle ended after dark with Billy Yank holding firm and Johnny Reb being roughly handled once again.

The 49th PV suffered 5 killed and 15 wounded during the engagement. Overall, the brigade had 189 casualties compared to more than 430 attackers who fell during the fruitless assaults.

At 8:30 a.m., June 28, Jake's company and three others were selected to serve as rear guard for the withdrawal to Savage Station. They had just gotten settled into a line of battle in a ravine when shells started pounding their position, killing one man. When the shelling stopped, they readied themselves for a ground attack, which came minutes later. What the unknowing assaulters faced was a milestone in the progression of military armament.

At least one Agar gun, mounted on a caisson and drawn by a mule, supplemented the defense. The rapid-fire weapon, nicknamed the Coffee Mill Gun, was fired by turning a crank. The hopper-fed gun was invented by Wilson Agar and could fire about 120 rounds a minute. Westbrook wrote that the gun, "did good work," taking a heavy toll on the charging rebels. The initial fighting went so well that Union fighters captured the colors of the Eighth Georgia Regiment.

The tide of battle began to turn as the Rebels continued to send in reinforcements, while the Bluecoats had to work with what they had. The situation became grim when the 33" New York Regiment fell back, leaving the 49th PV alone and in a precarious position. Westbrook penned that the New Yorkers unexpected withdrawal, "caused our boys to pay their respects to the New Yorkers in terms more forcible than elegant." Unable to defend the position alone the remaining companies of the 49th PV were ordered to fall back. Our diarist noted that, "we did some fine running in order to save ourselves."

This was not running because of fear as revealed by the shouted declarations of Joe Robbins, Company H, 49th PV. Westbrook described Robbins as a, "rather old man," but there's no age limit when it comes to grit. As Robbins was busting brush to the rear, nearby Rebels shouted for him to surrender. "Surrender hell," he answered as he continued to run. He was then told to stop or be shot. "Shoot and be damned" was his reply. They shot, and he was hit, but not captured. He died of his wounds August 14, 1862.

As Jake plodded his way back to Savage Station, he likely felt angry and disillusioned. How could all their hopes and hard fighting have come to nothing? I had similar feelings when I realized that in spite of years of sacrifices in Vietnam we had been foiled by events beyond our control. Countless acts of bravery, loss of America's finest young men and women, and all the life-altering injuries, mental and physical, hadn't altered the outcome. The waste was not limited to life and limbs.

Near the end of my first tour in Vietnam I passed a junkyard of war-torn military vehicles tilting awkwardly on broken axles, busted tracks, and flat tires. In a neighboring field were fuselages of Huey helicopters that had crashed and been retrieved. Tattered and broken rotor blades, their honeycomb innards exposed, laid about like broken windmills. Skeletal remains of cannibalized artillery pieces littered another section. On the edge of the debris-covered acres was a towering stack of unsheltered cases of C rations. Some of the rain-soaked cardboard boxes had split open, spilling green cans of food onto the ground where they rusted in the weeds. The waste was incalculable, but I was seeing a drop in an ocean.

What Jake witnessed when arriving at the Union supply depot at Savage Station was far beyond anything I had seen. Immense stores of everything needed by an army in the field was set ablaze to keep from being captured by the Rebels. Mountainous piles of flour, hardtack, clothing, ammunition, and sundry goods were torched. Westbrook wrote that, "the contents of mail pouches were emptied on the ground in a pile as large as a load of hay, ready to have the match set to it, and every person was destroying as much as he could." Two trains with boxcars loaded with supplies, including explosives, were set on fire, and smashed into one another resulting in a tremendous blast. Other trains were run off a destroyed bridge into the Chickahominy River.

Far more tragic was the abandonment of 2,500 sick and wounded Federal soldiers, crammed hip to head, in the field hospital at Savage Station. Selfless doctors and medical personnel stayed behind with their patients and were captured with them. The retreat was so hasty that naked, bloating corpses were left unburied, as were piles of amputated body parts. In an attempt to mask reality, Little Mac called the retreat "a change of base," but Union soldiers knew the score. They called it, "the big skedaddle," and Savage Station became the funeral pyre of the Peninsula Campaign. The retreat was incomprehensible to many Union officers.

Brig. Gen. Edwin Sumner, commander of II Corps, was incensed when he received orders to continue to fall back. A veteran of the Blackhawk War and Mexican-American War, he was the oldest field commander to serve on either side during the war. Age hadn't dulled his will to engage the enemy.

"I never leave a victorious field," Sumner bellowed in the stentorian voice that earned him the nickname Bull. "Why, if I had 20,000 more men, I would crush this rebellion."

Jake and the others hadn't lost their fighting will either. On June 29, on the outskirts of Savage Station, they helped stop determined Confederate attacks. They also repelled attacks on June 30, during the Battle of White Oak Swamp. The battle-a-day pace and road marches in withering heat was exhausting, but they didn't falter. On July 1, the climactic Battle of Malvern Hill was waged two miles north of the James River. Once again Confederate forces repeatedly charged across open fields toward strongly defended positions bristling with cannons. The results were predictable.

At first light the following morning a Union officer set to paper what he saw on the sloping field in front of the Federal defenses. "A third of them [Rebels] were dead or dying, but enough of them were alive and moving to give the field a singular crawling effect," he wrote. The Confederates had lost 5,650 dead, wounded, or missing. The Union loses were put at 3,000.

The 49th PV was near enough to hear the roar of battle but were held in reserve and didn't participate in the Union victory. Neither had McClellan who was safely tucked away on the USS *Galena*, a gunboat on the James River. At times the vessel was bobbing in waters 10 miles from the battlefield. In essence he had deserted his army, and if not for the fact that his troops were victorious, he would have likely been court-martialed for dereliction of duty.

Although the Forty-ninth wasn't drawn into the Battle of Malvern Hill, they continued to share in the misery that had plagued the campaign from the outset. Spirit-sapping rain started to fall shortly after midnight on July 2nd and didn't let up. The footsore Pennsylvanians marched all day through mud that at times reached mid-calf. When they arrived at Harrison's Landing on the James River, they were out of food and, "hungry as dogs." Slumping to the ground, they slept in the syrupy soil.

Being ordered to retreat after winning major victories had a souring effect on the morale of Union forces. After the Battle of the la Drang Valley, even though we won, our base camp at An Khe was subdued and quiet for days. Thousands of Americans, North and South, had drank hot blood during the Peninsula Campaign, and neither side was inert to the mental effects of such carnage. Civilians were horrified by lengthy casualty lists being tacked up in public places. Those who participated in the killing would live with the sights and sounds of it for a lifetime.

In the words of Westbrook, the regiment, "was about played out. If this duty lasts much longer there will be no Forty-ninth, the men are very weak from exposure, every person has diarrhea." The failures and setbacks that marked the first year of war had a wearing effect on them and their president. After the failures on the Virginia peninsula Lincoln said he was, "as nearly inconsolable as I could be and live." Adding to his mental anguish was disconcerting reports that the Army of the Potomac was being brought low by illness. Diseases such as typhoid fever and dysentery were responsible for filling more graves than shot and shell. Bombarded by conflicting reports, Lincoln decided to check out the situation himself.

On the evening of July 7, 1862, Lincoln and Secretary of War, Edwin Stanton, boarded a steamer and headed for Harrison's Landing, arriving the following afternoon. The hastily organized visit came as a surprise to most. It was announced by a thunderous salute from a gunboat and urgent orders for the men to ready themselves for a presidential review. More than a few men in the ranks pursed their lips to hold back giggles and outright laughter when their gangly leader paraded by on horseback. From eyewitness accounts it appears that Lincoln's mount was too small for his 6-foot 4-inch frame, and he had trouble getting synchronized with its gait. This caused him to bounce, and whenever he lifted his stovepipe hat to salute his troops it seemed he was in danger of becoming unseated.

It was dark when Lincoln rode by the 49th PV with McClellan in tow. If the men were becoming disenchanted with their commanding general, their love for the president never wavered. He might look ridiculous on horseback, what with his feet nearly touching the ground, but he was a man they could trust and admire. After the impromptu review the president dismounted and stood on a fence rail to address the men who had fought so bravely. In expressing his feelings toward them he said, "The country owes you an inextinguishable debt for your services."

The country also owed them an apology for being so poorly led in the field. They had killed twice as many Rebels as they had lost and won nearly every engagement during the failed campaign. The circumstances are similar to the Vietnam War, during which we won every battle of consequence and killed far more of the enemy then we suffered ourselves. The outcome of my war will haunt me to my grave, and I suspect Jake and his pals were heartsick from the bitter defeat they were forced to stomach.

Having every right to be demoralized, the men in blue remained steadfast in their resolve to defeat the Rebels. On the plus side of things, they had proven to themselves that they were the equal of their Southern foes. French immigrant, Regis de Trobriand, rose to general rank during the war, and was the commander of the 55th New York Volunteer Infantry during the Peninsula Campaign. He heaped praise on the Union army for, "not allowing itself to be destroyed by Robert E. Lee, nor by George B. McClellan." Tragically, the leadership the army needed so desperately in the field was months away. Nearer in time was the war's bloodiest day.

Chapter Six

For more than a month the Union army lingered at Harrison's Landing, doing little more than holding dress parades and keeping the Rebels at bay. In spite of the galling retreat, It remained a disciplined fighting force, made evident on August 12. That evening during dress parade, charges of cowardice and, "absenting himself without leave from the 49th PV regiment while in the face of the enemy," were brought against a man named Tyson. The offense was punishable by death, but a lesser sentence was handed down.

According to Westbrook the man was sentenced, "to have one-half of his head shaved and have a board tied upon his back with the word, 'Coward,' inscribed on it in large letters; and be marched before all the regiments in the brigade. In addition to this, he was to forfeit $10 out of wages due him by the United States and be confined in prison at hard labor for two years."

The following evening Tyson, with hat in hand and the board of shame on his back, was marched in front of the brigade as the drum corps played "Rogues' March." The worst example of public humiliation I witnessed occurred during my first week in Jump School. A student decided to quit after being continuously "dropped" to do push-ups for what the cadre perceived to be lack of motivation. The entire class was standing in formation as the student was brought before us.

"Tell them what you want to do," an instructor yelled, pointing toward us. "I want to quit," the kid said in a barely audible voice.

"What?" the Black Hat yelled. "They can't hear you."

The guy ended up screaming that he was a quitter. He was crying by the time the instructor allowed him to head for the building where he would be terminated. It was awful to watch, and I vowed that I would die before I'd put myself in that position. I guess that was the purpose behind it, but other guys quit and weren't put through anything like that.

The Army of the Potomac hadn't quit during the Peninsula Campaign, but their commanding general had. On August 14th the 49th PV received orders to march the following morning. They were up at 3 a.m., and soon ready to move out, but the order to do so didn't come. That entire day and well into the evening they watched troops and wagons pass by on their way off the peninsula. The wagon train, said to be 50 miles long and consisting of 12,000 wagons, was still squeaking, and swaying by the regiment on August 16. Being designated as the rear guard the regiment didn't get under way until supper time. Before their departure they propped dummies with sticks for rifles along the breastworks at 50-foot intervals.

It was well past dark when the regiment came to a stream about four miles south of Charles City. The men had spent a rare day without having to slosh through mud and water and nobody wanted to get wet before bedding down for the night. Jake was probably among others in Company D who milled about while discussing possible ways to ford the stream without getting wet. As they pondered the situation a voice from the darkness wheedled; "Men, step into the water, you will camp soon."

"Damn you, get in yourself," shouted Sgt. Cunningham who clearly had gotten enough advice for one day. The man in the dark was wearing waterproof gum boots and obediently complied with the NCO's suggestion. They heard later that the unidentified man was said to have been McClellan.

For several more days the 49th PV continued marching toward Fort Monroe. When they reached Yorktown on August 19, they camped on the banks of the York River. Some of the men hunted for oysters as others stripped a peach orchard clean of fruit. Westbrook estimated there had been a thousand bushels of peaches on the trees when they arrived, and not a single one left on a branch when they departed the next day. When they reached Hampton on August 21, they were issued rations of soft bread, the first they had enjoyed in four months.

During my tour in Vietnam with the 1st Cav., we didn't get any fresh food for nearly the entire year. Everything we ate was either C-rations from a can or B-rations prepared by cooks when we were in base camp. B-ration powdered eggs scrambled up green and were as unappetizing as they looked.

Toward the end of my tour, camp life had improved to the point where we were sleeping on cots inside large CP tents. One morning a guy came through the tent announcing fresh eggs were being served in the mess tent. I thought he was joking and went back to sleep. He had been telling the truth, and I gave myself hell for not believing him. After that, fresh eggs for breakfast became quite common.

Around the same time fresh eggs started showing up, a huge pile of barbecue spareribs was laid out on a long table in the mess tent. It was the first fresh meat we had had in almost a year, and we were told to eat as much as we wanted. By the time I had eaten my fill I was smeared with barbecue sauce from forehead to waistline. I've never tasted anything so delicious, and every time I order ribs at a restaurant, I remember that feeding frenzy at An Khe in the late spring of 1966.

On August 22, 1862, the Forty-ninth reached Fort Monroe and boarded the steamer Montreal.

Two days later they docked at Alexandria and the Peninsula Campaign became history. They were different men from those who set out on the endeavor. Their dedicated diarist saw them as, "a hard looking lot of soldiers and very dirty." Despite their appearance, and having been cheated out of accomplishing the mission, they weren't defeated soldiers like those who had beat feet back to Washington after the Battle of First Bull Run. After months of hardships and vicious combat they'd been transformed into veterans and had whipped the Rebels soundly during nearly every engagement. Yes, they had retreated from the peninsula after being at the doors of Richmond, but it was through no fault of their own.

For the first time since leaving Alexandria in March the men had an opportunity to read current newspapers. What they read was largely depressing accounts of Confederate gains and Union ineptitude. President Lincoln had had enough of McClellan after the fiasco on the peninsula and on July 11 relieved him of command. Maj. Gen. Henry Wager Halleck was appointed General-in-Chief of all Federal forces and Maj. Gen. John Pope was given command of all Union troops north and west of Richmond, with the exception of McClellan's men who were still moving off the peninsula.

Pope's boastful nature and condescending remarks resulted in him being disliked by troops on both sides of the conflict. Because of family connections - he was a collateral descendant of George Washington and through marriage related to the wife of President Lincoln - he enjoyed a place on the promotional fast track. His first leg-up was a leap of grades from captain to brigadier general on June 14, 1861.

Initially, it appeared that the star was deserved when Pope was instrumental in opening large sections of the Mississippi River for Union navigation. This earned him a second star, which also seemed will placed when his men helped win the Battle of Shiloh on April 6-7, 1862. Lincoln rewarded his in-law with the new posting, but it wasn't long before he regretted the trust he put in the man that Lee described as, "a miscreant."

Pope fancied himself a field general and often bragged that his headquarters was in the saddle. To further the puffery he signed his messages, "Headquarters in the Saddle." The signage caused a distractor to remark that, "General Pope doesn't know his headquarters from his hindquarters." The bombast might have been overlooked if not for the language in his first general order address to his troops.

"Let us understand each other," Pope began. "I have come to you from the West, where we have always seen the backs of our enemies;

from an army whose business it has been to seek the adversary and to beat him when he was found. Dismiss from your minds certain phrases, which I am sorry to find much in vogue amongst you. I hear constantly of 'taking strong positions and holding them,' of 'Lines of retreat' and 'bases of supplies.' Let us discard such ideas. Let us look before us and not behind. Success and glory are in the advance, disaster and shame lurk in the rear."

Pope had publicly criticized McClellan's handling of the Peninsula Campaign, and there was much for him to find fault with. Nonetheless, the troops loved McClellan and they didn't like this newcomer disparaging him, and them, in his accusatory address. Pope's words are reminiscent of remarks I heard made by a new commander who took over Command and Control North after our popular commander left. Word quickly got around that although he wore paratrooper wings on his uniform, he had only made three jumps, and not the required five needed for graduation from Jump School. Neither was he a qualified Special Forces officer, which made it unlikely we would accept him as one of our own. Whatever remote chance he had of being welcomed into our ranks was dashed when he gave his introduction speech to those of us in Recon Company.

The gut-sprung newcomer said we were some of the sorriest looking soldiers he had ever seen, and he was going to shape us up. To be fair we did dress however we wanted to, and we didn't spend much time in the barber chair. In our defense we were conducting the most dangerous missions of the Vietnam War and we felt this earned us considerable slack and preferential treatment. We obeyed orders and we felt that was sufficient.

Aside from the new colonel's martinet nature was the fact that he was a phony, and we saw right through him. Worse than that his oversized ego made him dangerous. As if what we were doing was some kind of parlor game, he said he was going to break the record for cross-border missions conducted in a month. At the time the number stood at 30, and it incensed those of us running the targets that we would be thrown out there for such a frivolous reason.

He further jeopardized lives by demanding that the launch site commanders got an OK from him before pulling a recon team out of Laos or North Vietnam. That would take additional time when every second counted. The launch site teams quit rather than comply, and the colonel replaced them with people who didn't know what they were doing. This almost caused the death of my entire team. When we got to the launch site all the personnel I knew and trusted were gone, replaced by people I didn't know.

The replacement Covey rider, who would coordinate our insertion, was a lieutenant I had never laid eyes on. I showed him my map and told him to avoid this particular valley, because it was full of antiaircraft guns. He said he would, but he seemed distracted, and I didn't get the sense he got it. A few minutes later I mentioned it again to him and he bristled. I didn't bring it up again, but I still didn't think he understood.

Heading into the target a few hours later I was busy on the radio when my assistant team leader nudged me and yelled there were fires on the ground. What he thought were fires were 37 mm antiaircraft guns firing. The lieutenant was flying us straight down the valley I had told him to avoid at all cost. The only way we survived was nosediving the Hueys down to treetop level. The after-action report stated we were taking fire from more than 50 positions. That's how incompetence and stupidity can get you killed. That was the last mission I ran. I told the idiot camp commander I didn't mind dying, but I did mind dying stupid. His reign came to an end when he fabricated a story in order to be awarded a Silver Star medal for valor. When his lies were discovered, he was forced to retire from the Army, but was allowed to keep his retirement benefits, which I find disgraceful.

During my nine years in the Army, I was blessed with wonderful leaders, and that one noxious poseur proved the exception. When I was assigned to the 7th Special Forces Group at Fort Bragg in 1973, I checked in with the group sergeant major. He told me, "If you're right, don't come bothering me. But if you're wrong, that's when you need to come to me, because that's when you'll need my help." That's an example of the caliber of leaders I served with.

It's tragic that in war hubris and incompetence is paid for with the blood of men honor bound to follow orders, no matter how ruinous. Jake and his regiment would soon pay a price for their commander's recklessness, but fate spared them from the Second Battle of Bull Run fought from August 28-30, 1862. The struggle took place on the same ground as the battle fought July 21, 1861. This time the strapped Confederates were after the Union's bountiful supply depot at Manassas Junction.

Critical to the success of the endeavor was Gen. Thomas "Stonewall" Jackson's so-called foot cavalry. His infantry earned the complimentary nickname during the spring of 1861 when their speed and stamina on long marches bewildered the Federals and tied up Virginia's Shenandoah Valley like the lacings of a boot. During a five-week period, Jackson's infantry and cavalry raised dust and hell along nearly 650 miles of roads and trails.

At times Jackson's men marched more than 30 miles in a day. Thanks to an SF officer, I got a taste of what Jackson's men accomplished. We had spent a few weeks training at a Marine Corps camp about 100 miles from Fort Bragg. During a bout of drinking in the officers' club after the conclusion of the training a Marine asked our guy how we were getting back to Bragg. "We're going to march back," he said. Because he said it, we had to do it. To give a rational reason for it they said it was going to be a test to see if modern-day soldiers could replicate what Jackson's legendary foot cavalry had done.

With full rucksacks, web gear and weapons we were tasked with covering the 100 miles in four days. It was stinking hot, and the heat radiated up in visible waves from the black asphalt back roads we skirted during the march. By the time we finished the first 25-mile leg I wondered if I could do it again the next day. I was surprised to find the second-day march easier than the first. That wasn't true for everyone. One of my teammates had blood oozing from patches of skin on his inner thighs that had been rubbed raw. By the third day I felt great and was enjoying the walk through the countryside. That afternoon a van of hippies drove by waving and shouting. One of them tossed a joint of marijuana out the window, and I saw it land on the shoulder of the road just ahead of us. My A-team commander who was leading the march with the team sergeant turned back to the rest of us and said, "Don't even think about it."

Some of us felt so good on the final 25 miles to Fort Bragg that we ran part of the way. When we got back to our company area we sat on the grass and reviewed our experience. My team sergeant removed his boots and socks and held his feet up, revealing deep blisters on both soles. He told me he would have rather died than fall out of the march. We had roughly reenacted what Jackson's men had done, but it was easier for us. We were well fed, well equipped and had all the fresh drinking water we wanted.

Jackson's men were malnourished, ill-equipped and often had to drink brackish water. Some of them had no footwear, and country boys or not, they had had to suffer. During their march to the supply depot at Manassas Junction in late August 1862, they covered 62 miles in two days, much of it on rough roads strewn with sharp stones. Adding to their misery was the lack of cooling rain to provide relief from the heat and dust kicked up by thousands of men and animals on the move. I don't think Civil War soldiers handled adversity any differently than we did a century later. You lean forward, shut out the pain best you can, and endure.

When I was 8 or 9 years old, I was given the job of digging up a row of potatoes in our large garden. I scowled at what appeared to be an impossibly long row of plants. I angrily stomped the forked spade into the ground and turned up the first russets. I kept my eyes on the ground, digging and imagining heroic escapes from my perceived bondage. Before I knew it, I sidestepped onto the headland at the edge of the patch and realized my work was done. Turning up that long row of spuds taught me to tackle a difficult job head on and get it done. Years later, when I was being pushed beyond exhaustion, I mentally stepped into the wheelhouse of my mind, disconnected myself from my body, and concentrated on the task at hand. My mantra became, "Everything ends. I might die, but it will end."

For Stonewall and his men, it ended on the morning of August 27, 1862, when they reached Manassas Junction. Spread before them was an oasis of plenty to quench every want their tortured bodies fevered for. Only a small contingency of Union troops troubled them with pestering cannon fire as they rushed the banquet table of Union goods. The square mile of milk and honey was filled with delicacies and sundries of war from buttons to belts and bullets. Crammed warehouses built of fresh sawn wood smelled of leather, foodstuff, and oiled metal. Scores of loaded boxcars stood on half-mile long track spurs like grab bags for the taking.

A blanket, canteen, perhaps new shoes were snapped up by the needy, but the loadstone that drew the Rebels full attention was a large assemblage of sutler wagons. These were the mobile equivalent of the modern PX, offering goodies from candy to tobacco. The civilian owners of the wagons had fled, knowing they didn't have a prayer of saving their goods. With the abandon of pie-eating contestants, famished men crammed their mouths with canned lobster, pickled oysters, cured ham and soft bread. Pockets were filled with nuts, hard candy, cigars.

Jackson, mindful of the dangers posed by inebriated soldiers, said he feared the barrels of whiskey more than he did Pope's army. He ordered every barrel and demijohn of strong spirits broke open, but his wolves of war thwarted the effort. Some dipped their canteens in puddles of booze as others drank from cupped hands.

When a semblance of military order was reestablished, the Confederates hauled away what medical supplies and needed items they could transport. Jackson then allowed his men to continue their scavenger hunt and take what they wanted. What couldn't be consumed on the spot or lugged away was put to the torch or ruined. The Rebels were nowhere to be found when Union troops arrived at the devastated supply depot. What they found was a vast field appearing as if a tornadic wind had swept through. Most of what hadn't been carried off was defaced or burned. Stirrups had been cut off new saddles. Flour, salt, meat, cornmeal, and other perishables were dumped in piles on the ground. War is waste, but surly some who witnessed it on such a shameful scale must have felt at least a tinge of guilt.

The 49th PV was camped a mile west of Alexandria when they received news of the Confederate raid on the supply depot. The following day, August 28, they got marching orders, but spent the day waiting for word to move out. While they lounged against their packs and fiddled with busy work, the opening act of the Battle of Second Bull Run was playing out not many miles to the south. The war had moved on after the first chaotic clash, and many of the dead were left unburied. Now, greeting the new combatants were sun-bleached skeletal remains swaddled in winding sheets of decaying rags.

Jake's regiment was spared participation in the battle that concluded August 30, with the Confederates logging another victory. The engagement cost the Union about 14,000 casualties. The Confederates, mostly fighting from strong defensive positions, suffered about 8,000 casualties. Pope had been outfoxed at every turn with his men paying for his mistakes with their blood. As far as Union troops were concerned, the only good that came from the three-day clash was that Pope had been exposed as a blustering incompetent. When the fighting ended, many of the men in blue were unable to stifle sneers when they saw him.

The depth of contempt soldiers reserve for commanders like Pope is bottomless. Every war has these pompous pretenders, and as often as not their unveiling costs lives. The most prominent fraud I encountered during the Vietnam War was a major who worked in the TOC at CCN. He was constantly second-guessing decisions made on the ground by recon team leaders and expounding on what he would have done. This was particularly hard to digest because he had never been in combat, much less run a mission across the fence.

The major got his chance to show what he could do when he was sent into Laos with a company-size unit called a Hatchet Force. It was made up of Vietnamese and Montagnard mercenaries led by a handful of Special Forces soldiers. They came under fire as soon as their boots hit the ground. I wasn't there, but I read messages generated during the event and talked to survivors.

Initially, the major ordered the men to create a perimeter, and put M-14 toe-popper antipersonnel mines in front of their fighting positions. The plastic casing of the puck-sized mine was colored olive drab to be difficult to detect. An eight-digit coordinate of its location was supposed to be recorded. I only used them to booby trap Claymore mines to keep the enemy from sneaking up during the night and turning them around toward us. We always recovered them when we moved out the next day. I was very careful with them, and never left any behind. That wasn't true for everyone. Some target areas became closed off to recon teams when they became dangerously seeded with the mines.

When mortar shells started raining down on the Hatchet Force's position the major ordered them to move right through where they had placed the toe-poppers. Several guys got their feet blown off. After a few hours on the ground the major was screaming for an extraction. I heard that he actually radioed back, "Get me out of here. I didn't know it was like this." The operation became a complete mess, and a number of good men were killed and wounded. They were extracted the next day, and the major left camp in disgrace.

Pope had failed just as miserably, and it came as no surprise that Lincoln relieved him of command. The Army of Virginia was merged with the Army of the Potomac, and despite strong opposition, McClellan was again placed in command of this powerful force of nearly 90,000 men. By then Lincoln knew McClellan was no fighting general, but he did have a genius for organization, which the exasperated Union soldiers desperately needed. Inexplicably, the men in blue, for the most part, retained confidence in their Little Mac.

Perhaps it's best that fighting men aren't privy to the beef-witted decisions made on high by derelict commanders. Duty, after all, remains duty and soldiers are obliged to obey orders without question. At the squad and platoon level one can try to talk sense to a greenhorn leader about to make a foolish, life-threating mistake. An example is the infantry platoon in Vietnam that refused to walk down a trail into a possible ambush after a newly arrived officer ordered them to do so. It was an article of faith in Vietnam that trails were channels of death. I would have balked, too, but if the platoon leader, after being schooled in the dangers of such a move, insisted on doing it I would have obeyed. That said, I would have ensured there were flankers on each side of the trail.

The Civil War is rife with examples of men unhesitatingly obeying orders they knew would almost certainly lead to their deaths. By this stage in the war the men of the 49th knew their commander, Col. Irwin, was a reckless inebriate. They also had to have doubts about McClellan, considering his performance during the Peninsula Campaign. The Rebels harbored no doubts about their top commanders. Lee, flushed with victory, set his eyes northward on Maryland. If he could win a decisive battle on northern soil, it could prompt France or England to support the rebellion. Spill enough Union blood and antiwar politicians in Washington could garner the votes needed to win the November elections.

Another check mark on the plus side of the strategy sheet was that Lee's marauding army would gain access to Maryland's bountiful larders. This would allow Virginia to replenish its storehouses with the autumn harvest. And there was an outside chance some Marylanders, many of whom demonstrated favor for the Confederate cause, would throw their lot in with the triumphant Rebels. Additionally, Richmond would remain safe while Federal troops concentrated their efforts on the invasion force.

For all that, there remained the unpredictable, intangibles of war. In early September 1862, superbly confident Rebels waded into the slow current of the Potomac River about 20 miles south of Frederick, Maryland. To win favor from the populace Lee instructed his troops to sing, "Maryland, My Maryland," as they marched into the state. His hope was this would win support and draw volunteers into Confederate ranks. The recruiting effort was largely a failure because those who wanted to fight for the Confederacy had already traveled south to do so. Instead of being welcomed with open arms the Rebels were held at arm's length, farther, if possible, because of the "strong-smelling" body odor they put off.

The bedraggled invaders didn't look like the formidable fighting force Northerners had been hearing about for months. One disgusted Marylander penned, "I asked myself in amazement, were these dirty, lank, ugly specimens of humanity the men that had driven back again and again our splendid legions with their fine discipline, their martial show and colour {sic}? I felt humiliated at the thought that this horde of ragamuffins could set our grand army of the Union at defiance. Oh! They are so dirty! I don't think the Potomac River could wash them clean."

Another onlooker wrote, "They were the dirtiest men I ever saw, a most ragged, lean, and hungry set of wolves." The observer also noted that the Rebels had an elan and swagger about them that their Northern foe seemed to lack. If they assumed the fight had gone out of the Yankees, they were wrong. Lee thought the Union army, demoralized and in disarray after Second Manassas, would be incapable of posing a threat to his men for at least a month. What he didn't realize was that most of the men in blue knew in their hearts that it wasn't their fighting ability, or lack of courage, that lost them battle after battle. They had been out generaled, not outfought. Whatever damage Second Manassas had done to Union morale was largely neutralized by the reappointment of McClellan.

Soldiers love commanders who demonstratively love them. Perhaps the biggest reason for the troops adoring McClellan is that he was careful with their lives. Lee, whose appraisals of McClellan's capabilities were generally spot-on, underestimated his organizational abilities. In just a few days Pope's Army of Virginia had been assimilated into the new Army of the Potomac and was on the move.

On September 5, the day after Lee's men, wet to the waist, started fording the Potomac River into Maryland, the 49th PV received orders to prepare rations for three days, and each man was issued 60 rounds of ammunition. The day was pleasant and some of the men walked over to where the 126th Pennsylvania Volunteers were camped and spent time visiting. Rain started falling late that night, and cooler temperatures set in. The rain ended around noon, and it wasn't until late afternoon that Jake and the others received orders to break camp and prepare to move out. The sun was low on the horizon when they formed ranks and started marching toward Washington.

By 10:30 p.m. they had crossed the Long Bridge and were in the nation's capital. The sound of marching woke many citizens. Groggy with sleep they crowded sidewalks to watch the troops pass by. The overcast skies had cleared, and the features of the men could be seen in the moonlight. Shouts from the sidelines repeatedly asked the question, "Where are you headed?" The reply was all that was known. "We are going to meet the Rebels."

It was 1 a.m. when the 49th halted outside Tennallytown, now spelled Tenleytown. They rested until 6 p.m., then resumed the march. They tromped through the darkness until 9:30 p.m., when they made camp about six miles south of Rockville, Maryland. The Union troops were moving well, but the Rebels were having a tough go of it. The feasting done at Manassas Junction was days in the past, and now they were subsisting on mostly corn and apples pilfered from fields and orchards. The predictable result was widespread diarrhea.

Thousands of Rebels fell along the wayside, too sick or exhausted to continue. And there were those who joined the Confederacy to protect Southern soil and refused to participate in fighting done on Northern ground. Within days of crossing into Maryland, Lee had lost 15,000 troops for reasons unrelated to combat. About 50,000 soldiers remained, and they were eager to whip the Yankees in their own territory.

McClellan left two corps behind to safeguard Washington. This gave him six corps, about 85,000 men, to counter the Confederate threat. By September 7, Lee's Army of Northern Virginia was massed near Frederick, Maryland. He had his sights set on Harrisburg, capital of Pennsylvania, about 70 miles to the north. This called for moving his supply lines west of the Blue Ridge Mountains so as not to be in danger of being cut by Union cavalry. To pull this off, 12,000 Union troops at strategically important Harpers Ferry, as well as 2,500 soldiers in Martinsburg, had to be eliminated. To accomplish this, Lee opted to divide his army. How all this was to work was detailed in Special Orders No. 191, which he distributed to his commanders on September 9.

The complicated special orders were so sensitive that Maj. Gen. James Longstreet memorized his copy, tore it to bits and chewed the fragments into pulp. Despite safeguards to keep the ultra-secret document from enemy hands, fate came into play. In this case destiny chose Maj. Gen. Jackson as the patsy. Renown for keeping his own counsel, Jackson nonetheless made a copy of the orders and sent it to his brother-in-law, Maj. Gen. D. H. Hill. He wanted to let Hill know that his division had been selected to act as rear guard for Lee's army. When the copy of the orders generated at Lee's headquarters reached Hill's headquarters, an officer, known but to God, knew that Hill had already received a copy from Jackson. The officer, supposedly realizing that the orders would make a terrific souvenir, wrapped them around three cigars and stashed them in a pocket.

On September 12, Jake's regiment was camped at the northern base of Sugarloaf Mountain, a 1,282-foot-high elevation about 10 miles south of Frederick. When McClellan received word that day that the Rebels were leaving the strategically important crossroads city, he ordered troops forward to occupy it. When he rode into the municipality the following day he was greeted by mobs of well wishers. He and his mount, Dan Webster, were draped with garlands of flowers as adults and children reached out their hands to touch him. McClellan later crowed that he had been, "nearly pulled to pieces," by his admirers.

Among the Union troops occupying Frederick that day was the 27th Indiana Regiment. They were ordered to make camp in a meadow on the outskirts of the city. The Rebels had used the area for their campgrounds, leaving it littered and laced with fetid, slit trench latrines. After searching for a habitable area, a grassy spot near a fence line was chosen. After pitching tents, the men brewed coffee and socialized. Sergeant John M. Bloss and Corporal Barton W. Mitchell were chewing the fat when Mitchell noticed a thick envelop in the grass. Upon inspection he discovered it contained a sheet of paper wrapped around three cigars. The heading of the paper read, "Headquarters, Army of Northern Virginia, Special Orders, No. 191." Following were surnames including Jackson, Stuart and Longstreet. The name of the most prominent Southern foe of all graced the bottom of the official-looking document that ended, "By command of Gen. R. E. Lee; R. H. Chilton, Assistant Adjutant-General."

The two men dutifully handed the find, cigars and all, over to their company commander, Captain Peter Kop. After quickly moving up the chain of command the orders were in the hands of Brig. Gen. Alpheus

Williams. The paper might have stalled there for lack of authenticity, and the warranted assumption that the all-too fortuitous find was a Confederate ruse. At this point fate ushers forward Union Col. Samuel E. Pittman who had served with Chilton before the war and was familiar with his handwriting. After assuring Williams that the orders had been penned by Chilton, they were on their way to McClellan's headquarters along with a note explaining how they were found and why they should be accepted as genuine.

It was nearing noon, Saturday, September 13, 1862, when McClellan read the orders. In his elation he shouted, "Now I know what to do." Prior to receiving Lee's strategy and disposition of forces he had been predictably cautious. Buoyed with confidence, he proclaimed to his staff, "Here is a paper with which if I cannot whip Bobby Lee, I will be willing to go home."

The day the key to victory landed in McClellan's lap, Jake had been on the march since sunrise. The 49th moved in a northwesterly direction to Buckeystown and crossed the Monocacy River via the covered Baltimore and Ohio Railroad bridge. A short distance beyond the span the men came to an abandoned farm. An orchard was too enticing to pass up, and for the next several hours the men picked apples and peaches at their leisure.

Serving with the 7th Special Forces Group at Fort Bragg in the early 1970s, I learned how delicious found fruit can be. For two weeks the A-team I was on had to live off the land as we paddled an RB-15 rubber boat down the St. Johns River in Florida. We were given five M-16 bullets and permission to shoot any wild game except deer. I was made the designated shooter and used three rounds to kill two water moccasins and a feral pig. The snakes were swimming in the river, and one of them sank before we could retrieve it. We roasted the one we got, and it was big enough to provide the 12 of us with sizable portions.

We hemmed and hawed about shooting the pig, because we had seen several of them rooting in the woods and thought they might belong to a local farmer. We were three or four days into the exercise and basically starving so the decision was made to shoot one. I had drawn a bead on one of them when our team leader changed his mind.

He hadn't completed the word "wait" when I pulled the trigger. I got a dirty look from our West Point captain, but he scarfed down the ham with the rest of us.

A week into the survival exercise we spotted a deserted house near the riverbank and decided to spend the night in it. Scouting out the area around the house we discover a grapefruit orchard. The fruit was ripe and sweet as oranges. After making ourselves at home in the two-story house I took a walk along a nearby dirt road. I hadn't gone far when I came upon a small convenience store. I bought a box of powdered doughnuts and returned to the house. I thought the guys would be thrilled, but when I produced the goodies, somebody noted that if we ate the doughnuts, we would be breaking the rules of the exercise. Buying food wasn't living off the land. I hadn't thought of that, and after discussing the matter for a few minutes we agreed not to eat them. The ants got the doughnuts, but we left with several dozen grapefruit.

The exercise taught me that it takes two or three days without eating for a modern man to revert back to a primitive hunter-gatherer. That means a person spends nearly every waking hour either looking for food or thinking about how to get it. We had gotten a lot of survival training, but until the stomach is completely empty it doesn't mean much. During SF training we were given a deck of cards with color photographs of eatable plants on one side and information about them on the other.

When we dug up some wild potatoes, we knew we were supposed to boil them twice before eating. We were hungry and tried to eat them after one boiling. They were bitter and uneatable. Boiled twice they were as good as store-bought spuds, maybe better. A week into the exercise we had more food than we could eat. What started out as an ordeal became a wonderful voyage down a beautiful river. One day we were catching fish in our general-purpose nets that also serviced as hammocks.

Standing in the warm, waist-deep water I reminded a teammate that we were getting paid for having so much fun.

One night as we paddled down the river, we sang old rock 'n' roll songs. People living along the shore probably thought we were drunk.

Another night we laughed uproariously as we navigated a fast moving stretch of river filled with snags. The guy with the flashlight on the prow of the boat would yell, "Starboard, starboard," and everyone on the right side of the boat would paddle like mad. Then we'd hear, "Port, port, more port." We probably hit as many snags as we missed that night, but the tough RB- 15 bounced off them and we'd continue merrily along.

After the exercise was completed, we enjoyed a greasy breakfast at an Air Force base prior to boarding a C-130 for the flight back to Bragg. We were going to parachute in, because the Air Force would then have to pay for the flight. If we landed, the Army would have to pick up the tab. Somewhere over South Carolina the breakfast turned on me. There wasn't a restroom on the aircraft or even a bucket. As the situation grew desperate, I considered hanging my butt over the end of the partially open tailgate. My understanding team leader said I could be the first out the door, and he'd also hook up my static line so I wouldn't have to stand sooner than necessary.

The instant the green light came on I was out the door. I was worried that the jolt of the parachute opening would override my pressing defense, but it held. Nonetheless, I was in agony and desperate to get on the ground. So desperate, in fact, that I dumped air out the back of my maneuverable chute nearly all the way to the ground. When I landed, everyone else was still hundreds of feet in the air. I was out of the parachute harness in a few seconds and squatting in heartfelt relief. It wasn't until I was hiking up my pants that I realized I was about 50 yards from bleachers filled with spectators.

Jake and the others wouldn't have cared about onlookers either as they picked the orchard clean. After retiring to a nearby meadow they feasted and rested until 8 p.m. Then, with the landscape illuminated by a crescent moon, they marched over a ridge and made camp at Jefferson, Maryland. That day, as part of Lee's battle plan, Jackson's forces opened their attack on Harpers Ferry. The strategically important junction town was defended by mostly inexperienced soldiers under the command of Col. Dixon S. Miles. He had been convicted by a court of inquiry of being drunk during the First Battle of Bull Run.

After eight months of inactivity, he was given command of a brigade and tasked with the defense of the "Godforsaken, stinking hole," that would change hands 14 times during the war.

At first light on September 13, 1862, screaming Rebels broke cover and charged Federal positions defending Maryland Heights overlooking Harpers Ferry. The determined attack was shattered by Union gunfire coming from behind hastily thrown up abatis obstacles. Once, then again, the attackers were repulsed by greenhorn troops led by Col. Eliakim Sherrill. The former New York Congressman was a steadying influence on the men, many of whom had been in uniform less than a month. He was readying them for another onslaught when a Confederate bullet tore through his cheeks and tongue. The sight of their commander being carried from the field rattled the young soldiers. When veteran Rebels launched another attack, the defenders lost their nerve and headed to the rear. Attempts to rally the troops failed, and by mid-afternoon an order to retreat to Harpers Ferry was issued.

By nightfall the enemy was firmly in control of the high ground on Maryland Heights and Loudoun Heights. In order to take advantage of the hard-won positions they had to manhandle cannons to the summits. The agonizing effort included clearing lanes through dense woods. The exhausting work wasn't combat, but the pain it caused was probably imprinted for a lifetime on those who suffered through it. The cannons, each weighing nearly a ton or more, pitted men against gravity. Ultimately, rope-burned hands were raised in triumph when dozens of cannons arrayed along Maryland Heights opened fire on the town below.

On Sunday, September 14, 1862, the 49th PV started marching at 9 a.m. to the small town of Burkittsville. Arriving about 2 p.m. they rested in a cemetery and listened to distant sounds of explosions coming from Harpers Ferry about 11 miles away. While they waited for orders to march toward the besieged town, Henry Minnichan amused his buddies by making a captured chicken take the oath of allegiance.

Not everyone in VI Corps was lallygagging that afternoon. Six miles south of South Mountain, fighting raged at Crampton's Gap where about a thousand Rebels manned defensive positions behind a stone wall. The VI Corps commander, Maj. Gen. William B. Franklin, was as cautious as McClellan, and grossly overestimating the strength of the enemy. Although his force outnumbered the Confederates 12 to 1, he believed just the opposite was true.

For a few hours the belligerents exchanged fire, and then Franklin sent for reinforcements. He was content to wait until the next day before resuming the attack. Maj. Gen. Henry W. Slocum, commander of the First Division, was disgusted by Franklin's hesitant manner, and ordered an all-out frontal attack on the Confederates.

The order to charge came around 4 p.m., and the Union troops responded with enthusiastic shouts. Their morale had been bolstered by citizens in Burkittsville who had given them water, baked goods, and verbal support. It was a much-needed lift after the deflating string of defeats. On that hot afternoon as they rushed across freshly harvested cornfields their steps neither faltered nor slowed. The Rebels poured heavy fire into the advancing ranks but started to break and run when the charging Yankees neared the stone wall. Many of the Southerners left their knapsacks and rifles behind as they fled. The pursuit didn't end until the Graycoats had been driven beyond the summit of South Mountain.

The victorious charge had been costly with more than 500 Union troops killed or wounded. The Rebels suffered nearly 900 casualties and had about 400 men captured. Particularly painful for the Confederate troops was the loss of four battle flags. The 49th had been held in reserve, never leaving the cemetery. The following day, September 15, they marched through Crampton's Gap and set up camp in a field near the western base of the mountain.

Harpers Ferry fell to Jackson and his men that day, but the regiment wouldn't receive that news until six days later. While resting on September 16, they heard sporadic cannon and rifle fire coming from the nearby farming community of Sharpsburg. Lee had chosen a ridge line east of the town of 1,300 citizens to anchor his 18,000 men. To his front was Antietam Creek, which the following day would be colored with blood.

When Jake awoke in the early morning of September 17, 1862, a fog had settled on the area. It was to be the bloodiest day in United States history. At 6 a.m. the regiment started marching in a southwesterly direction toward the sound of fighting. The clamor of fierce combat grew louder as they neared Boonsboro at the foot of South Mountain. When they reached the summit of a hill near Keedysville, it became clear that a colossal battle was being fought. The elevation afforded a "fair view" of billowing smoke flashing red with fire.

Jake and the regiment would be doubly fortunate this day as shattered men fell in windrows. McClellan, who had initiated the fighting at first light by attacking Lee's left flank, decided to hold VI Corps in reserve near his headquarters. The Pennsylvanians' second stroke of luck came days earlier when their drunkard commander was put in charge of the Third Brigade of VI Corps' Second Division. Jake's outfit was part of the division's First Brigade, which nullified Irwin's influence on them. Tragically, this wouldn't be the case for the 7th Maine Infantry Regiment.

As the 49th PV waited for orders to move forward, Brig. Gen. Winfield S. Hancock, who had masterfully maneuvered them during the Peninsula Campaign, spoke to them. "Boys, do as you have done before; be brave and true, and I think this will be your last battle."

For 13-year-old Charles "Charley" King, the general's words proved prophetic. The youngster had caught the attention of Jake and the others months before when they were raw recruits drilling on a parade field. The patriotic youngster stood on the edge of the expanse, beating a small drum in time with their footsteps. When he was approached, he furnished his name and said he wanted to join the regiment as its drummer boy. After the reluctant parents were assured their son would be well cared for, and kept as safe as possible, they gave their permission for him to enlist.

Charley was 12 years, 5 months and 9 days old when he raised his right hand and took the oath. He served with such dedication during the Peninsula Campaign that he received the honor of being made drum major of the regiment. Drummer boys were noncombatants and were generally kept in the rear to help with the wounded. Charley was of another mind, and he moved forward with the 49th PV when it was ordered into a whirlwind of vicious combat near a whitewashed house of worship named Dunker Church.

Major Tom Huling, the new commander of the regiment, led the men into the fray. They were soon forced to, "kiss the ground," as Westbrook put it. With little protective cover the position became untenable, and Hancock ordered them to fall back a short distance. As they did, Huling's horse, Sam, was hit by a piece of shrapnel and went down. Gus Heller was also hit and lost one of his feet. Then Charley was hit by a piece of shell and collapsed into the arms of a fellow soldier. For three days he struggled to live, but the wound was too severe. Accounts differ as to where he was buried. What is certain is that drum major Charley King was the youngest soldier to die in combat during the Civil War.

The luck of the 49th PV held at Antietam with three men wounded and two killed. Overall, the toll for the Union was more than 12,400 dead, wounded, captured, or missing. The tally for the South was more than 10,300. If Irwin had been commanding the 49th during the battle the regiment might have suffered as grievously as the 7th Maine Regiment did. His foolhardy order to the ill-fated unit the afternoon of the battle was said by the 7th Maine's commander, Major Thomas Hyde, to have been, "an inspiration of John Barleycorn," a reference to whiskey.

Addled by strong spirits or a vainglorious impulse, Irwin ordered the 166 men and 15 officers of the 7th Maine to charge across open ground in an attempt to dislodge a much larger force protected by a stone wall. The ensuing carnage was as predictable as it was needless. Less than 70 men managed to limp and stagger back to friendly lines. The others laid dead or wounded.

Hyde, who would later be awarded the Medal of Honor for his bravery that day, wrote how survivors after reaching the relative safety of the Union lines were, "crying like children," because of the unnecessary waste of human lives. The following day Irwin was removed from command of the brigade and returned to the 49th PV

Antietam is widely considered a strategic victory for the Union in that the Confederates retreated back to Virginia. Others have argued it was a draw. When the fighting ended, the Union held the contested ground and by definition that made them the victor. But the cost in human lives had been terrible. Every house, barn and shed for miles around was turned into makeshift hospitals, and that wasn't enough. The number of casualties overwhelmed all efforts to provide adequate aid, and many men died of wounds without receiving the comfort of a caring hand or swallow of water.

The day following the battle the 49th PV waited for orders. Wherever they looked the ground was covered with dead men and horses. The warm temperature hastened decomposition, necessitating a truce so bodies could start being buried. There were far too many. When the regiment started marching toward Sharpsburg on September 19th, the widespread butchery became sickeningly evident. They had to skirt the road for some distance because it was paved with blackening corpses. As Jake passed the wreckage of swollen, discolored bodies he likely tried to breathe with shallow sniffs, as I had done. My introduction to the stench of death came in the trampled, blood-splattered elephant grass in the la Drang Valley. Days later, back at base camp, in fresh air and sunshine, the smell mysteriously returned for an instant.

In terms of casualties there would be worse bloodlettings than Antietam. Gettysburg, Chickamauga, Chancellorsville, and Spotsylvania Courthouse head that list. Yet, more Americans died in battle outside Sharpsburg, Maryland, on September 17, 1862, than on any other day in the nation's military history. When the shooting sputtered to an end around 5:30 p.m., more than 3,650 men had died violently. During the ensuing days many of the wounded also died.

The Rebels could take comfort in knowing their generals had largely performed brilliantly. McClellan's generalship was so lacking as to make one wonder what side he was on. Perhaps his greatest fault was not attacking Lee's vulnerable forces before Jackson and his men had time to reinforce them. Nor did he pursue Lee's army as it withdrew back to Virginia.

Fed up with his overly cautious general, Lincoln relieved him of command of the Army of the Potomac on November 5, 1862. A few days later Maj. Gen. Ambrose Burnside was given command of the principal Union army in the Eastern Theater. Under his leadership it would soon come to grief at a Virginia riverfront town called Fredericksburg.

Chapter Seven

As Jake trudged back to Virginia, he had time to mull over his first year of war. Reality had likely dispelled any daydream notions he had prior to the fighting. He had learned that glory, if it even exists, was as fleeting as simple comforts had become. The punishing rains, needless suffering, and distressing retreats from victory during the Peninsula Campaign had tested his fortitude and caused him to doubt many of his leaders. Only the righteousness of the cause remained inviolate. That kept him going, step after weary step.

I was certain our cause in Vietnam was just, too. It was only toward the end of my time there that cynicism crept in. It didn't have anything to do with our reason for being there, but how we were being kept from winning. I had gotten my first inkling of this in late November 1965 when we weren't allowed to pursue retreating NVA into Cambodia during the Battle of the la Drang Valley. During the decades after the war damning revelations, and in my mind treasonable conduct by high-ranking politicians and military brass, have turned my stomach.

Robert S. McNamara, Secretary of Defense from 1961-68, admitted in 1995 that as early as 1965 he knew the Vietnam War, as we were fighting it, was unwinnable. And yet in 1966 he was responsible for lowering mental requirements for induction into the armed forces, resulting in large numbers of low IQ men being sent into combat. This conveniently filled vacancies that otherwise would have had to be filled by those with college deferments, Reservists or National Guards. Then there's the reported admission by former Secretary of State, Dean Rusk, that during the war the United States, through the Swiss embassy in Washington D.C., routinely alerted the North Vietnamese to the next day's target locations to be bombed. His explanation was that it was done to reduce civilian casualties.

Jake would have been spared most knowledge of McClellan's shortcomings, but not the disorientating shakeup they caused. News that McClellan had been relieved of command reached them on November 8, 1862. On that snowy, bitterly cold day they were camped near a depot in White Plains, Virginia. The following day, a Sunday, they learned that Maj. Gen. Ambrose Burnside had assumed command of the Army of the Potomac. He hadn't wanted the job, afraid that he wasn't up to the task. His misgivings would prove accurate during the upcoming Battle of Fredericksburg.

A large battle like Fredericksburg is dizzyingly complex, made all the more so by one-sided interpretations and conflicting accounts. Like many students of the engagement, I had judged it as another example of Union ineptitude verses brilliant Southern generalship. In this case Burnside was the moron and Lee, once again, the genius. However, recent scholarship suggests it's far from that simple. Burnside will likely never look good, but he may in time emerge as a tragic figure rather than a bumbler with needless blood on his hands. There certainly was plenty of blame to go around on the Federal side.

Political pressures on Lincoln had been exacerbated by McClellan's failures as a field general. A Union victory was imperative to renew Northern confidence and to quiet the clamor of defeatist Democrats who wanted to allow the South to go its own way. Because of this, Burnside had no choice but to go forward with a winter campaign despite its inherent dangers. To a large extent he inherited McClellan's plan to plow through Fredericksburg, and before Lee could mass enough troops to stop him, move on Richmond. Victory hinged on speed and surprised.

After assuming command, Burnside organized the Army of the Potomac into three Grand Divisions and a reserve force. The Right Grand Division was commanded by Maj. Gen. Edwin V. "Bull" Sumner, Center Grand Division by Maj. Gen. Joseph Hooker, and the Left Grand Division by Maj. Gen. William B. Franklin. The 49th PV was under Franklin's command, and on November 15, 1862, it received orders to march at 8 a.m. the following morning. It proved to be a hike of 18 miles, and it was long after dark when they went into camp between Bristow and Cattle Station near the Orange and Alexander Railroad.

The highpoint of the day was receiving word that Col. Irwin had departed for Pennsylvania. After a 15-mile march the following day, they bedded down beneath tall pines in Stafford County. Another day of hard marching carried them to within five miles of Stafford Courthouse. Relentless rain was making travel difficult and caused supply trains to flounder and fall far behind the marchers.

Insistent hunger compelled the men to forage for food wherever it was likely to be found. Farms were obvious targets, and the relative civility shown noncombatants during the early days of the war was largely gone. Food, intended to carry already impoverished Southern families through winter months, was commandeered. Helpless civilians seethed with rage as their milk cows and beef cattle were slaughtered, quartered, and carried off by unapologetic men.

Temperatures continued to fall during the night, and industrious Federals shored up their tents with logs. Shivering men fed wood to campfires and hoped for orders to settle into winter camp. As much sense as going into winter camp made, overriding factors, political and military, ensured that wouldn't happen. At 8 a.m. on December 2nd, a quiet Tuesday morning in camp was transformed into a swirl of activity when the 49th PV received word to decamp and prepare to move out. Two hours later the order was countermanded, and muttering men reset their tents. One can imagine the griping that ensued, but something was afoot. In the early morning of December 4, the men broke camp and marched until they were about two miles south of Brooke Station near Stafford, Virginia.

The following day the Pennsylvanians trudged through pelting rain to reach a nearby pine woods, which afforded a measure of relief from worsening conditions. By mid-afternoon it was snowing and growing alarmingly cold. When the march continued the next morning there were 4 inches of snow on the ground. Slipping and tripping on ruts and divots hidden beneath the snow made the trek torturous. Westbrook noted in his diary that the frigid 10-mile march, "tried our best and strongest men." When they went into camp at 2:30 p.m. they were near the dark waters of the Rappahannock River. On the far side could be seen the looming outline of Fredericksburg.

The underpinnings for disaster had already been laid. Key to the attack plan was the rapid fording of the river, which required bridging materials and pontoon boats to support planking.

Misunderstandings, lack of urgency and blundering incompetence led to days of delay. While the massive army of 120,000 Federal troops awaited the arrival of the boats, the Rebels gathered strength and built strong defenses on the heights south and west of town. There was little for the Bluecoats to do but wait and suffer.

On the morning of December 7, Jake and the others heard that six men in the division had frozen to death during the night. Food had become so scarce that one man in the regiment ate corn intended for mules and horses. The distribution of a ration of hard tack and two rations of coffee on Monday, December 8, was the first since the previous Saturday. Men wondered if the patriots at Valley Forge during the Revolutionary War had it as hard.

The temperature was well below freezing the morning of December 11, when the bridge building finally started in predawn darkness. There would be six pontoon bridges in all, three across from the town and the rest farther downriver to the south. Initially the bridge builders were hidden by a thick fog rising from the river. As the morning sun burned away the protective veil, the workers became easy targets for sharpshooters firing from buildings on the opposite side. Federal cannons on Stafford Heights pounded the town with a continuous barrage that some veterans thought was louder than the heaven-splitting roar during the Battle of Antietam. By mid-afternoon, fire and smoke rose from houses and public buildings that had been reduced to jagged ruins. Despite the bombardment the Rebels continued to pick off pontoniers whenever they tried to resume work.

Time and again engineers leapt to their task, only to add more dead and wounded to the river and banks. As semi-submerged corpses drifted languorously downriver, Burnside watched his plans being unhinged by the Rebels' stalwart defense. When belching cannons failed to stop the murderous fire coming from cellar windows and lower-floor apertures, he was at a loss as to what to do. Not so West Point trained engineer, Brig. Gen. Daniel P. Woodbury, and artillery chief, Brig. Gen. Henry J. Hunt. They suggested pontoon boats be used to ferry a landing force across the river to clean out the sharpshooters.

Burnside initially balked, believing the effort suicidal. Brave men of the 7th Michigan and 19th Massachusetts were willing to give it a shot, answering Burnside's misgivings with shouts to let them try. The enthusiastic response resulted in permission being given. The number of men said to have participated in the historic crossing varies from as few as 70 to more than 130. They piled into three, blunt-nosed pontoon boats designed as heavy support platforms rather than sleek, water-parting vessels. Some men frantically paddled, as others hunkered low in the boats as Minie balls whizzed overhead and blew splinters out of the thick, wooden gunnels.

When the boats reached the midway point in the river the sharpshooters, firing from high points on the Fredericksburg side of the river, lost sight of them. This contributed to the Federals making the first successful water crossing, under fire, as well as establishing the first bridgehead, in American military history. In their eagerness to get at the Confederates, some of the Yanks jumped into the icy water before the blunt bows of the boats ground ashore. The attackers swarmed up the barren slopes and started pushing the Rebels back from the waterfront. House to house fighting soon ensued. This was a novel brand of warfare neither side was experienced in waging.

The defenders had the advantage, firing from windows and behind every manner of cover.

Water and Caroline streets became shooting galleries as charging Federals presented easy targets. As casualties mounted and the fighting grew in savagery, the mannered act of taking prisoners was largely replaced by plunging bayonets and merciless pointblank blasts from firearms. The no-quarters fighting littered streets with dead and wounded. By early evening Rebels grudgingly withdrew from the town and fell back to strong entrenchments.

Townsfolk, for the most part, had been evacuated prior to the heavy shelling on December 11. With the Rebels gone, the town was defenseless. The Confederates had made the Yanks pay for every yard of Fredericksburg real estate, and now the Federals exacted their vengeance. The sacking of Fredericksburg is one of the most egregious episodes of the Civil War. Looting private homes, smashing family heirlooms, throwing libraries of books into mud and countless other wanton acts of destruction is indefensible. And yet, within the context of the moment, it's understandable.

The glaring eyes of a defiant Southern citizenry had touched raw nerves in the psychic of Union soldiers, and with their dead stiffening in the streets many felt a stern retribution was justified. It's telling that many, if not most, of those who participated in the pillaging of the town felt no shame for their actions. In a carnival-like atmosphere they gleefully cavorted through abandoned homes, smashing a parlor piano here, an antique keepsake there, and leaving wardrobes of clothing trampled in their wake.

The 49th had no part in this, having spent the day in line of battle on the opposite side of the river. Much of the time was spent watching a pontoon bridge being built in fits and starts as Rebel fire allowed. When the span was finally in place and troops started crossing, the regiment received orders to withdraw a mile to a wooded area. They spent another miserable night doing their best to keep from freezing as the temperature dropped to 30 degrees. My own memories of being outdoors in killing cold gives me an idea of what that must have been like. Stinging fingers and toes impart no fear when warmth is nearby. It's another story when one is stranded beneath a leaden, frozen sky and night is coming on.

When I was with the 7th SF Group, the A-team I was on was participating in a winter field exercise. We had been pushed hard through the night by aggressor troops with the 82nd Airborne Division. Around 4 a.m. we had put enough distance between us and them to grab a few hours of sleep. Exhausted, we crawled into our sleeping bags without bothering to rig up a shelter. I stupidly left my boots outside my bag, and a few hours later when we needed to start moving again, they were frozen solid. It took a few minutes of working the leather back and forth with my hands to make the boots pliable enough to get my feet into them.

With only enough time to make one canteen cup of coffee, we huddled together around the flaring fuel tablet heating the brew. Then, as the coffee was passed hand to hand, I noticed that as each teammate bent their head forward to take a sip, a drop or two of snot dripped from their nose into the cup. Conditions being what they were, all 12 of us drank from the cup without a word said.

On December 12, 1862, a Friday, reveille for the 49th PV sounded at 4 a.m., and by 8 a.m. Jake and the others were on the march back to the river. An hour later they were tromping across the pontoon bridge that men had sacrificed their lives to construct. On the far side they made a left turn and marched a half mile to the vicinity of a large stone house where they formed a line of battle. They were a half-mile from the river and near the Old Richmond Stage Road.

Jake's Company D, as well as three other companies from the regiment, were tasked with supporting an artillery battery. There were exchanges of artillery and skirmishing between Union infantry and Rebel cavalry, but no serious clashes. But there was little doubt that the following day would bring a major battle between men eager to get at each other's throats. The Confederates had the advantage of fighting from behind formidable defenses. The heights west of town bristled with tangles of slender tree trunks, their sharpened tips facing eastward. There were breastworks, too, fortified with logs. Bordering the lower slope of Marye's Heights was an innocuous 4-foot-high stone wall. The workers who built the free-standing barrier decades before, couldn't have imagined the terrible role it would play on December 13, 1862.

The Battle of the la Drang Valley in November 1965 stands alone in my wartime experiences. It was one of the bloodiest battles of the Vietnam War, but a pinprick compared to what happened outside Fredericksburg on December 13th. With bridges across the Rappahannock and the town occupied, the entire Army of the Potomac, more than 120,000 strong, was brought to bear against 78,500 Confederates massed on high ground west of town. The day of slaughter dawned with a dense fog shrouding the soon-to-be contested ground to the west and south of the violated river town.

At 7 a.m., Company D was relieved from guarding the battery and returned to the regiment's position. Burnside's battle plan, as laid out to his commanders on December 12, was vague. It called for Franklin's Left Grand Division to conduct the main attack south of town where the 49th was located.

Franklin and the others wanted firm orders for the morning attack so they would have time to position their forces accordingly. Their leader hesitated, choosing to return to headquarters and hash things out a bit more.

When Franklin received the awaited orders sometime after 7 a.m. on December 13th, they weren't at all what he expected. He had been under the impression that he would be attacking with the entire Left Grand Division of about 60,000 men. Instead, as he understood Burnside's inexact wording, he was to send out only a single division, with another in support, to strike the right flank of Lee's forces on Prospect Hill. Franklin chose Maj. Gen. George G. Meade's division of about 4,500 men to spearhead the attack, and a division under the command of Brig. Gen. John Gibbons in support. Maj. Gen. Abner Doubleday's division was selected to protect Franklin's left flank and was arrayed facing south between the river and the Richmond Road.

With the fog masking enemy forces from one another, Meade started moving his men out at 8:30 a.m. When the fog started to clear around midmorning, Union troops attracted the attention of two Rebel cannons that started lobbing shells into their massed ranks. Counterfire soon knocked out one of the cannons, but the other continued to pour round after round into Union ranks. Federal cannoneers blazed away at the lone gun that was stalling the advance and throwing off the battle's timetable. Quick maneuvering frustrated the effort, and only when ammunition ran low did the Rebel cannon pull back.

While the maverick cannon was successfully dodging shells, other rounds were blowing bloody gaps in Rebel ranks. They took it without much reply, because the dozens of cannons hidden in the woods had been ordered to hold their fire until the Yankees moved within range, about 800 yards.

When they closed to within 400 yards, canisters filled with marble-sized iron balls could be added to the murderous menu. In Vietnam our version of this type of scatter-gun munition was the M546 Beehive anti-personnel round fired from a 105 howitzer. Each shell contained 8,000 steel flechettes resembling 3 penny nails with stabilizing fins. The barrel of the artillery piece would be leveled like a shotgun and fired directly into the ranks of charging NVA.

On the night of December 27, 1966, Beehive rounds were used with devastating effect against an estimated 1,000 NVA trying to overrun LZ Bird in South Vietnam's Binh Dinh Province. The artillery base was supporting ground operations being conducted by the 1st Cavalry Division. Despite its importance, LZ Bird was defended by less than 200 men. It was on the verge of being overrun when Beehive rounds were fired pointblank into swarms of attackers. An eyewitness said the tiny projectiles "shredded" the bodies of the enemy soldiers, abruptly ending the attack.

Rockets filled with flechettes were also fired from helicopter gunships. Because they made little noise, we often prepped LZs with flechette rounds prior to our recon teams being inserted. I got to see the effectiveness of what we called "nails" during a recon mission in Laos. A Cobra helicopter fired several flechette rockets at a large group of NVA moving toward my six-man team as we waited for extraction helicopters to arrive. The rockets were fired during a pause in the shooting, enabling me to hear the tiny projectiles hitting the leafy jungle canopy. Thousands of needle-sharp darts impacting thick foliage creates a sizzling hum similar to the sound of heavy rainfall. Decades later at a Special Operations Association reunion in Las Vegas I met the Cobra pilot who made that gun run. He claimed I radioed him saying, "Keep it coming, you're nailing them to the trees." I don't recall saying that, but I can still recall the unique sound of that murderous murmuration.

Jake would have likely never forgot the tremendous artillery exchange the morning of December 13. The 49th had moved across the road to support an artillery battery and was being protected by an embankment. Around 1 p.m. the Federals resumed the attack, heading up Prospect Hill toward a wooded area concealing about 35,000 troops under the command of "Stonewall" Jackson.

The fabled general had more than 50 cannons and nearly a dozen soldiers for every yard of defensible soil. There was also a potentially fatal flaw of neglect in the Rebel line that if properly exploited could have resulted in a Union victory. The Achilles heel was a 600-yard-wide section of marshy ground and thick underbrush that had been left unmanned, possibly because it was thought the Bluecoats would skirt the difficult terrain. The Confederates were mistaken.

Meade's First Brigade, under the command of Col. William Sinclair, and consisting of all Pennsylvanian troops, spearheaded the attack. Brig. Gen. C. Feger Jackson's Third Brigade was to the left, and the Second Brigade, commanded by Col. Albert L. Magilton, followed in close support. As they raced across railroad tracks, they were met by a maelstrom of bullets and exploding shells. Sinclair was wounded straight away, but the men continued to surge forward, albeit in a herky-jerky manner due to rough terrain and heavy fire.

Disorganized and rattled, the attackers struggled through tangles of brush and over broken ground. Their fortitude was rewarded when they stumbled into the gap and started turning the Confederate's flanks. A brigade of Rebels about a quarter mile behind the undefended opening was overrun, and for a time it appeared Burnside's hope of tearing Lee's army in two was coming to fruition. It was not to be. The Confederates quickly brought up reinforcements, while the Union's response to the golden opportunity was maddingly slow. Federal troops fought courageously but were unable to hold their ground. When they ran out of ammo, they were left with only their fists and bayonets to fight with.

Once again, the 49th was fated to remain on the sidelines during the battle, resulting in only one man in the regiment being wounded. Although Burnside repeatedly ordered Franklin to send his entire force forward, the commander of the Left Grand Army ignored the order, falsely claiming all his men were employed. Westbrook's diary entry revels the frustration felt at the slow reaction of Union reinforcements.

"This evening the troops on our left have fell back," Westbrook wrote. "They could not hold the ground, and we could not leave our position to assist them. Burnside's troops are marching to their assistance past us, but oh! they are slow. Some of our boys went to their ranks to learn what troops they were and did some swearing to their officers because they were not moving faster to help the Pennsylvania Reserves."

The bravery of the Federal soldiers who advanced up Prospect Hill was remarkable but availed nothing. Disjointed movement, ignored orders, miscalculations and a slew of other shortcomings resulted in one area of intense combat being dubbed the "Slaughter Pen." The slope itself was christened "Dead Horse Hill," strewn as it was with carcasses.

Fighting in the southern sector ended as darkness fell, but not the suffering. Thousands of wounded men laid throughout the night on frozen ground. Enough men, in fact, to populate a small town. Franklin had lost about 5,000 soldiers, the Rebels 3,400. This, of course, was only half the Battle of Fredericksburg. To the north Union forces were experiencing what Burnside's generals had warned him would be tantamount to, "murder, not warfare." They were speaking of Marye's Heights, and their ignored prophecy came to pass on that grim, winter's day.

The stone wall, shored up with dirt and timbers, proved unbreachable. Three thousand Confederates saw to that. The rock bulwark hemming the heights was fronted by Telegraph Road, thereafter, to live in history as the, "Sunken Road." The Rebels, stacked behind the wall in ranks three and four deep, had the front-line firing and the others reloading rifles and passing them forward. This relay system resulted in an unrelenting torrent of musket fire that decimated the attacking Federals.

On higher ground behind the wall were batteries of cannons that swept the entire field below with a steady barrage of explosions. Divisions were sent into the meat grinder piecemeal throughout the afternoon with tragic results. After several attempts without a Federal soldier getting to within 40 yards of the wall it was obviously hopeless. Burnside was strongly counseled to give up the frontal assaults, but he stubbornly persisted. Perhaps he had no choice. A Tour-guide's narration at the battlefield suggests the last three assaults were sent forward to keep the Confederates from counterattacking and pushing the Army of the Potomac into the river. By the end of the day 6,000 to 8,000 Bluecoats, some accounts claim more, laid dead and wounded on Marye's Heights. Confederate losses were about 1,200.

It had been another crushing defeat for the Union, brought about largely by incompetent leadership, backstabbing and Lincoln's insistence for action. Overall, Federals suffered more than 12,500 casualties, while the Rebels sustained less than half that number. The carpet of carnage spread across the pastoral hillsides defies the ability of words to describe. After visiting the battlefield, Pennsylvania governor, Andrew Curtain, told Lincoln, "It was not a battle, it was a butchery." Most every imaginable horror had been visited upon the soldiers, including fire when a blaze started by explosions incinerated wounded men unable to escape. Throughout the night mournful cries of pain and pleas for water created a macabre drone that made men cover their ears to shut it out.

A story has been passed down through the years that on the morning after the battle Confederate infantryman, Richard Kirkland, serving with the Second South Carolina Volunteers at the stone wall, could stand the cries of anguish no longer. After receiving reluctant permission from his commander, Brig. Gen. J. B. Kershaw, the young sergeant is said to have gathered several canteens and gone out among the Union wounded, providing them with water and what comfort he could.

Although official accounts report both sides firing at one another whenever a target presented itself, Kirkland was apparently given a pass. He was said to have ministered to the wounded in his area for more than an hour without being shot at. Because of his courageous action he became known as the "Angel of Marye's Heights." The story became widely known in 1880 via a letter Kershaw wrote that appeared in the Charleston News and Courier. Kirkland was killed September 20, 1863, during the Battle of Chickamauga. Without his input the veracity of the story continues to be debated. Nonetheless, in 1965 a statue memorializing his alleged humanitarian act was placed on the battlefield near the stone wall.

Whether the story is apocryphal or not, it serves as a reminder that bitter enemies can be moved by human compassion. I saw a painting commemorating Kirkland's deed in Eldon's office when he was the commander of 1st Special Forces Operational Detachment Delta. It depicts a Confederate soldier cradling a wounded Union soldier in his arms while giving him a drink of water from a canteen. After Eldon retired from the Army as a major general, he hung the painting in a prominent hallway of his home.

A less inspiring work would have been painted of Burnside and his senior officers on the evening of December 13, as he castigated them for failing to follow his orders and causing the carnage. Tempers were short and the accused shot back that the debacle was completely Burnside's doing. In a fury the indignant commander vowed to lead his former IX Corps in a frontal attack on Marye's Heights the following morning. He was talked out of the suicidal assault, but even proposing such a calamitous venture is an indication of his frayed mental state.

Although both sides were expecting the battle to resume December 14, neither side had the will to do so. Except for light skirmishing and brief cannon fire in the morning, Westbrook reported an, "unusually quiet," afternoon. He used the word "pleasant" when describing the weather. Nothing else could have been agreeable that day. The 49th remained in line of battle, continuing to support a battery of cannons. As the hours passed, word began to circulate that Federal losses had been exceptionally heavy. With afternoon shadows lengthening, white flags of truce rose here and there. Soon the scrap and scuff of picks and shovels were heard as the work of burying the dead commenced.

I've never seen killing on that scale, nothing close to it. When the dark heavens began to glow and undulate eerily along the northern horizon shortly after 6 p.m. on December 14, many soldiers thought God was casting a judgmental light on the open-air mortuary. Men stood dumbstruck, cowered in fear, and dropped to their knees in prayer as the light grew in radiance and spread across the dome of the sky.

It's likely that a few troops from northern climes, and perhaps a handful of learned Rebels, realized the startling eruption of shimmering lights was a presentation of the aurora borealis. But most were ignorant of the phenomenon, certainly Southerners. Northern lights, as commonly referred to, are seldom seen below the Mason-Dixon line. Compounding the psychological shock was the intensity and striking colorations associated with this particular event, thought to have been caused by an unusually large solar flare. Shafts of multicolored rays were described as dancing and swirling across the sky. One battlefield witness wrote that the sky, "turned as red as blood." Clearly, as noted in the accounts of eyewitnesses, this was one of the most spectacular aurora borealis in recorded history.

Northern lights occur when charged particles discharged from the sun strike atoms in the Earth's atmosphere. Red, blue, and white seem to have been dominate colors that night. The colors of the national banner suggested to some Federals that the display was a favorable omen. A writer for the Richmond Daily Dispatch interpreted it differently. He wrote that the crimson columns of light signified, "the blood of those martyrs who had offered their lives as a sacrifice to their native land." Elizabeth Lyle Saxon included the awe-inspiring event in her book, "A Southern Woman's War Time Reminiscences." The author recalled that an elderly woman told her, "Oh, child, it is a terrible omen. Such lights never burn, save for kings' and heroes' deaths."

Many soldiers thought the world was coming to an end. A Rebel witness wrote in his diary that a Florida unit that hadn't wavered on the battlefield ran off in a panic when the "remarkable brilliancy," appeared. When I was a youngster, I was camping with a few friends next to Round Lake in central Minnesota. One night we were sitting around our campfire when the sky lit up with bright, swirling colors of green and gold. We had never seen anything like it, and quickly concluded the end of days had arrived. We got down on our knees and started praying like we had never prayed before. When the lights faded and we realized we would live, a feeling of relief and gratitude swept over me. It was a feeling I would experience time and again in Vietnam.

When darkness returned to the skies above the Fredericksburg battlefield a hush settled on the land as men composed themselves and tried to understand what had happened. Then, shaken soldiers on both sides, started singing hymns and continued on into the night. It was, perhaps, a fitting conclusion to a battle in which valor was squandered. After the Federal army retreated back over the river the bridges were drawn in, "and swung around to our shore."

As Westbrook put it, "We think Burnside has been outgeneraled." The men knew they had been terribly misused. An army of lesser men would have folded camp and called it quits. Not surprisingly, the desertion rate did rise dramatically. But Jake and others stayed the course, continuing to believe in themselves and their cause. But Burnside wasn't done with them yet, and within weeks he would literally lead them into a quagmire of misery.

For the time being, Jake's spirits could be lifted by the hope that surely now they would be allowed to rest and revitalize in winter camp. But, in spite of all they had been through, petty injustices persisted. Less than a week before Christmas a man in Jake's company, possibly Jake himself, had his blanket stolen causing him to nearly freeze. When he went to Col. Irwin requesting an order that would allow him to draw a new blanket from the brigade quartermaster he was turned down. Westbrook quoted Irwin as saying he wouldn't, "give a damn for a soldier who couldn't get a blanket." He concluded the account by writing, "Scarcely had it gotten dark until the colonel was short one blanket."

The men could right such indignities themselves, while others, such as a persistent shortage of food, were beyond their abilities to correct. Westbrook noted that since Burnside took command, they had been without rations half the time. While winterizing their quarters on Christmas Eve near White Oak Church, Virginia, the men cynically speculated about what they would be feasting on the following day. What they had was pork and hard tack, and not a drop of liquor. Westbrook wrote that nearly all the headquarter officers managed to get drunk. The one-sided festivities were repeated New Year's Day. I recall the animosity felt by us enlisted men in the early months of my first tour in Vietnam when our officers got a club long before we did. The saying that leaders eat last doesn't always hold true.

The day after Christmas, Jake listened to a letter from the president being read. Dated, December 22, 1862, it was addressed to the Army of the Potomac. "I have just read your Commanding General's preliminary report of the battle of Fredericksburg," Lincoln wrote. "Although you were not successful, the attempt was not an error, nor the failure other than an accident. The courage with which you, in an open field, maintained the contest against an entrenched foe, and the consummate skill and success with which you crossed and re-crossed the river, in the face of the enemy show that you possess all the qualities of a great army, which will yet give victory to the cause of the country and of popular government. Condoling with the mourners for the dead, and sympathizing with the severely wounded, I congratulate you that the number of both is comparatively so small. I tender you, officers and soldiers, the thanks of the nation. Abraham Lincoln."

For the next few weeks, the men worked on improving their living quarters and speculating on scuttlebutt about the regiment being consolidated from 10 down to four companies. This rearrangement came to pass January 11, 1863. Surplus officers and NCOs were sent back to Pennsylvania to recruit more soldiers. Irwin was among those departing, which certainly gladdened the hearts of many.

The following days were described as "cold and frosty" in the mornings, then often becoming pleasant by afternoon. Squad drills and inspections kept the men somewhat busy, but there was plenty of time to mull over the disastrous battle and disparage Burnside's handling of it. What they weren't aware of was the general's secret plan to redeem himself with a surprise attack against Lee's army. In spite of winter conditions, Northern politicians and newspaper columnists were clamoring for military action.

Considering what they had just been through, and worsening weather, made a move on the enemy unlikely. So, there was considerable surprise on the evening of January 16, when orders were issued for the men to march the next day with 60 rounds of ammunition and three days rations. When the order was postponed for three days, Westbrook figured Burnside would, "play hob this time," and mess things up again.

It wasn't Burnside playing hobgoblin, but his own officers, two of whom were actively conspiring against him. Brig. Gen. John Newton and Brig. Gen. John Cochrane, both of whom were with VI Corps, told Lincoln that they and others had lost faith in Burnside and if the Army of the Potomac suffered another defeat on par with Fredericksburg it would likely collapse. Learning of this, Burnside traveled to Washington to give Lincoln his take on things. This delayed the attack and necessitated a change in the battle plan. The weather up to then had been unseasonably mild and would have afforded a favorable window in which to launch the operation. The postponement provided the time needed for a meteorological disturbance off the southeast coast to develop into a powerful nor'easter storm.

When the 49th PV moved out during the late morning of January 20, the air was cold, and the overcast sky was dark and menacing. The rain held off during the 12-mile trek that ended in a wooded area five miles above Fredericksburg. The objective was to rapidly throw pontoon bridges across the Rappahannock River and strike Rebel forces with a haymaker blow they didn't see coming. Around 7 p.m. the dreaded rain began drumming on tent canvas. The pitter-patter soon gave way to the ominous hiss and pop of heavy rain driven by strong winds. The downpour continued through the night, and by morning gave no indication of letting up. Men who managed to fall asleep woke up in muddy water. The temperature was just above freezing, but cold enough to cause hypothermia. As the land melted into a slurry of mud, it became impossible to start fires. The absence of a heat source or fortifying dipper of hot coffee must have been agonizing.

As the torrential rains continued, Burnside insisted on pushing forward. Wagons, cannons, and caissons were sinking to their axles in mud. Mules and horses lurched and lunged in hopeless efforts to dislodge them from the muck. Additional teams were added to the traces until two dozen or more creatures were straining to move a single wagon or artillery piece. Horses broke legs, blew out their hearts and died from exhaustion or a merciful bullet. Mules, realizing the futility of what they were being driven to do, brayed their contempt of lash and curse.

Burnside's desperation kept him from admitting that any meaningful forward gain had become hopeless. Splattered with red mud from hat to heel, he rode hither and yon exhorting his men to greater efforts. When no more mules and horses were available to move a single cannon, soldiers were added to the tug lines. As many as 150 men laid hold to ropes, then put their backs into it. The muscle-straining efforts might move their burden a short distance, but when they paused to rest it sank again.

The Sisyphean labor was made more torturous by jeering Rebels on the south banks of the river gleefully deriding their floundering foe. Darkness brought an end to the inhuman tug-of-woes, but not the discontent of the soaked-to-the-skin sufferers. When Burnside ordered a renewal of the futile folly for the next day the mood became mutinous. Shortly after sunrise on January 22, as rain continued to fall, he directed his officers to issue a ration of whiskey to the men in hopes of easing tensions. The liberally poured booze went into empty stomachs, turning anger and frustration into clutched fists. Long fuming animosities between units erupted into brawls. By noon Burnside bowed to the obvious and ordered an about face.

It had rained for 30 hours, dropping more than 3 inches of precipitation on nearby Washington. For two days the winds had reached gale-force levels. The official record dubbed the disaster, "The Mud March," and it was as calamitous as the recent battle, albeit without the frightful human casualties. Still, droves of sick men became sicker as the ambulances they were crammed into were unable to move rearward. The route of advance, and then retreat, was marked by the carcasses of valuable draft animals that had been worked to death.

The operation had accomplished nothing positive, but the negative side of the ledger was filled. When Jake and the regiment managed to slough back to camp near Falmouth on January 23rd, they found their "quarters full of water." Their shanties had been occupied by others or torn down for firewood.

Boys hawking newspapers from horseback shouted out the headlines - "Burnside Stuck in the Mud." Westbrook penned that they weren't stuck in the mud, but the artillery certainly was.

The Mud March was the last straw for some Union soldiers who threw away their guns and headed home. Lincoln was also disgusted, and on January 26, Maj. Gen. Joseph Hooker became the new commander of the Army of the Potomac. Burnside had never wanted the job he was given, and correctly insisted he wasn't up to the task. And instead of helping their commander, a number of officers conspired against him. An honest reading of Burnside's overall war record suggests he was a tragic figure rather than a bumbling fool. His loyalty to the Union is unassailable, and although his battlefield legacy is marred, he did the best he could. Now, it would be "Fighting" Joe Hooker's turn.

Chapter Eight

On January 27, 1863, Jake stood in a pay line to receive money due him for July, August, September, and October. Extra clothing costs were deducted from his total take. At the time a private in the Union army made $13 a month, while his counterpart in gray drew $11. Each side paid their corporals $13 a month and sergeants $17. During my first year in Vietnam, I was a specialist 4th class, which is equivalent to the rank of corporal. My base pay was $238 a month, in addition to $65 a month combat pay. On my return to Vietnam in 1968 I quickly rose in rank to staff sergeant, and with four years in the service my monthly salary was $344.70. Add $55 a month jump pay, in addition to $65 combat pay, and I had money to burn.

Neither Jake nor I joined the military to get rich. When I enlisted in 1963 my base pay was $83.20 a month. When I arrived at the Reception Center, I was given $10, referred to as a "flying ten." The ten spot was to be used for the purchase of military necessities such as shoe polish and Brasso to shine our belt buckles. Unlike Jake I was assured three meals a day, and when we weren't in the field, a dry, warm place to sleep. This didn't apply when serving in a combat zone, but I didn't have to worry about freezing to death in Vietnam.

Jake's food supply was iffy at best, especially during the first two years of the conflict. During winter months they had to make their own semi-permanent shelters. After the debacle of the Mud March the exhausted Yanks were allowed to go into winter camp. They wasted no time in walling up tents with whatever material was available, be it mud, rough timbers or sawn lumber. The shanties, humble as they might be, were home.

While serving with the 1st Cav., I eventually upgraded from a pup tent to a larger CP tent when in base camp at An Khe. Since I spent most of my time in the field, I rarely enjoyed the comfort of sheltering tent canvas. When I returned to Vietnam as a Special Forces soldier in August 1968, it was a completely different experience. Comparatively speaking, I was dropped into the lap of luxury. My camp was on the beach just outside Da Nang with Marble Mountain on our southern perimeter.

I shared a single-room hooch with two other Americans on my recon team. The exterior plywood walls were banked with sandbags up to the level of the screened windows that were hinged with shutter flaps that could be raised or lowered depending on the weather. The tin sheeting on the roof was held in place by nails and sandbags. Spaced around the room were three bunks, as many foot and wall lockers, a small refrigerator, Jerry Plank's desk and an air conditioner. That plainest of dwellings was my refuge, and when I closed the door behind me, I shut out the war. A mission never ended until I was back within the protective embrace of those four walls. I loved that hooch as much as I've loved any place I have lived.

In time, the floor became pockmarked with holes big enough to drop a golf ball through. The holes resulted from an evening amusement involving mice. After supper, several of my friends would drop by my hooch and sit on the bunks. As the master of ceremonies, I'd fashion a paper cone around a flashlight suspended by a string from a rafter. Inside the small, circle of light on the floor would be placed a claymore blasting cap topped with a piece of C-ration cracker smeared with peanut butter.

Attached to the blasting cap was a detonating wire I'd string back to my bunk. All lights were extinguished except for the flashlight beam illuminating the bait. Within a minute or two a mouse would cautiously approach the morsel, peeking in and out of the light. As it grew braver with each incursion the tension mounted until the cringing onlookers were tittering with anticipation. By the time the mouse was eating the cracker the suspense was nearly unbearable. I'd drag it out as long as I could before squeezing the plunger of the hand-held detonator. Within the close confines of the room the flash and bang were pronounced. The light would come back on, we'd all laugh like idiots, and then someone would suggest we do it again. The explosive pastime ended when we noticed gummy flecks of atomized rodent on the walls and furnishings.

Mother Nature provided an exciting pastime for VI Corps troops a day after Jake and the others received most of their back pay. Snow fell throughout the day until nearly a foot of it covered the ground. Organized snowball fights between units filled the air with hand-packed missiles. Officers weren't exempt from being targeted and were pelted without mercy. Snow in Virginia doesn't last long, and it soon melted turning the ground into deep mud.

Living in filthy, close quarters, and often being wet and cold, sent many men to sickbeds and the graveyard. On February 2nd, the 49th PV was ordered to provide 150 men for picket duty, but only 100 could be mustered. Those who marched out to man listening posts and guard the perimeter suffered terribly from the cold. In addition to the miseries of the weather there was the uncertainty brought about by the continuing fallout resulting from the Fredericksburg fiasco.

On February 5th, Union soldiers were informed via a letter written by Maj. Gen. William F. Smith that he was no longer commander of VI Corps. Although he didn't say as much in his farewell letter, he was paying the price for playing a part in the palace intrigue that went on behind Burnside's back. Maj. Gen. John Sedgwick, a brave and well-liked commander, ascended to the vacated command slot. "Uncle John," as he was affectionately called by his troops, had missed the action at Fredericksburg, because he was recovering from wounds to his leg, wrist and shoulder suffered at Antietam.

The leadership changes instituted by Lincoln, especially the ascension of Hooker, proved beneficial to the common soldier. Hooker immediately took positive measures that markedly improved the quality and quantity of food being fed his troops. The importance of this was momentous. Until he put an end to it, crooked purveyors of foodstuff to the army held back fresh and dehydrated vegetables from the supply chain in order to sell them at a higher price directly to the soldiers. These unscrupulous merchants rivaled the enemy in doing harm to the nation's defenders.

Widespread lack of produce among cash-strapped troops drained their bodies of vitamin C, which ushered in the ravages of scurvy. The initial symptom for this deficiency disease is usually an overall feeling of listlessness. At first a soldier might attribute his lethargy to the taxing nature of military life. Not so easy to dismiss were bleeding gums and loosening teeth that wobbled with a probe of the tongue. As weeks passed without greens or fruit, joints began to ache, wounds didn't heal, headaches persisted, and daylight became nearly unbearable. Without the healing properties of an occasional apple, carrot, or a handful of greens the despairing body began to shut down. Starved of a single, readily available vitamin, soldiers died slow, agonizing deaths.

Hooker's mandate that his men regularly receive freshly baked bread and vegetables was an instant boon to health and morale. Within a few months, cases of scurvy plummeted from alarming levels to a handful. Deplorable camp conditions and lack of sanitation standards were addressed just as vigorously. With garbage piled in heaps throughout winter encampments, they were petri dishes for diseases. Closed off from sunlight and fresh air, and filled with unwashed soldiers, the huts were often foul dens of pestilence.

Dr. Jonathan Letterman, an enlightened physician for his day, understood the benefits of healthy food and clean-living conditions. As soon as he was appointed medical director of the Army of the Potomac on July 4, 1862, he set to work changing mindsets and conditions for the fighting soldier. McClellan gave the young surgeon a free hand to bring about needed changes. Initially, change came slowly, because the war took precedence and bullheaded officers dug in their heels, opposed to what they considered spurious thinking.

It was only after Hooker took the helm that change began to happen quickly. By then Letterman had convinced most of his doctors of the benefits of personal hygiene and sanitary camp conditions. He preached the need for moving camps periodically, and this innovation benefited the 49th PV. In mid February they abandoned their befouled camp near White Oak Church and relocated to a wooded area about a mile away. Letterman also focused on the implementation of proper latrines or sinks as they were then called. He said the slit trenches needed to be eight feet deep, with the deposits being covered daily by six inches of soil. Poles or slender logs held about one and a half feet above the ground were used for seats.

During the first days at our base camp at An Khe our latrine was a slit trench near where our pup tents were pitched. I was resting outside my tent one night, unable to sleep, when I noticed in the light of an illumination flare one of our guys waddle-walking toward the shit pit. He never made it. His desperate shuffle ended mid-stride. His head drooped, and he became as motionless as a statue. I turned away. It was one of the saddest things I've ever seen.

Within a week or two an outhouse was cobbled together with several toilet seats placed above 55-gallon fuel drums that had been cut in half. A few inches of gasoline or diesel fuel would be poured in the receptacles so the crap would burn. Stirring the shit was a detail I never got, but plenty of guys did. One of the pervasive smells in Vietnam was burning feces. Of course, there were the cautionary tales of guys dropping lighted matches or cigarette butts into the cut-down drums and getting their fannies fried.

By the time I returned to Vietnam in August 1968 the headquarters area at CCN had flush toilets. Recon Company never got that luxury and had to rely on an outhouse located on the north side of our living quarters. We hired Vietnamese to burn the shit, but there was always someone gripping about having their hooch downwind of the offensive smoke. I didn't mind our four-holer, but once in a while I'd walk up to the headquarters' area to enjoy a seat on a flush commode.

Hooker also instituted a fairer and more liberal furlough system for enlisted men. Then, in order to instill pride in individual units, each corps got its own insignia to wear on the uniform. VI Corps' insignia was a white cross with blue background, and its badge was a red cross with black-over-white border. Napoleon has been quoted as saying, "A soldier will fight long and hard for a bit of colored ribbon." Of course, it's what that bit of colored ribbon symbolizes that gives it worth and meaning.

The changes Hooker brought about, as well as improving weather conditions, served to right a lot of wrongs suffered by Union soldiers. Although clear skies soon clouded over, and a cold snap put an end to balmy temperatures, the men were out of the mud and under protective canvas. March was more of a lion than a lamb, occasionally teasing the men with just enough sunshine to make them believe spring had arrived. April was little better. Throughout the month Westbrook penned comments like, "Cool and cloudy," "It rained all day," "Morning cloudy, afternoon rain."

It was raining the afternoon of April 28, when Jake, with eight days of rations in his pack and a basic load of fresh ammo, marched with his regiment to within a mile and a half of the Rappahannock River. It was 6 p.m. when they reached their destination, almost directly across from Fredericksburg. The area held ghastly memories for those who had fought there the previous December, but most were eager to have another go at the Rebels on the far bank. Time is a wonderful rejuvenator of the fighting spirit. I would come back from a recon mission in Laos and say to myself, "Never again." After a few days of rest, I'd be eager to go again.

An hour before midnight the 49th PV was ordered to pack up and march to the river's edge. Their brigade had been selected to cross the river via pontoon boats and attack Rebel positions on the far shore. The successful crossing of the river by this means previously had proven its worth, but during the interim nobody had thought to create watercraft better suited for such endeavors. Members of the Sixth Maine Regiment got stuck with the detail of dragging 40 blunt-nosed, heavy-timbered vessels to the riverbank where they were arranged 20 feet apart. One exasperated Irishman gripped, "A damned pretty piece of business for the Sixth Maine to be carrying heavy pontoon boats for the Forty-ninth Pennsylvania Volunteers."

As Jake and the other assaulters waited for orders to launch the boats, they quietly speculated on their chances of making it across the river alive. When morning's first light revealed river fog so dense that the opposite bank couldn't be seen, the riverine force knew the odds had greatly improved in their favor. As soon as the boats were shoved into the river, men started paddling for all they were worth. With the exception of the ever-vainglorious Col. Irwin who stood upright in the boat, the assaulters squatted low to give the Rebs less of a target.

The vessels were halfway across the river before pickets spotted the flotilla emerging from the fog. The 49th PV, manning boats on the far right of the ragged line of vessels, were the first to reach the steep embankment. As luck would have it, the surprised pickets were congregated just above where Jake and the others were making landfall. As boat after boat emerged from the dense haze it became apparent to the defenders that they couldn't be stopped at water's edge. After firing hastily aimed shots at the wooden armada, the Confederates fell back about 100 yards.

The rattle of gunfire induced a Union soldier in one of the boats to do some retreating of his own. Over the side he went, swimming purposefully back to friendly shores. Well, not so friendly as it turned out. He paid for his act of cowardice by having his head shaved and serving out his term of enlistment at the Dry Tortugas prison in Fort Jefferson, Florida.

When the boat carrying Irwin ground to a halt he jumped into waist-deep water. He hadn't taken 10 steps before being shot in the leg. I doubt there was much hand-wringing when he went down. The Confederates, caught flatfooted and undermanned, had no choice but to retreat. When the Pennsylvanians stormed into a house near the river, they captured the captain in charge of the pickets and several sleeping men. With a bridgehead firmly established, the pontoon boats were soon supporting a span across the river. By 4 p.m. when the 49th was relieved, the Rebels had been pushed back to strong emplacements just outside Fredericksburg.

With their fighting done for the day, Jake's regiment marched back to the river and set up camp. The men woke the following day to the sound of rain drumming on their tents. After enduring the miseries of the Mud March, a warm springtime rain was a minor inconvenience. Except for mustering for pay, the regiment remained inactive during the day. The muffled sound of distant cannonading to the right of their position fueled all sorts of speculations. Initial reports reaching them said Hooker's forces were attacking the Rebel's rear about 20 miles away near a town called Chancellorsville. In contrast only light skirmishing marred an otherwise quiet day at Fredericksburg.

The far-off rumble of battle continued to growl during daylight hours of May 1. Jake stood ready to move out but no orders came to do so. Their front remained eerily quiet with only occasional shots being exchanged. Rumors sparked and sputtered, igniting feelings of hope one moment and doom the next. With evening darkness came the sound of cheering from Rebel positions. VI Corps responded by sending its bands forward to perform near the front line. Rousing martial music probably did little to placate the general feeling among Union troops that things weren't going well at Chancellorsville.

In fact, Lee was orchestrating what many students of the Civil War consider his greatest victory. But the win came at a terrible price in casualties that he could ill afford to lose. More than 13,000 Confederate soldiers were killed, wounded, or missing during the battle that started April 30 and ended May 6. The loss in irreplaceable manpower was greater than that suffered during their defeat at Antietam. One casualty in particular, Stonewall Jackson, mortally wounded mistakenly by his own troops, removed one of the South's finest warriors from the battlefield.

At first light on May 2, things began heating up along the Fredericksburg front. During the early morning the 49th moved up near the Old Richmond Road south of town. Hunkered below a protective rise, they were held **in** reserve as other units moved forward. Heavy fighting flared whenever Union skirmishers advanced to probe Rebel defenses. Fighting intensified during the afternoon when the

Yankees successfully pushed the enemy back from the contested road, and the 49th PV moved forward to ensure the gains wouldn't be lost. As Jake passed dead and wounded soldiers lying in trampled weeds and brush, he would have known that just months before many others had died fighting for the same ground.

Fighting hard for ground that would be quickly abandoned was a hallmark of the Vietnam War. Trying to imagine what Jake was seeing and thinking that afternoon brings my thoughts back to May 1969 and Hamburger Hill. From May 10-20, men with the 101st Airborne Division, the famous Screaming Eagles, supported by ARVN troops, fought to reach the summit of Hill 937 located little more than a mile from the Laotian border. The NVA had strongly fortified the hill with bunkers and hundreds of troops.

The hill is located in the infamous Ashau Valley, a place I became intimately familiar with while running recon missions on the Laotian side. The valley served the NVA as a primary funnel point for men and material into South Vietnam. The area became so saturated by enemy troops traveling down the Ho Chi Minh Trail that by 1968 it was very difficult to keep a recon team on the ground for any length of time. Those of us running Ashau targets jokingly dubbed ourselves the "Ashau for lunch bunch." It was a take-off of the Metrecal diet drink commercial seen on television in the '60s that used the phrase, "Metrecal for lunch bunch." Our time on the ground was often limited to the time it would take to enjoy a leisurely lunch.

The paratroopers finally took Hamburger Hill on May 20, but only after 72 Americans lost their lives on the steep slopes. Nearly 400 more were wounded. By body count the NVA lost 630 men killed, and likely many more were buried beneath collapsed bunkers or carried back into Laos. The savage fighting had been at close range and largely on steep, muddy terrain that made movement muscle burning difficult. The pain and suffering that took place there is immeasurable, and yet the hill had no strategic value and was abandoned soon after it was conquered.

The battle should stand as another proud achievement of the legendary division, and not as a tragic example of squandered valor like the Union defeat at Fredericksburg in December 1862. Of all the things Jake and I have in common, I think disillusionment is perhaps the most painful. We pledged our lives to causes we felt were worth dying for, only to have greed, hubris, incompetence, and political intrigue betray our efforts.

On the morning of May 3, 1863, it looked as if the bloody failures of the previous December were about to repeat themselves. The stone wall on Marye's Heights again blazed with rifle fire, shattering Union ranks as one charge, followed by another, was stopped. During a ceasefire to allow Union wounded to be removed from the field, observant soldiers noticed that the Rebels manning the wall weren't nearly as plentiful as in the past. This information resulted in a third attack that succeeded in carrying the position. The taking of the hated wall brought jubilation to the men of VI Corps, and they set to the job of pushing westward toward Chancellorsville.

The 49th had been tasked with guarding the pontoon bridge in case Rebels attacked the Union's left flank. Now, with the enemy retreating, they rejoined the corps. The commander, Maj. Gen. John Sedgwick, planned to use the Orange Plank Road to link up with the Army of the Potomac at Chancellorsville. Things went according to plan for several miles until the Rebels decided to make a stand at Salem Church. The sun was nearing the western horizon as Jake watched the regiment's sister unit, the 119th Pennsylvania Volunteers, as well as other regiments, charge forward.

Thickets of shrubs and undergrowth tripped and harried the attackers as they rushed toward a two-story brick church that had been used as a hospital and refuge for civilians during the First Battle of Fredericksburg. The Baptist church, situated on a low ridge, provided excellent fields of fire for Confederate marksmen shooting from first and second-story windows. Union troops, buoyed by the recent victory, and pumped up with hot-pursuit adrenaline, continued to surge forward into the heavy fire.

The onrushing blue wave was nearly to the church when a tremendous explosion of gunfire sent a gale of bullets tearing through the ranks with the devastating force of a bomb blast. The shattering blow was delivered by a large force of Rebels who had been lying in wait, concealed behind a fence and along a road depression less than 100 feet away. For 15 minutes some of the fiercest fighting of the war ensued. Try as they would to hold their ground the exposed Yankees were being shot to pieces.

When the Rebels counterattacked, the Bluecoats grudgingly fell back leaving hundreds of dead and wounded behind. As remnants of the 119th PV Regiment passed the 49th PV, its commander was asked where his regiment was. His answer, "All gobbled up." The phrase became a by-word for heavy casualties.

Darkness found Jake helping to hold a line near the church, uncertain as to how close or far to his front the Rebels were, or how many there were. Cries and moans of the wounded seemed to come from everywhere, and not a clue to know if they were friend or foe. When I read Westbrook's entry about their sleepless night, I remembered being helicoptered into LZ Columbus during the Battle of the la Drang Valley. It was night, and as we neared the LZ we could see lines of red and green tracer bullets flashing below. Myself and others were in a Chinook helicopter with a 105 howitzer and boxes of artillery shells. Within seconds of landing, the gun, ammo and personnel were off the chopper, and it was gone.

The silence in my roar-deafened ears was as absolute as the darkness I blindly stared into. I didn't know if there was a defense perimeter in front of me, or if I was on the perimeter. I'm sure I was scared, but I don't remember that. I only remember how long that night was and being surprised at first light to find myself in a clearing of foot-high grass with 105s on either side of me, and infantry manning a circular perimeter in the wood line.

Later, when there were wounded inside the perimeter, I don't recall them making any sound. I've remembered one of them countless times: the fish-belly pallor of his face, blood-soaked bandages tied across his bare chest, the upward tilt of his chin as I helped him smoke a cigarette. Next to him were others, still and unseen beneath olive-drab ponchos. When they were loaded onto the helicopters there was no hurry. The door gunners helped us slide them in without a bump or bounce.

Like Jake and the others on the line, Sedgwick didn't know what they were up against. He believed they were battling a single brigade, but he was mistaken. As soon as word reached Lee that the Federals had carried Marye's Heights and were on the march toward Chancellorsville, he sent reinforcements. By the morning of May 4th, the Bluecoats, having received no additional support, were outnumbered. Making matters worse, soon after sunrise the Rebels retook the heights west of Fredericksburg and started fast-stepping it along the plank road toward the stalled VI Corps.

By late morning less than 23,000 Union troops at Salem Church were facing about 25,000 Confederate soldiers who were attacking from the west, south and east. During one exchange of gunfire a herd of cattle got between the 49th PV and the enemy. The terrified cows ran in one direction, and then another, their tails "straight out." The Northerners fought valiantly, repulsing several attacks, but their situation was untenable. Ultimately, with no reinforcements coming, retreat across the Rappahannock River at Banks' Ford became necessary.

The 49th PV arrived at the river at 10 p.m., as red and yellow flashes of exploding shells illuminated their battle-blackened faces. Forced to wait their turn to cross the jammed pontoon bridge the exhausted men resigned themselves to fate and slumped to the ground. It was after midnight when they crossed, the bombardment never abating. The regiment had again been fortunate, suffering few losses. Not so the VI Corps overall, having lost more than 4,600 men killed, wounded and missing. The Confederate blood bill was even higher with nearly 5,000 names of dead and wounded stricken from the rolls.

Most of the blame for Federal defeats at Salem Church and Chancellorsville can be placed on Hooker's shoulders. Despite being outnumbered nearly two-to-one, Lee dominated the battlefield and rattled the walls of the White House. Lincoln was said to lament, "My God, my God, what will the country say?" As dark as the situation appeared, Lee realized a truth most elated Southern citizens and wildly confident troops chose to ignore. He had lost Jackson, one of his best commanders, and more than 13,000 irreplaceable officers and men. And for what? The Army of the Potomac had escaped relatively intact to fight another day, and the Federal losses in men and materials could easily be replaced.

The fight at Salem Church usually rates little more than a footnote in the overall treatment of the Chancellorsville campaign. Nonetheless, it hints at something more telling than wins and losses. The Yanks had fought the Rebs to a standstill, only giving way when their depleted numbers made further fighting impossible. Outnumbered during the second day of fighting, they still managed to stop cold several Rebel attacks, which allowed them to successfully retreat. In fact, it was a textbook example of how to retreat in the face of an enemy. There was little if any panic, and certainly no loss of fighting spirit.

Jake and the others knew that if properly lead they were the equal of the celebrated Rebels. Southerners would have spit on such an assessment, and likely growled that one of their own could whip 10 Yankees. They held their foe in contempt, and each victory fed their hubris. They were magnificent soldiers, true enough, but they weren't invincible. They would soon find that out in and around a small Pennsylvania town named Gettysburg.

Chapter Nine

Battle weary and exhausted after days of marching and fighting, Jake enjoyed the rare luxury of sleeping in. After crossing the Rappahannock River at Banks' Ford in the early morning of May 5, 1863, the regiment retreated another mile until reaching the protective cover of a woods. There they sank to the ground and slept. Spared the jolt of bugled reveille, the men woke at their leisure and ate breakfast. Afterward, they drew three days rations, and while waiting for orders, busied themselves by pitching tents, cleaning rifles, and tending to equipment.

Word circulated that they would be moving back to winter camp, but when that would be was anyone's guess. When it started raining around 4 p.m., the men crawled into their tents to wait it out. It wasn't a passing spring shower, but a drumming soaker that continued through the night and into the next day. With the river rising faster than quick bread, the pontoon bridge was taken up. There was now no question that the campaign was finished. For the next few days there was little to do but listen to camp rumors and wonder when the persistent rain would end.

On May 8th, the regiment received orders to march back to their abandoned camp. Jake and his mates were pleasantly surprised to find their quarters as they had left them. Drills, inspections, and dress parades keep them active, and warming temperatures helped improve moods. On May 13th, an afternoon thunderstorm blew in with tree-toppling winds that sent soldiers scrambling for open ground.

Afterward, they made the best of the resulting jackstraw clutter by trimming branches from downed trees and building elaborate arbors throughout the regimental area. Others used their time and skills for projects such as building additional ovens for the brigade bakery.

As the Army of the Potomac languished in a state of inertia, the camp was taking on the appearance of a permanent installation. With too much time on their hands the men started acting up. The first serious incident occurred the night of June 1, when a number of men in the 49th PV got stupid drunk and started throwing empty whiskey bottles at officers. Captain Hutchinson, serving as officer of the day, drew his sword when confronted by a bottle-wielding inebriant. The unnamed assailant was dissuaded from his intended assault by a friend, whereupon they were both placed under arrest.

Two days later a group of officers leaving camp were pelted with stones thrown by soldiers hiding in the woods. This infraction resulted in hours of extended drilling and being awaken at 4 a.m. to stand in formation, "like dummies," for the better part of an hour. While these shenanigans and retributions were going on, Lee was quietly slipping his army northward. The commander of the Army of Northern Virginia had put into action an audacious plan.

Stunning losses posted day after day in northern newspapers gave Peace Democrats, disparagingly referred to as Copperheads, a sharper pitch to their already shrill voices. Before the first shots of the war were fired, they favored allowing the Confederates to secede. As the rap and tap of hammers nailing coffins shut grew into an incessant drumming, they demanded an end to the war at any cost. Their clamoring insistence made Lee hopeful that another Federal defeat of the magnitude of Chancellorsville, especially on Northern soil, could tip the balance in their favor.

Additionally, an incursion northward would keep the Yankees

out of war-ravaged Virginia, giving it time to heal, plant and reap. Abundant foodstuff on Pennsylvania farms would fill hollow bellies, and well-stocked stores and warehouses would provide needed sundry items such as tack, clothing, and footwear. Growing pressure on besieged Vicksburg, Mississippi, might be lessened, too, if Union troops were syphoned off to deal with Southern marauders in the north. Of course, Lee hadn't forgotten the "tactical victory" the Union had won the previous year at Antietam. But subsequent victories had nursed a dangerous notion into a perceived truth. He had come to believe his army was invincible. For a time, it appeared he was right.

The shrewd Southern general left men behind to provide harassing fire, thereby masking his army's northern movement. On June 7, an enemy shell took out Sedgwick's mobile bake oven, resulting in a short retaliatory exchange. Two days later the largest cavalry confrontation of the war occurred at Brandy Station near Culpeper. The day-long battle didn't produce a clear winner but did reveal a noticeable uptick in Union capabilities.

Prior to the clash at Brandy Station the Confederate cavalry was clearly superior to Yankee horse soldiers. However, time and training had transformed this previously neglected arm of the Union military into a formidable force. On that early June day, as more than 20,000 men shot, slashed, and swirled on horseback, Federal cavalrymen proved they were on a par with their Southern foes. Their unmounted counterparts would soon do the same.

Outgeneraled at Chancellorsville, Hooker spent weeks regrouping and pondering his next move. He was jolted out of his paralysis by word that Lee's army had stolen a march and were heading north. Union camps were thrown into an uproar as the ponderous Army of the Potomac, with its more than 100,000 men and implements of war, prepared to move out. Throughout June 13, momentum built like a driving wheel gaining speed. The railroad depot swarmed with activity as boxes, crates, hardware, provisions, and sundry supplies were manhandled from wagons into boxcars. Steam-spewing locomotives huffed in and out of the station as troop formations marched northward.

VI Corps drew rear guard duty, which allowed Jake to spend the day witnessing the magnificence of a disciplined army heading to battle. The immense army train stretched for miles, so it wasn't until 10 p.m. that the 49th PV got under way. Except for the occasional flicker of a torch, brooding overclouds sealed the night in darkness. Curses rang out as men stumbled and blindly groped their way along, their outstretched hands fanning back and forth. Arrival of a pelting rain heightened dangers and difficulties as half-crazed horses and mules bucked and plunged through deepening mud.

Wagons, caissons, limbers, and cannons battered men like threshing flails. A slip, fall or blindside blow from the rump of a whirling horse sent unfortunates sprawling. Groans, shouts, and screams rose and faded as men were stomped and crushed beneath metal-rimmed wheels. Heedless of the agonies being suffered, the army moved relentlessly forward. What was endured that night went far beyond anything I experienced.

Because much of the direct-action work Special Forces does is conducted during hours of darkness, I've spent many nights moving through woods and jungles in all kinds of climatic conditions. But I didn't have to worry about being run over by a wagon or trampled to death by draft animals. We moved in small groups, and when there were lightning bugs about, we'd catch one, wait until it lit up, squash it, and rub the luminescent goo on the back of our heads for the guy behind to see. We had the benefit of flashlights with red lenses to retain our night vision. Obviously, we only used flashlights to check a map or compass when covered by a poncho.

In late August 1965, a group of Viet Cong weren't nearly as cautious with their light discipline as they made their way up the side of Hon Cong Mountain, just outside our base camp at An Khe. A platoon of troops with the 101st Airborne Division secured a radio relay site on the summit. I had been helicoptered up there to serve as a radio operator. Shortly after dark on the first night I was up there we saw a light moving up toward our position. I guess they thought the jungle was dense enough to shield the glow from us.

We watched the bobbing beam for a good half hour before it went out. The final 50 yards to the top was open ground with short grass, rocks, and small boulders. When we heard movement below, I radioed for illumination flares. When they popped overhead and flooded the area with light, we saw a dozen or more crouching figures dart for cover behind rocks. We started shooting, but quickly realized grenades were much more effective. The steep slope allowed us to easily lob the grenades downhill.

Realizing their position was untenable the survivors slipped away. The next morning, we dragged five or six bodies and some weapons to a collection point, and a Huey ferried them away. The body I handled looked like a frail old man, and his rifle was a piece of junk I couldn't identify. I later heard the bodies were placed outside the village for relatives to claim. I naively thought the war would be over in six months if that was an example of the enemy we were facing. A few months later in the la Drang Valley I learned there were NVA that were tough, smart, well-armed, resourceful, and brave.

Another great benefit we had in Vietnam that Civil War soldiers couldn't have dreamed of were night vision scopes that amplified ambient light from a night sky. The first Starlight Scope I saw was during Operation Masher/White Wing in early 1966. On a moonless night near Bong Son, I looked through one for the first time and saw the landscape in front of our position illuminated with a greenish tint. A few years later while serving with SOG I saw a small handheld device that didn't need ambient light to work. "It'll work in a dark, windowless warehouse," I was told. I never saw another one, and I suspect that one was sent home in someone's baggage.

During Jake's time, night was night, and only the degree of darkness changed. On the night march of June 13-14, 1863, darkness was about as absolute as it gets. I've been under triple-canopy jungle at night and couldn't see my hand pressed to my nose. I suspect it was like that. Fortunately, for Jake and those floundering about that night, the road eventually widened when the forest gave way to open land. The ordeal ended at 3 a.m., when they reached Potomac Bridge above Brooks Station.

Bruised and bushed, the soldiers laid down where they stopped, sleeping until the morning sun was well above the horizon. The men rested throughout the day, and being it was Sunday some of them walked over to where the Fifth Vermont Regiment was camped to listen to what a preacher had to say. Although VI Corps wouldn't resume the march until evening, the rest of the army was racing northward. Wagons, at times four and five abreast, pulled by froth-flecked draft animals, rolled by in a seemingly endless parade. Yells and hoots from teamsters mixed with the crack of whips and creak of stressed wood. Coloring the cavalcade was the russet rub of dust boiling up from pounded earth.

Daylight was beginning to pale when news started circulating that Lee and his army were farther ahead than previously thought. They had used the Shenandoah Valley to mask their movement, and now the underbelly of the North was exposed to the spear. Maryland, Pennsylvania, and Washington were suddenly potential targets. The news further strengthened the Bluecoats resolve to catch up to their foe and turn them back. VI Corps started marching at 9 p.m., along a rough stretch of road that in the darkness twisted ankles, tangled feet, and sent heavily laden men stumbling to the ground.

When the march was halted for a few minutes most of the men remained standing, not wanting to have to make the effort needed to get back on their feet. As they passed deserted winter camps, burning arbors illuminated the way. Sunrise came without the anticipated order to halt. As the temperature rose, the motionless air provided no relief. Men fainted, pitching headlong onto the ground. Out-on-their-feet marchers, incoherent and blinded by delirium, were collared by regimental surgeons, and put in ambulance wagons. When the wagons were full, men with barely the strength to breathe crawled under any bit of shade they could find.

Regiments lost cohesiveness as soldiers faltered and fell by the wayside, red-faced, panting and wracked by nausea. Scattered among them were dry-skinned figures without the will or strength to take a sip of water. Noon came and went without a break, and those still on their feet continued moving forward in a mindless shuffle. It was nearly 3 p.m., when the ordeal ended in a large field on the outskirts of the deserted town of Dumfries. Too tired to utter even a faint cheer, the soldiers plopped down and rested until regaining enough strength to brew coffee and pull rations from their pack.

For the Army of the Potomac the 18-hour march would be remembered as the most harrowing of the war. Heat and stagnate air resulted in a number of soldiers dying from sunstroke. That the march hadn't been halted even as men died demonstrates how desperate the Union was to catch up to the Rebels. When the call to "fall in" jarred Jake awake at 2 a.m., June 16, the urgency to continue the march was such that there wasn't time to brew a cup of coffee. Without the restorative pick-me-up, the day was starting out wretchedly.

Jake's eyes may have still been blurry with sleep when he and the others in the regiment received a small blessing that would have seemed infinitely larger in light of the circumstances. Being they were the rear guard they stood idle for more than an hour as the army moved forward. This gave them time to brew coffee and savor the humble pleasure while waiting to join the march. The pleasurable, predawn sips must have been exquisite, and enjoyed with gratitude.

The new day proved as hot and dusty as the previous, though not as long. In the early afternoon the marchers were given a break after reaching the Occoquan River at Wolf Run Shoals. During the rest stop thousands of men raced into the cooling water, splashing, and hooting as they joyously washed away grim and sweat. Around 4 p.m., after a refreshing dip and satisfying meal, the advance continued. The respite, and news that Lee's forces had entered Pennsylvania, rejuvenated wilting spirits. Here and there along the serpentine weave of blue, songs, laughter and exuberant shouts rose from the ranks.

This was not a demoralized army dulled by repeated defeats. A grim resolve tightened already set jaws as they marched northward through town after looted town.

On June 28th, camped a mile west of Hyattsville, Maryland, Jake learned that Maj. Gen. Hooker was no longer their commander. He had offered his resignation during a squabble with superiors, and Lincoln readily accepted. The president chose Maj. Gen. George G. Meade to fill the vacancy. As the commander of V Corps, Meade knew a major battle was imminent. That he didn't fold like a party chair speaks well for his, "high character," especially when his appointment wasn't met with hat-tossing enthusiasm.

Meade's irascible nature and sharp, flesh-flaying tongue prompted one detractor to call him, "a damned old google-eyed snapping turtle." But as McClellan proved, popularity doesn't win battles.

Neither does inflexibility and blind adherence to a battle plan, which Burnside was guilty of when he sent wave after doomed wave charging up Marye's Heights. Even a well thought out plan will likely fail if the commander loses confidence in himself as Hooker did at Chancellorsville.

Just a few days out from the largest battle ever fought in the Western Hemisphere, Meade was thrust into the leading role of a historic event, the outcome of which could decide the future of the nation. Lee, who probably gauged Meade's capabilities from his service during the Mexican-American War, knew he was no Hooker. When he learned of the command change it's been said he made the observation that, "General Meade will commit no blunder in my front, and if I make one, he will make haste to take advantage of it." As accurate as that assessment might have been, the ultimate measure of a field commander's worth is how well he adjusts on the fly to the ever-changing dynamics of battle.

On July 1, neither Lee or Meade wanted, or were ready, for a full-scale engagement. They were still pulling together their forces when the trumpets of destiny sounded, and the curtain began to rise. Gettysburg, with 10 roads radiating out from it like tentacles, drew the enemies toward it like opposing currents into a whirlpool. One flow consisted of a division of Confederate infantry tramping purposefully eastward on the Chambersburg Pike. The other, a small Union cavalry division under the command of Brig. Gen. John Buford, was arrayed along three ridges west of the awakening market town.

Clouds shielded Rebel eyes from the glare of the rising sun and contributed to the pleasantly cool temperature. Around 7:30 a.m., Yankee outriders spotted the advancing Rebels. Lt. Marcellus Jones dismounted, borrowed a Sharps carbine from a nearby corporal and used a fence rail as an aiming rest. He drew a bead on a man astride a light-colored horse. He assumed the rider was an officer, but at more than 500 yards he couldn't be certain. The shot he fired could have been the first of an estimated 7 million rounds expended during the three-day battle.

That lone shot three miles west of Gettysburg initiated fighting that grew in intensity as the day wore on. Throughout the morning, commanders in blue and gray, fed troops into the fray. The Confederates, despite heavy losses, continued to assault Union forces. By afternoon the outnumbered Yankees were being forced back through the streets of Gettysburg to high ground south of town. The names of the rocky rises where the Federals chose to make their stand became indelibly imprinted in the annals of history. During the following two days Cemetery Hill, Cemetery Ridge, Culp's Hill, Devil's Den, Round Top, Little Round Top, and a peach orchard would be washed with blood.

In contrast to the hellish struggle occurring that Wednesday in and around Gettysburg, VI Corps was enjoying a day of rest in fields on the outskirts of Manchester, Maryland. During the previous three days, Jake had marched more than 60 miles in an effort to catch up to the Rebel invaders. Footsore and weary he gratefully lazed about as curious locals came calling. To show their gratitude the civilians arrived laded with drink and copious servings of home cooked food and baked goods. Blankets were spread beneath an untroubled sky, and soldiers and townsfolk enjoyed picnic fare and friendly conversation. Neither general or private had an inkling of what was transpiring less than 40 miles away.

Toward supper time the visitors started drifting back home with empty jugs and baskets, while well-fed troops prepared to bed down. Shades of night were darkening as a galloping horse, blowing frothy spit, and spurred on by its rider, charged up to Fort Hill School where Sedgwick was headquartered. The cavalry officer, likely as played out as his mount, handed the commander of VI Corps a message that pitched the camp into a flurry of activity.

The dispatch from Meade told Sedgwick to immediately move his command toward Gettysburg by the shortest route possible. Within minutes buglers were sounding the rousing notes for assembly.

Commands and shouted replies to urgent questions were punctuated by brays and whinnies of animals unnerved by the sudden turmoil around them. By campfires and torchlight, soldiers scrambled to secure belongings and prepare to march. By 8 p.m. the 49th PV was moving along Baughman's Road on the way to the Baltimore and Gettysburg Pike.

VI Corps fielded nearly 16,000 men, consisting of 36 infantry regiments and eight artillery batteries, making it the largest corps in the Army of the Potomac. Tip to stern the columns of marchers and wagons stretched for 10 miles. As the men pushed hard through the night, messages were received to alter the route. This caused considerable backtracking, which didn't go unnoticed by the infantrymen. They placed blame on some unnamed, "blundering officer," and pressed on.

The absence of a rest stop for breakfast was remedied at farmhouses and crossroads where people offered food and water to the flagging soldiers passing by. When the 49th PV crossed the Mason-Dixon Line into their home state, Westbrook wrote that the outpouring of emotions was, "indescribable." Men cheered wildly and sent their hats sailing into the air. Energized by being on home turf, and with the sound of musketry and cannon fire growing louder with every step, the pace quickened.

By early afternoon the temperature had climbed to 81 degrees, and many of the men were as parched as the dust clouds kicked up by their feet. When the columns of approaching soldiers were spotted by Union troops on Little Round Top, they feared it might be Confederates closing in on their rear. When they were able to make out the red Greek Cross on battle flags identifying the VI Corps, the beleaguered troops were ecstatic. Here at last were the desperately needed reinforcements being prayed for.

Jake and the others had marched nearly 40 miles in 17 hours. They had gotten to the fight, but they arrived on wobbly legs and gasping for breath. Their appearance on the battlefield was inspiring to those already engaged, but they were in no condition to enter the fray. They needed time, if only an hour or so, to regain strength. To this end they were held in reserve behind Little Round Top south of town.

Later, with darkness settling on the battlefield, the 49th PV moved to the front. It was aswarm with soldiers and mounted officers shouting orders in attempts to stabilize lines. A few hours earlier less than 300 soldiers with the 1st Minnesota Volunteer Infantry Regiment helped ensure the Union had a line to defend. During the three-day struggle that transubstantiated the Gettysburg landscape into hallow ground, several pivotal events occurred that ultimately determined the outcome of the battle. The sacrificial charge 1st Minnesota made in order to buy the Union a handful of priceless minutes stands among them.

A battered Fort Sumter in Charleston Harbor was smoldering on April 14, 1861, when Minnesota governor, Alexander Ramsey, pledged 1,000 men to fight for the Union cause. In the following days farmers, lumberjacks, merchants, and others stepped forward to make good on the governor's promise. Lincoln's initial call was for 75,000 volunteers to serve for three months, but this soon changed to a three-year commitment. The men who joined 1st Minnesota, like Jake and his outfit, were in it for the long haul.

At the Battle of First Bull Run the boys from the North Country proved their mettle, fighting tenaciously and being one of the last units to leave the battlefield. And when they did so they retreated in an orderly fashion, unlike many Union troops who panicked and ran. They further distinguished themselves during the Battle of Antietam, and by the time they reached Gettysburg they had earned a reputation for standing their ground and fighting like the devil. By then combat and sickness had reduced the regiment to less than half its original strength.

When 1st Minnesota's hour of truth arrived in the early evening of July 2nd, most of them were guarding a battery of six cannons on Cemetery Ridge. Earlier that afternoon Maj. Gen. Daniel Sickles, commander of III Corps, had ignored orders and moved his 10,000 men about a half mile forward to what he assumed was a better position. This opened a large gap in the Union line, and because it increased the area to be defended it stretched his forces dangerously thin.

That afternoon when thousands of Confederates slammed into Sickles' two divisions, the Minnesotans were moved forward to a rise in the terrain. From this vantage point they could see vicious fighting in a peach orchard a half mile away. Some of the most murderous fighting of the war took place in the vicinity of this normally tranquil grove of fruit trees as each side raked the other with shot and shell for hours. Around 6:30 p.m., the battered Union line bent and then shattered like a splintering branch. The moment Union troops began turning their backs to the enemy, panic began spreading as fast as men could run until III Corps was in full flight.

As onrushing Rebels pushed fleeing Yanks into their ranks, 1st Minnesota was given the task of stopping the stampede to the rear. Col. William Covill, commander of the Minnesota regiment, realized the impossibility of this, and ordered his men to allow the wild-eyed rabble to continue on its way. That Covill's men didn't waver as routed, terror-stricken troops streamed by is commendable in itself. If they too had turn tail and ran; the charging Southerners would have had an unopposed route to the opening in the Union line. As it was, only these Minnesotans stood in their way.

Maj. Gen. Winfield Scott Hancock, commander of II Corps, rode up on the chaotic scene.

Keeping a tight rein on his horse in the midst of a hailstorm of bullets and exploding shells he looked into the eye of the approaching catastrophe. Churning up the slope was a tidal wave of Confederates hellbent on capturing Cemetery Ridge and destroying the Union army. The hard-fighting general had ordered reinforcements to plug the breach, but it would take several minutes before they arrived. He needed a substantial force to meet the onslaught, but all he saw was the sparse ranks of 1st Minnesota.

"My God, are these all the men we have here?" Hancock yelled. "What regiment is this?"

"First Minnesota," Covill shouted back. The square-jawed colonel was probably at least vaguely familiar to the general. A few days before, Covill had been relieved of his command and put under arrest for allowing his men to cross a creek on logs and boards rather than wade through the water. The thoughtful gesture drew the ire of Col. Charles Morgan, Hancock's chief of staff, because he felt it slowed other marchers. On the eve of battle the petty offense was overlooked and Covill was granted permission to resume command of the regiment.

Now, in the stinging smoke and thunderous mayhem of close combat, the Minnesotans stood as one. In moments such as these it's difficult to know exactly what is said. It's been reported that Hancock pointed at the flag of a nearby Alabama regiment and ordered Covill and his men to capture it. The exact words spoken aren't as important as the uncontested fact that everyone of those men, each knowing with near certainty they would be killed or wounded, quickly formed a battle line along the slope.

Eight undermanned companies, some with less than 40 men, dressed their ranks on the color guard standing at their front. As the final pieces moved unerringly into fated place, men faced their unvarnished self, void of pretense and dripping raw. Each of them, without exception, determined they would give their lives for something inexpressible in words, but felt as surely as they felt the pounding of their hearts. In that ennobling moment of decision, they became more than ordinary men.

"Forward, double quick," Covill's voice rang out from where he stood immediately behind the colors. With a great roar the men surged forward, racing down the rock-strewn slope toward immortality. The Alabamians in their front were momentarily stunned by the sight of a few hundred Union troops sprinting toward them with purposeful menace. The veterans quickly shook off their disbelief and began decimating the oncoming Yankees with murderous fire. Scores of men fell, but those as yet unharmed drove on without a hesitate step.

First Minnesota's battle flag went down five times, and each time it was lifted back aloft and carried forward. When the fragmented Union lines were within 30 yards of the Rebels, Covill ordered his men to halt and fire. The broadside sent dozens of Rebels crumbling to the ground. With no time to reload, Covill ordered his men to renew the charge. The sight of leveled bayonets glinting in the half light of dusk unnerved some of the Rebels who turned and barged into the men behind them. The surviving Minnesotans drove into the jumble of Confederates with the force of a splitting wedge.

Enveloped in the pocket they created, the Minnesotans were taking fire from front and flanks. They fought on even though Covill laid seriously wounded in a shallow gully, and all but a few of their officers were dead or wounded. Hancock needed five minutes, and had been given 15, enough time to fill the gap with soldiers. Only 47 men of the First Minnesota answered roll call that evening. They paid a terrible price for that quarter hour, but it stopped the Confederate advance.

The following day the survivors helped hold the center of the Union line against the all-out onslaught of Lee's army, remembered as Pickett's Charge. In the decades that followed, some have credited 1st Minnesota with saving the Army of the Potomac, and even the Union, at Gettysburg. It's impossible to know what the results would have been if they hadn't made the charge. What is certain is their valorous sacrifice earned them an honored place in the annals of military gallantry.

What those men did that day was a considered act, rather than a knee-jerk response in the heat of combat. They knew, to the man, the consequences they would suffer by carrying out that order. A similar moment of decision came for me during my first recon mission in Laos. We were to search for a suspected underground complex that possibly held American POWs. We went in with three Americans and three Chinese Nung and Vietnamese mercenaries. David Badger was the team leader, Jeff Junkins the assistant team leader and I was the radio operator.

We were inserted by an H-34 helicopter flown by Vietnamese pilots. When I jumped out of the chopper the weight of my rucksack threw me off balance, and I landed on my back under the chopper's right tire that was yo-yoing up and down an inch or so above my chest. I hadn't been on the ground three seconds and was nearly crushed like a peanut.

We quickly moved off the LZ into single canopy jungle. While the team paused a moment for Badger to radio a, "team OK," our tail gunner, Pau, nodded his head toward something he spotted. I couldn't see anything, but the look of exasperation on Pau's face told me to focus harder. As I stared unseeingly into the spindly thatch, the horizontal rails of a containment fence for small animals materialized. As I marveled at this visual sleight of hand, we received word that our insertion helicopter had been shot down nearby and we were to move to its location.

We hadn't taken 20 steps when we learned the downed crew was safely aboard another chopper and we were to continue our mission. After moving a short distance, we started smelling soup, and I could feel a slight vibration on the soles of my boots. When we came across a tin, ventilation stack sticking out of the ground it became obvious that we were on top of something. Nearby was a concrete bunker with screening over the firing aperture. Leaning against the side of the bunker was an M-16 rifle, which we brought with us.

At that point we started hearing the sound of bamboo sticks being hit together, and poor imitations of bird calls. The signaling was intended to channel us in the direction the NVA wanted us to go. Our covey rider, Buddha Grant, was still nearby when Badger called a Prairie Fire Emergency, meaning the team was in imminent danger of being captured or killed. As soon as Grant arrived overhead, he spotted a large number of NVA moving toward our position.

All I remember of what followed was busting through thickets as Grant guided us to an LZ. My memory returns when the Huey came flaring in, and we started sprinting toward it. Not a shot had been fired prior to that, but the instant we broke from cover, shooting erupted from seemingly everywhere. As I neared the right side of the ship, I noticed the calm expression on the face of the pilot as he turned his head to survey the wood line sparkling with gunfire. I made sure our three little people were aboard before I dove on.

The rule, without exception, dictated that the team leader was the first on the ground and the last off. This led to something akin to a Keystone Kops routine. In proper order Junkins followed me, diving in on the port side of the chopper. Not seeing the team leader, he jumped back off. Then Badger jumped on from my side, but not seeing Junkins he jumped back off. The pilots, thinking everyone was onboard, lifted off just as Junkins jumps back on. As the chopper surged upward, banking to the left, Junkins was only halfway on. I grabbed his rucksack and as I struggled to pull him inside, he starts screaming. I thought he had been shot in two, but it was only a leg cramp.

We were all sighing with relief when we realize Badger was back on the LZ, alone. We had to go back. As our shot-up Huey turned back toward the LZ everyone knew we were headed for the afterlife. No one spoke. I felt cold and scared. The little people were bowed in prayer. An indescribable feeling of gratitude swept through me when we got word that another Huey had spotted Badger and swooped in and picked him up. More than 40 years passed before I became aware of the significance of that event. I was walking my dog, Nell, and mulling over shortcomings in my life. Then, in my mind, I was back on that helicopter, resigned to dying for an ideal. In that moment of remembrance and understanding, I realized that weighed in my favor.

When the 49th PV arrived on the front lines after dark on July 2nd, it was hard to know which side was favored. The rush and roar of battle slowly ebbed into a jumbled rattle of movement and settling in. The regiment got orders to rest under arms and be ready for an emergency. The long march had taken a lot from them, but not their spirit. They were eager to get at the freebooters who had invaded their home state, picking farms and stores clean like scavengers on a bone.

With dawn came the guttural cough of Union cannons firing on Confederate positions on Culp's Hill, about two miles to the right of Jake's location. The 49th had been moved to the left of Round Top to support cavalry in their front. After an early and hurried breakfast, they fashioned rifle pits best they could in the rocky ground and waited. If things had gone according to Lee's plan for July 3rd, they would have seen plenty of action. As it was the fight for Culp's Hill forestalled the planned attack on the Federal's left, and that sector remained quiet.

Around noon heavy firing along the line prompted the movement of the 49th to a wooded area to the right of Little Round Top. About an hour later more that 150 Rebel cannons opened fire on the right center of the Union line on Cemetery Ridge. The two-hour barrage was intended to soften, if not shatter, the Federal's line for an infantry assault to follow. When the ill-advised charge came, there was too much smoke for Jake to witness the fighting. Of the estimated 12,500 Rebels who raced nearly a mile across mostly open ground during Pickett's Charge, nearly half went down either wounded or killed. It was a slaughter akin to Marye's Heights, and Union troops were heard shouting, "Give them Fredericksburg."

As Confederate survivors filtered back dazed and disbelieving that they had been bested by the hated Yankees, Lee muttered, "It's all my fault." He was right. The field of torn bodies was a testament to the limits of human will. On that final day of battle Lee asked too much of his men, and ground to dust the myth of Confederate invincibility.

The 49th endured the tremendous artillery barrage preceding Pickett's Charge but were spared from direct fighting. On the Fourth, they moved to the summit of Big Round Top where they spent the day on edge and hungry, as skirmishers exchanged potshots with one another. Toward nightfall they moved back to near where they had rested the previous evening and bivouacked. That evening fresh beef from a hastily butchered heifer supplemented issued rations. With full stomachs the men settled in, and probably didn't stir when rain started falling around 2 a.m. and continued through the night. As they stretched and kneaded sore muscles the following morning they received word that the Rebels were retreating. The deadliest battle of the war was over, and the Union had prevailed.

Moving across the battlefield that day, Jake witnessed the price that had been paid. Swollen corpses, looking like over-stuffed scarecrows, carpeted the ground like throw rugs. Among them laid dead mules and horses, appearing all the sadder for their blameless innocents. Everywhere the hum of flies and sweeping shadows cast by circling vultures. An unimaginable stench grew fiercer by the hour and would persist until winter's freeze. Westbrook simply noted that the sight of blackened bodies and "fearsome" smell would be long remembered. His entry that day was largely about the people of Gettysburg unfurling the Stars and Stripes, and how they came up to clasp their hands in gratitude as they marched by. He closed the day's account by penning, "We halted and camped for the night in a field of clover."

Exhausting marches, day and night, followed as Union troops pursued the retreating Rebels. Rations were sparse, and the only consolation was that the Confederates were having it tougher. Their wagon train of wounded stretched for miles, and the fat days spent gorging on the bounty of the Pennsylvania countryside were in the past. In retreat they were a wounded beast, proud, snarling, and capable of striking hurtful blows.

An exchange at Funkstown, Maryland, was stiff enough to be called a battle, and showed the Federals that there was still plenty of fight in Lee's men. The Rebels crossed the Potomac River back into Virginia on July 13-14. The Gettysburg Campaign ended with both battered armies reeling with exhaustion. It would be several months before the 49th PV would again see any appreciable action. Jake had heard the passing sweep of death's scythe and seen its bite. As the war ground on toward its third year, he must have wondered how long his luck would hold.

Chapter Ten

If Jake had taken stock of himself as he neared the two-year anniversary of his enlistment, he would have found himself a much different man than the lumberjack who raised his right hand and swore allegiance to the Union. Suffering beyond telling had revealed to him an inner reserve he couldn't have previously imagined. He had participated in 14 battles and, like myself, had probably mastered to some degree a kind of self-induced amnesia.

More than 30 years after the fact, a friend of mine recounted a story about a harrowing event I had been involved in during the war. I hadn't thought about it since it happened. Hours later when trying to remember what he reminded me of, I couldn't, and to this day it remains as buried as before. Another example of this phenomenon of repression occurred around the same time. It was a winter evening and I had gone out to the woodpile to fetch an armload of logs for the fireplace. Returning to the house the top log rolled off and fell to the sidewalk. The sound it made striking the concrete stopped me mid-stride. Some incomprehensible switch in my head flipped on and a scene I hadn't remembered since I happened upon it by chance years before appeared in my mind. Two Vietnamese men were pitching dead Vietnamese soldiers off the back of a parked truck. The bodies fell several feet before landing on a slab of cement. The sound the skulls made hitting the hard surface was the exact sound the log had made. Memories, alive, buried, or halfway so, make up who we are. The darkest ones mostly settle deep, out of sight and knowing, like subterranean rivers. Unfortunately, they don't all return to the underground once they resurface.

Jake's war had changed, too, just as mine had. Death, injuries, and countless unjust acts create bitterness lasting generations. When the Army of the Potomac returned to poverty-stricken Virginia after the conclusion of the Gettysburg Campaign, the soldiers felt justified in turning the Old Dominion on its head. Westbrook wrote, "We are destroying everything as we go. They destroyed plenty in Maryland and Pennsylvania and we desired to retaliate." Orders were handed down for the men to stop burning and stealing, but it did little good.

"We are in the enemy's country and don't care much what we do," Westbrook wrote in his entry on July 24, 1863. To illustrate his point, he related a story about an elderly farmer being held at gunpoint as his geese and chickens were carried away. For spite, sacks of his grain were set on fire. To ensure no repercussions would be suffered, a few geese were dropped off at the officers' mess.

Most officers were quick to turn a blind eye to foraging if the bounty was shared with them.

Desertion was a different story, and a major problem for both sides. Several hundred Union and Confederate soldiers were executed during the war, the majority of them for desertion. That's more than the combined total in all other American wars, but still a small percentage of those guilty of leaving their unit with no intent of returning. Most of those captured and returned were subjected to lesser punishments than death.

These lighter sentences included spending the rest of the war in work camps, having the letter D branded into the skin, having the head shaved or being publicly humiliated. If a case was compelling or happened to reach Lincoln, who usually had a soft heart in such matters, one could receive a pardon.

When the ultimate punishment was meted out it was usually done to set an example for others. On the evening of August 13, 1863, Jake learned that he, along with the entire Second Division, had been ordered to witness an execution the next day.

After company inspection the following morning, Jake's brigade marched a few miles to a hillside halfway between Warrenton and New Baltimore. Westbrook's account of the execution differs somewhat from that of E. M. Woodward's in his book, "Our Campaigns; Marches, Bivouacs, Battles, Incidents of Camp Life and History of our Regiment During It's Three Years Term of Service," published in 1865. According to Westbrook the men of the 49th PV witnessed only deserter, Thomas Jaret of the Fifth Maine Regiment, being executed.

After the doomed soldier was paraded before the division, he was seated on a coffin and shot. The men were made to view the body before marching back to camp. Westbrook called it, "a sad spectacle and quite different from seeing a man shot in battle." He further noted that the officer in charge of the firing squad loaded the rifles. All the firearms, save one, was loaded without a bullet, ensuring the man firing the fatal shot would be anonymous.

I have an idea of what Jake might have felt as he looked at the dead man sprawled on the bloody coffin lid. While at CCN three friends of mine got miffed when they were sent on a recon mission and missed a New Year's Eve floor show. After being inserted into Laos they got lax, let their guard down, and ended up dead. To make an indelible impression on us of the consequences of not taking a mission seriously, our camp commander made all of us in Recon Company view the bodies laid out on the helipad. It was an ugly affair, but on later missions when I'd catch my focus slipping, I'd remember those faces framed in body-bag black and get back on the bounce.

Woodward reported seeing five, "substitute deserters," executed on or near August 14, 1863. He was with Second Regiment Pennsylvania Reserve Volunteer Corps, assigned to V Corps Army of the Potomac. The deserters were members of V Corps, whereas Jaret had been with VI Corps. It's likely the only executions soldiers were made to witness were of men from their own corps. Substitute deserters, more commonly called bounty jumpers, were generally dealt with more severely than a man who simply had enough and went home. During the Civil War, men who got drafted could pay someone to take their place. The price was steep, so only those with money could take advantage of the unfair practice. Bounty jumpers would take the money, enlist, and at the first opportunity desert. Some made a business of it by repeatedly enlisting and deserting.

The V Corps author described a "death procession," consisting of a priest, rabbi, guard, prisoners and firing squad. As a band played mournful dirges, the five deserters were marched in front of the assembly and halted by coffins arranged next to open graves. The music ended as the men were seated on the wood boxes and blindfolded. A brief prayer followed, likely audible to all in the numbing silence. Then the order, "Ready, aim, fire."

As the reverberating boom of rifle shots faded, a detail of soldiers stepped forward to arrange the bodies for burial. For the next few minutes only the wind and tap-bang, tap-bang sound of hammers driving sealing nails into coffin lids disturbed the quiet. After ropes were placed under the rough-wood biers the boxes were seesawed into the ground. With the last spade of dirt patted down, the band struck up a lively tune, and the men marched back to camp. Woodward wrote, "Men who sell their blood for money and then desert, deserve no sympathy."

Confederate guerrillas got less sympathy from Union troops than bounty jumpers. During the weeks following the executions, guerrillas under the command of Col. John Singleton Mosby kept Jake and the others on their toes. The previous January, Mosby formed the 43rd Battalion Virginia Cavalry and quickly started earning the title, "Gray Ghost," for his elusiveness and daring exploits. The nickname was doubly appropriate, because Mosby operated in a gray area that provided him and his men considerations other guerrillas didn't enjoy.

Most Confederate guerrillas, called bushwhackers, were civilians operating independently and weren't affiliated with the army.

Considered illegal combatants, if captured they could be shot outright. Mosby and his command were partisan rangers. Although they employed unorthodox tactics and operated independently, they were led by commissioned officers, wore Confederate uniforms, and had to keep their higher-ups abreast of their actions. These distinctions placed them in the category of legitimate soldiers, and if captured gave them all the rights given to prisoners of war.

Although U.S. Army Special Forces has many capabilities, guerrilla warfare is our specialty. SOG recon teams operated as guerrillas deep within enemy territory, carrying out operations such as ambushes, trail watches, prisoner snatches, tapping into communication wires, blowing up cache sites and general reconnaissance. These were sterile missions, meaning we carried nothing that could identify us as American soldiers, because we were operating in so-called neutral countries.

Our cover story if captured was that we had mistakenly strayed across the border into Laos, Cambodia, or North Vietnam. The joke was that this would buy us a few minutes, because the NVA would be laughing too hard to shoot us. The truth is, we wouldn't be captured. The Special Forces Creed states, "I will never surrender though I be the last." We were never issued suicide pills or told to commit suicide if our capture was imminent. That said, I carried extra morphine for the Americans on the team to overdose with when all means of resistance was gone. The indig planned to dispatch each other with their final bullet, avoiding suicide and thereby having a chance to get into heaven. My assistant team leader and I discussed the pros and cons of various methods and decided on the overdose. Our hope was that the Lord would be understanding.

The partisan rangers were active in northern Virginia during the late summer of 1863. On July 24, three men with the 49th PV ventured outside the camp perimeter to pick blackberries. Engrossed in their pick-one-eat-one pursuit they failed to notice a few of Mosby's finest sneaking up on them. When they found themselves looking down the barrels of six-shooters it was too late. They were taken prisoner, and likely spent the rest of the war in a squalid prisoner of war camp.

Nearly every day one or two Union pickets would be nabbed. On

August 30, three VI Corps soldiers strayed beyond the picket line while attempting to trade coffee and tea for hoe cakes with the locals. They were captured by five of Mosby's men, who relieved them of $63 before marching them away. Woodbrook witnessed the capture but wasn't robbed or rounded up himself. The guerrillas had no compunction about taking money from their prisoners, but honored Westbrook's neutral status as a "safeguard."

Several days before the incident, Westbrook was summoned to brigade headquarters where he received orders to guard a house belonging to a "red hot Secesh (secessionist)." Despite the elderly farmer's dislike of Yankees, his request for a Federal soldier to guard his place from vandals and trespassers was granted. Woodbrook wasn't happy about the assignment, because the house was located a mile outside Union picket lines. The three captured men had talked with Woodbrook just minutes before being collared.

When the guerrillas ordered Westbrook to surrender, he explained he was safeguard of the house. When the secessionist verified this the guerrilla leader muttered, "all right," and didn't take him captive. The diarist identified the guerrilla leader as Capt. William "Billy" Smith, a Mosby confidant. A few days later two of Westbrook's friends dropped by the house to visit. When the watchful partisans swooped in on horseback the friends bolted into a nearby cornfield. Running headlong through a maze of towering cornstalks with cavalry in hot pursuit had to have been terrifying. The guerrillas tried to flush their quarry out of the field like partridge, but the fugitives successfully evade their pursuers and made it back to camp. The following day Westbrook watched the determined partisans searching, "down in the cornfield," until evening.

Being pursued by people bent on capturing or killing you is quite an experience. The NVA dedicated more than 50,000 troops, including specially trained hunter-killer teams, to counter SOG recon teams. These units would sometimes use tracker dogs, which we thwarted by sprinkling a powdered form of tear gas behind us. Only once did I hear the resulting yowls of a dog getting a nose full of CS powder. Especially harrowing were the nights when we'd be huddled together as nearby NVA searched for us. Once when the tension reached an unbearable point, a circuit breaker of sorts tripped in my brain and fear was replaced by calm. Although NVA were close enough to be heard talking and rustling brush, I briefly went to sleep.

In the early morning of September 5, partisan rangers were after bigger quarry than Union privates in a cornfield. After learning the location of Brig. Gen. William F. Bartlett's headquarters in New Baltimore, they hatched a plan to capture him. At 2 a.m. a squadron of about 30 guerrillas boldly rode up to a picket post. When a guard demanded the countersign, he was shot, and the raiders spurred their mounts into the Union camp. Bartlett was quartered in a house, and his staff officers were in tents pitched in a nearby orchard. The general was awakened by the sound of guerrillas firing into the tents. With no time to pull on his breeches, he grabbed his revolver and ran outside in his nightshirt. Dodging from tree to tree he emptied his pistol at the attackers, later lamenting he would have liked a bigger gun. The raiders were quickly driven off, leaving behind two wounded horsemen and countless Bluecoats marveling at their audacity.

On September 16, the 49th PV packed up and marched about 20 miles to a location about three miles outside Culpepper near Hazle River. For the next several day's Jake's company worked with other units on improving roads. On October 2, Col. Irwin returned to the regiment and spent time visiting men from his former command. His leg wound left him unable to remain in the army, and three weeks later his discharge papers arrived. His military career, such as it was, ended. It was probably none too soon for those familiar with his booze-induced conduct.

A heavy frost in late September set Jake and the others working on winterizing their quarters. With only routine camp activities breaking up the days, there was time to forage for building supplies and speculate on the possibilities of settling in until spring. That wasn't Lincoln's thoughts, and he kept pressure on Meade to follow up on the Gettysburg victory. Meade was reluctant to attack Lee, having had to send two corps to the Western Theater after the Union defeat at Chickamauga.

Lee didn't have any qualms about attacking the weakened Army of the Potomac and on October 10, he led his troops northward across the Rapidan River. The incursion didn't go as planned, resulting in a resounding Union victory on October 14, at Bristoe Station. After the defeat, Lee moved his army to the south banks of the Rapahannock River where he planned to spend the winter. The Army of the Potomac followed slowly, hampered by the damage Confederates had done to the Orange and Alexandria Railroad.

The 49th PV marched for 20 straight hours to get in on the fighting at Bristoe Station but didn't see any significant action. In spite of having been involved in major battles the regiment had suffered few casualties. Sam Wellers' luck was holding up, too. The member of B Company 49th PV, was sentenced to be executed November 6, for desertion. His head had been shaved a few days earlier, after which he had been, "drummed up and down," in front of the brigade. While sweating out his final hours he was told his execution had been postponed, because the regiment had received orders to prepare to march at first light the next day.

It had been getting progressively colder and in the crisp predawn darkness of November 7, a sleepy-eyed bugler would have been wise to hand rub a bit of warmth into the metal mouthpiece of his instrument before sounding reveille. By now seasoned veterans went about their early-morning routines by rote. Ash-dusted embers, pink and failing, were poked and kindled back to life. Soon campfires were boiling coffee, heating rations, and warming outstretched hands.

By the time edgings of light were coloring Jake's uniform he was on the march toward Rappahannock Station, about 13 miles away. By noon the regiment was nearing its destination, and within sight of Confederate pickets. As they sized up the earthworks, squatting on the horizon like a hickory stump, the clatter of heavy gunfire was heard coming from Kelly's Ford, five miles downriver. As planned, Federal forces under the command of Maj. Gen. William H. French, were attempting a river crossing there. After sharp fighting, the Yankees successfully crossed to the south side of the river and quickly laid a pontoon bridge for reinforcements to follow.

Learning of the fracas on his right flank, Lee sent the bulk of his army to meet the threat. He was certain the Bluecoats in his front won't have a chance of crossing the river there. To maintain a foothold on the north side of the often-bloodied waterway, he established a strong bridgehead with redoubts, rifle pits and connecting trenches. The defenses were manned by some of his best troops including hard fighting Louisiana Tigers. Rebel artillery batteries on the south side of the river added yet another menacing feature to the picture.

Confederates were so sure they couldn't be driven from the formidable defenses that they were busily building huts on the south side of the river to winter over in. Confident cavalry pickets with the "coolest impudence," on their faces steadied their horses within pistol range of the Bluecoats. When a brazen Rebel officer pranced his mount forward, feinting a charge, several bullets sent his way changed his mind and direction.

After a few hours of pokes and parries, Union troops started pressuring Rebel outriders and skirmishers back to their defenses. When Federal batteries positioned less than a mile from the river started pounding the redoubts, Confederate cannoneers replied. Their offerings were far from effective with many of the rounds overshooting their intended marks.

Around 4:30 p.m., the lone pontoon bridge across the river began bobbing beneath the weight of three regiments of Rebels rushing to reinforce the earthen fortress. In addition to the massed manpower, four cannons, primed with grapeshot and cannister rounds, awaited unwanted callers. A Confederate commander boasted that the entire Federal army couldn't take the position. The likelihood the Bluecoats would try was diminishing by the minute as the landscape darkened and their cannons fell silent.

Smug behind their protective berms and deriding the blue-clad men less than a half mile away, the defenders started to relax. Lee was convinced the huff-and-puff at his front was a diversion from the main thrust at Kelly's Ford. But the general and his men were viewing the situation from a perspective no longer guiding true.

The time had passed when the Federal army was as predictable as night following day. Neither was it an army of easily turned faint hearts as many Southerners supposed. An inkling of a change had come that spring at Brandy Station, followed by a stronger nudge at Gettysburg and yet another at Bristoe Station. In the gathering twilight of November 7, 1863, a half dozen VI Corps regiments stood posed to make all to see.

Lax Confederates were momentarily stunned as the inert phalanx to their front suddenly took on the appearance of a blue landslide rushing toward them. Perhaps 100 yards or more were covered by the charging Yankees before Johnny Reb realized they were being attacked. The 6th Regiment Maine Volunteer Infantry was spearheading the assault, followed by the 49th PV, flanked on the left by the 5th Wisconsin and on the right by 119th Pennsylvania.

As the Rebels regained their composure, they started firing volleys into the rapidly approaching ranks as their interior cannons flashed. The 5th Maine continued to barrel forward just as it had done months before when it overran Marye's Heights and broke the Confederate line at Fredericksburg. When Lee's finest refused to yield, hand-to-hand combat ensued. All four regiments were soon engaged, fighting the enemy cheek-to-jowl along berms and parapets. Bayonets, clubbed rifles, and any object that came to hand were used to stab, slash and batter. The Confederates fought tenaciously, but the Yanks proved the better that evening. With whoops and cheers, they pushed the defenders back into the fortifications, planting their battle flags as they progressed.

When two Federal brigades burst through the western side of the collapsing defenses the Rebels' situation grew as dark as the sunless sky. The north side of the bridge was being captured, while the main force concentrated on throngs of Graycoats yielding ground, but still fighting. The clatter of weapons falling on the ground increased as hands rose in surrender. Of the hundreds of Rebels who broke for the river, many drowned in the icy water or were shot as they sprinted across the bridge.

The brevity of the action, coupled with a stiff south wind that muffled the severity of the clash, convinced Lee that all was well at the bridgehead. When reports to the contrary started coming in, they were hard to believe, seemingly beyond reason. The keystone on which his plans and defenses revolved had been snatched away as if by magic. Loses were staggering, in fact unprecedented. Never before had more Rebels been captured at one time by the Army of the Potomac - 1,500 including 130 officers.

Another 349 Rebels had been lost at Kelly's Ford.

Confederate pride and weapon stockpiles were dealt painful blows. Four cannons, 2,000 rifles, ammunitions and eight sacred battle flags fell into Federal hands. Lee's aide, Col. Walter H. Taylor, called it, "The saddest chapter in the history of the army." The commander of the thought-to-be-impregnable bastion, Brig. Gen. Harry Hays, claimed to have been overwhelmed by 20,000 to 25,000 Federals, when the actual number didn't exceed 2,100. Excuses and recriminations couldn't mask the truth, although most Southerners continued to shield their eyes and hearts from it. The hated Yanks had whipped their boys in a fair fight.

Federal loses were relatively light, less than 500. The 49th PV had four men killed and 17 wounded. The 5th Maine paid the highest price with 43 killed and 107 wounded. On November 8, their bodies were laid out in a single row inside the fort. "Uncle John" Sedgwick, mastermind of the audacious attack, paid his respects. As he looked at the still forms lying shoulder to shoulder, he wept. As painful as the cost was, it couldn't dull the elation of the victors.

For two miserable years the common soldier marching with the Army of the Potomac had been mishandled, mistreated, and maligned. It had taken time and needless bloodshed to scour out incompetent poseurs, allowing abler men to take their place. No more telling evidence of this was the retreating Army of Northern Virginia and a chagrin Robert E. Lee.

The Rebels set fire to their side of the pontoon bridge to delay Union pursuit, but the damage was quickly repaired the following day. On the morning of November 10, Lee and his army crossed the Rapidan River and went to ground. That same day a contingent of soldiers and officers marched to Meade's headquarters and presented him with eight captured battle flags. Meade graciously acknowledged the trophies, then gave Brig. Gen. David A. Russell, who had led the charge and was wounded during the fray, the honor of taking the flags to Washington and presenting them to the government.

Russell was accompanied by Sergeant Otis O. Roberts of H Company 6th Maine. The sergeant was awarded the Congressional Medal of Honor the following month for engaging in hand-to-hand combat during the attack, and single-handedly wresting the battle flag of the 8th Louisiana Infantry away from its bearer. The windfall of battle flags powerfully reflected the momentous achievement of the courageous men who successfully captured the bridgehead. In spite of his painful wound, Russell traveled by train to the capital.

Arriving in Washington, Russell sent a message to Secretary of War, Edwin M. Stanton, requesting a convenient time for the presentation of the battle flags. After waiting hours without receiving a reply, Russell went to the War Department and asked to see Stanton. When informed the Secretary of War was too busy to see him, Russell handed the flags to the nearest office worker and walked out.

After rejoining his command, Russell was admitted to the hospital where he spent more than two months recuperating from his battle wound. Stanton was a lawyer and politician without military experience. Not understanding the significance of a battle flag is the only reason I can think of for him not giving Russell and Taylor a few minutes of his attention. In my experience the nearest parallel to the affront was when Gen. Creighton Abrams, commander of U.S. forces in Vietnam, came to CCN to pin medals on some of our guys. He didn't like paratroopers, and detested Special Forces. The award ceremony took but a few minutes, because as far as I know he didn't say anything to anybody. He was in and out of our camp so fast you would have thought it was on fire.

Stanton must have been educated on the significance of the battle flags and attempted to make amends. On November 19, Jake stood in formation and heard a letter read stating that the Secretary of War had received the flags, "with great satisfaction." Those listening probably received the message with less satisfaction and returned to their work erecting cold-weather huts. They were eager to close out campaigning for the year and settle into winter camp.

Meade wasn't finished with campaigning quite yet. He had worked out a solid plan to move rapidly and strike Lee's right flank before he could unite his separated forces. The housing boom was put on hold November 25th when orders were received to move out the following morning. The same day, 92 draftees assigned to the 49th PV arrived in camp. They got broke in hard the following day and received a taste of the old saying, "hurry up and wait."

The weather had become miserably cold and being roused from under warm blankets in predawn darkness was torturous. Nonetheless, Jake and his fellow Pennsylvanians dutifully turned out at the given hour, bolted down food and coffee and set out at 7 a.m., in the direction of Brandy Station. French's III Corps was scheduled to move out at first light with VI Corps following.

According to the timetable III Corps should have been on the march for at least an hour before VI Corps reached its camp. To everyone's wonderment that wasn't the case. Instead of finding a deserted campground, the field was covered with tents, inside of which were sleeping soldiers. Wagons stood as empty as discarded shoes, and unsaddled horses turned their heads toward the new arrivals in the hope of being fed and watered. Inevitably, there will be a few witless souls who don't get the word, but an entire army corps?

It exhausts the imagination as to how a slip up of this magnitude could have occurred, particularly when the timely departure of troops was vital to the operational plan. A few days previously there had been an all-day rain that left the ground saturated. Held at a standstill, VI Corps troops waited for hours in standing water as thousands of men packed up and prepared to move out. Generations can go by before a military unit lives down a blunder like this, if then. Some missteps are so egregious that the guilty unit is disbanded. Only the most charitable soldiers in VI Corps were going to forgive III Corps for the wasted hours spent milling about in mud. It wasn't until 11 a.m., that VI Corps was able to resume the march.

It has been my experience that when an operation gets off to a bad start it seldom gets back on track. Well behind schedule, the Union line of march stalled time and again causing the men to warm up and cool down in the bitter cold. Meade's plan had III Corps crossing the Rapidan River at Jacob's Ford by noon on November 26th. It was after dark before they arrived there, and then another wheel came off the proverbial cart. Engineers had underestimated the number of pontoon boats needed to bridge the river. Several more hours were lost as poles were used to jerry-build a makeshift span. It was well after 1 a.m., when the 49th PV crossed the river and bedded down. They had marched 25 miles.

A team sergeant of mine told me that it isn't one mistake that kills you, but two. While you're dealing with the first mistake the second one arises and does you in. I've seen the truth of that a number of times. The two delays had taken from Meade the all-important element of surprise and gave Lee the gift of time which he used to consolidate his forces. Meade's volcanic temper could have blistered saddle leather when he learned of the delays caused by French's corps. But with his army already in enemy territory he decided to press forward.

After a few hours of rest, Jake was up before daylight on November 27, and was soon forming a line of battle with the regiment. During the morning, artillery fire and musketry boomed and crackled off their right flank. The fighting was near Payne's Farm in nearly impenetrable brambles and thickets. As the hours went by the fighting continued to shift southward, until by 2 p.m., III Corps was engaged in front of the 49th PV.

The sun was low on the horizon when the regiment was ordered forward to support French's men. Moving ahead at double-quick pace they were greeted by Rebel shells, one of which wounded a captain and knocked another man senseless. When they encountered a road, they saw French astride his horse and not looking his best. When the general urged them forward into the fray the men didn't think he knew what he was talking about.

"Damn you, go in yourself," was heard, although the regiment dutifully continued to hurry toward the sound of battle. Gathering darkness ended the exchange of gunfire, and the regiment held the ground it was on. At 1 a.m., Jake and the others stiffly rose off the frozen ground and started moving through a forested area on their left. The six-mile trek through thickets of spindly pines and underbrush wasn't helped by a waning moon and dense fog.

It was daylight before they were given a break to brew coffee. No sooner had they started enjoying the first sips then urgent shouts of, "The Rebels are coming," were heard. Tin cups were quickly exchanged for rifles, and the men started running toward the defensive line. Brig. Gen. Albion Howe, commander of 2nd Division, was about to enjoy breakfast when the alarm sounded. His staff had spread a white tablecloth on the ground around which they were seated when the men of Company B, 49th PV came charging through.

"General, we can't help it, we're only obeying orders," one of the men shouted as breakfast utensils were booted into flight like flushed partridge and the clean table spread was trampled underfoot. The incident provided a bit of levity, especially when it was learned the Rebels were actually members of II Corps coming in from the picket line. There weren't any gleeful remarks later that morning when the enemy's defensives on the west bank of a stream called Mine Run came into view.

The Rebel's mastery of quickly throwing up strong defenses was boldly evident along a ridge skirting the Rapidan tributary. Sullen moods were further darkened by a steady rain that fell for hours. Throughout the day fleeting peek-a-boo sightings of friend and foe less than a half mile apart kept sharpshooters busy. As though to ensure nobody got too comfortable, Jake and the others were made to get up at 2 a.m., to draw rations for three days.

At noon on Sunday, November 29th, Meade rode along the Union's front line assessing the situation. Plans to attack the Rebels were going forward, and 32-pounder howitzers were moved to the front lines. Building breastworks for these pieces was particularly difficult and dangerous. Turning hard ground with a pick or shovel from a kneeling or crouched position was bad enough, never mind the snap of passing sharpshooter bullets. Making matters worse, the rain had been replaced by a biting wind that made men shiver and tents pop.

When word came down that the Rebel fortifications would be attacked the following day, men got busy writing their names on things they could carry into battle so their bodies could be identified. Early in the war a proposal was sent to Stanton suggesting every Union soldier be issued an identification tag. The idea never got further then the Secretary of War's desk, resulting in nearly half of the Union dead to rest beneath markers that read Unknown. It wasn't until 1906 that the army authorized the issuance of ID tags.

Breakfast on the morning of November 30, was a somber affair. Many of the men were probably on the verge of gagging as they tried to put something in their stomachs. I know the feeling, well. I never heard SOG recon missions referred to as suicidal, but targets such as Golf-Nine and A Shau Four were so "hot" they came close to qualifying for that distinction. As near as I can figure I ran 23 missions across the fence into Laos, and one into North Vietnam. The average was three.

Everyone who conducted SOG missions voluntarily put themselves at an extreme level of risk. Why I did it had been an impossible question for me to fully answer for decades. Of course, there were the easy-to-get-at reasons such as wanting to be with the best, which is why I volunteered for Special Forces. My first hint that there was a hierarchy of elites among the elite came in Training Group, when a few vague allusions were made by instructors to the possibility of a super-secret, super-dangerous SF unit in Vietnam.

The existence for such a shadowy unit became a bit less iffy shortly after I arrived in Vietnam for my second tour. I was at 5th Special Forces Group headquarters in Nha Trang, going through the Combat Orientation Course, and awaiting orders for my new assignment. One night in the NCO club I happened to strike up a conversation with a couple of scruffy SF guys who had flown in to get some administrative work done. They never said where they were based, or what they did, but they led me to believe that if there was a super-secret unit, they were part of it.

The next day I dropped by the sergeant major's office and said if such a special unit existed, I wanted to volunteer for it. He told me there wasn't any such thing, and not to bring it up again. When I returned the following day and made the same request, he practically threw me out on the street. When my class graduated from the three-week course, we gathered in a classroom and an instructor told each of us where we were going. There were about 20 of us, and when he read my name and said CCN, every face in the place looked at me. As near as I can recollect, he said something like, "God help you son." Although I can't remember his exact words, I clearly recall that his voice carried the solemnity of a deathbed confession.

The instructor probably knew that a few days previously, 15 SF guys had been killed at CCN when the camp was attacked. More Green Berets were killed that night, August 23, 1968, than during any other single event in the regiment's history. I found out about it when I was out-processing at the Nha Trang Air Base prior to catching my flight to Da Nang. The clerk going through my personnel records happened to be from my hometown. He told me I didn't want to go to CCN because, "A bunch of your guys were just killed there." He offered to change my orders to somewhere safer, but I declined.

When I learned what SOG was about, I immediately started lobbying to get into Recon Company with the guys who were running the missions. That decision introduced a dichotomy into my life that plagued me for decades. I hated war and the pain it causes, especially among the innocent. I was sickened by the shameful waste, and detested profiteers, be they a petty black marketeer or a corporate mogul. The mindless destruction of natural and manmade beauty filled me with sadness, and every loss of a friend left a wound that never heals.

I was also aware of another truth that contradicted all my professed hatreds. Yes, I hated war, but I also loved it. I loved the ritual of dressing for battle and feeling the reassuring weight of my ammo laden webgear heavy on my shoulders. The heft of my CAR-15, and its shrapnel-scarred carrying handle and front sight. Even today I'll pick up a hot, just-fired shell casing to smell its sharp, sulfuric scent. And I can't deny that there were times when I couldn't pull the trigger fast enough, or once yelling at a jet pilot for not firing on some NVA, even though it would have meant killing me, too.

For nearly 50 years I picked at this Gordian knot of contradictions without loosening a single strand. Then, while thinking about Eldon's elegy which I was honored to give, the answer came. My thoughts had gone back to a feature story I had written around 1990 about six Cistercian nuns, along with their two golden retrievers, Barnum and Bailey, who left an abbey in Massachusetts to find a new home snug against the Blue Ridge Mountains near Crozet, Virginia.

The nuns were living in two small log cabins and led a life of work and prayer. When they weren't making Gouda cheese to support themselves, they were praying. I understood the cheese making aspect of their lives but was a little baffled by the constant prayer. They explained that they saw the world in terms of light and darkness, good and evil. Their prayers were offered as a counterweight on the side of good.

Thinking of the sisters at Our Lady of the Angels Monastery made me realize that people like Eldon and myself are knights of the light. He had spent his life fighting dark forces, be they in Vietnam, Bosnia, Panama, Iraq, or places unnamed. It wasn't war that we loved but fighting the forces of evil and darkness in the world. Of course, where you stand determines what's light, and what's dark, but that's for each individual to decide. I have no doubt that I was fighting on the side of the light.

On that last day of November 1863, the big question in the minds of the soldiers on either side of Mine Run was whether or not they'd see the light of another sunrise. Men mumbled prayers and did what they could to steel themselves for what laid ahead. A Pennsylvania reserve regiment was slated to lead the charge against what most judged to be an impossible objective. Westbrook said they were in good spirits even though it was believed they would, "get cut to pieces."

Around 8 a.m. the Fifth Wisconsin and 49th PV moved forward at the double quick to support a battery of artillery. The Rebels opened up with cannon fire before the Union guns got into position. As exploding shells flashed and shook the ground, Union cannoneers returned fire best they could. When a caisson filled with artillery ammunition was hit by a shell it caused a tremendous explosion that shattered nearby gun carriages. Defenseless draft animals standing in harness were slammed to the ground by the concussion and fist-sized shards of metal.

The deafening duel crashed and boomed for a half hour. When it lifted, the Union soldiers waited for the expected order to charge forward. It never came. Meade, after conferring with his generals and staff, concluded that the defenses along Mine Run were unassailable. The 49th PV moved back into the woods and built fires, relieved that the attack had been called off. That night was terribly cold, and some of the men on picket duty died from exposure.

With options frozen as hard as the ground there was nothing to do but withdraw. On the night of December 1, the entire army crossed back over the Rapidan River at Germanna Ford. Two days later they were back in their old camp at Brandy Station. The movement that had shown such promise on paper had come to naught because of the sort of inept blundering that had hamstrung the Army of the Potomac since the outset of the war.

French was relieved of active field duty, because of his poor performance. Although his career was ruined, he remained in the army until his retirement in 1880. The Mine Run Campaign probably didn't measure up to the horrendous ordeal of the Mud March for sheer folly, but it was more deadly. In excess of 1,200 Union soldiers were killed and wounded, while the Confederates losses were about half that many.

Still, things had changed. The Confederates had lost their aura of invincibility during their foray into the North, and the Union had grown in confidence and competence. As the warring armies yielded to winter's grip, it was time to rest and wonder what the spring would bring.

Chapter Eleven

For several days after returning to the Brandy Station camp, orders were given to prepare to move out and then countermanded. The camp would buzz with rumors that the Rebels were crossing the Rapidan River in force, then fizzle like a damp fuse. Between being run out on alert and marching in dress parades, the men spent their time improving their winter quarters and working on roads. Even on sunny days it remained cold, but the frequent precipitation mostly fell as rain. Each time marching orders were rescinded, the men retired to their cozy shacks and burrowed in.

In the early afternoon of December 15, Jake's regiment was thrown into a dither when it received unexpected orders to march from camp under arms. No one seemed to know what was going on, but after tramping a short distance they were formed up for review. It was then explained that a group of Russian naval officers had dropped by to take a look at them. The Ruskies had traveled from Alexandria, Virginia, where their ships were moored.

The soldiers dutifully presented arms as the sailors passed on horseback, doffing their caps, and looking pleased. Westbrook wasn't impressed, remarking that they were poor horsemen who appeared, "to get ahead faster than the horse." He also noticed a rider's trouser leg had ridden up, exposing what he assumed had once been white hose. He didn't know where the officers were off to after the review, and he didn't care.

What the soldiers did care about were furloughs, which were being liberally issued as Christmas neared. It's likely Jake was given a 45-day leave to travel home. Other than a few east and west jogs along the way, the directional route from Brandy Station to Clearfield County, Pennsylvania, is almost a straight shot.

There's no way of knowing how Jake traveled the 240 miles from camp to the family farm. I can guess he spent a lot of time looking out the window of a train or stagecoach. He had experienced terrible things that singe the soul and can make one feel uneasy in social gatherings. That stiff, awkwardness has never completely left me.

When I returned home in June 1966 after my first tour in Vietnam, I couldn't have been less prepared. While in country I had lost track of time, one day melding into the next. I kept a short-timer's calendar during my previous year in Korea, dutifully checking off each day until my departure date. I didn't have one in Vietnam, and if I did, I wouldn't have been able to keep it dry.

I was in the field when a Huey landed, and our company clerk jumped out and jogged over to where I was. He handed me a thin folder containing my personnel file and told me I was going home. A few days later I arrived at Oakland Army base in California, still wearing the clothes I had on when I was plunked from the jungle clearing. I was fed a steak dinner with ice cream for dessert and told that my country was grateful for what I had done.

I hadn't slept since leaving Vietnam and was in a daze as I went through the process of getting discharged. While being issued a dress uniform, I came to a doorway at the same time as another guy heading in the opposite direction. I stepped aside to let him pass, and he did the same. When I stepped back into the doorway to proceed, he did, too. We aped each other's movements a few more times before we both started to laugh. When I took a good look at this guy, I realized I was standing in front of a mirror.

It was early evening when I arrived home unexpectedly. My dad's friend, Jim Sauer, had dropped by for an end-of-the-workweek drink. Jim was a colonel in the Army and was wearing his uniform. I thought, "What the hell, now?" Later, I caught myself opening and closing the refrigerator door, fascinated by the light that came on and being able to grab a cold drink just like that. I hadn't been home an hour before my dad said, "You're going to have to get a real job now."

On Monday I went to work for a roofing company. The owner said he hired me because he figured having just returned from Vietnam, I could stand the summer heat. I was a different person from the kid who left town in 1963, but the world had changed, too. A crew member my age told me I should stop putting Brylcreem in my hair. The long, dry look was the thing. And I was told I could attend a weekend party, but I couldn't talk about the war. Problem was, all I could think about was the war. Once while eating supper, I quietly started crying for no reason. My folks pretended not to notice. Less than a year after returning home I reenlisted.

Jake had been through much more than I had, and the war itself had come closer to home. My war had been fought on the other side of the world, whereas Gettysburg is less than 150 miles from Drifting, Pennsylvania. It must have helped a great deal for him to know there was a deep, sincere appreciation for what he and the others were doing to protect their countrymen and preserve the Union.

I can imagine Jake's family and friends sitting with him in the flickering light of a table lamp, prodding him for stories of battles and army life. I think of him, too, looking out a window framed with frost and feeling like the last man on earth. He knew he was part of a different world that he had to return to. He might have sighed with relief when the farm disappeared behind him, and he became one person again.

Back in camp the mud was as deep as ever, but Jake would have been happy to see the guys he had been through so much with. He would have quickly learned that the brigade band had reformed. There hadn't been much musical entertainment since the 49th PV's band had gone silent after being disbanded at Harrison's Landing in August 1862.

Evening music went well with campfire gab sessions, and thanks to Westbrook, many daylight hours were spent playing football.

On January 19, 1864, the diarist made a "football," out of boot leather. Their version of the game probably resembled soccer or rugby, with a great many more players. Officers joined in on the shin kicking, and according to Westbrook took their bruisings, "good-naturedly." The pastime was a hit, and by the end of January the entire regiment was getting into the action. Some days the game went on for hours, only breaking up when military duties, like dress parades, interfered.

On March 2, a momentous event occurred that would dramatically impact the war and the soldiers fighting it. Without having met Ulysses S. Grant in person and knowing him only through his major victories in the Western Theater, Lincoln promoted him to lieutenant general and gave him command of all Union armies. The ceremony on March 9, was as brief as the prepared remarks each man made.

After Grant read his three-sentence response to the president's words, he asked what special service was required of him. The answer, "Take Richmond." Grant told Lincoln that would be done if he was given the necessary manpower. The commander in chief assured him he would get what he needed.

As these consequential promises were being exchanged, Jake was either plodding through ankle-deep mud or helping prepare a hot meal for others in the regiment returning to Brandy Station after several days on the picket line. The guard duty had been made all the more miserable by freezing weather. The fortunate souls who remained in camp probably felt a tinge of guilt for having avoided the days of hardships. To make up for it they went to work gathering up all the beans, rice, and pork they could find.

That evening when the men returned after a 30-mile march, they were greeted with a hot meal consisting of baked beans, bean soup, crackers, pork, and coffee. Whenever we returned from a recon mission, regardless of time of day, we got a steak dinner. It was the only time the indig were permitted to eat in the American mess hall. There's nothing like a shared meal to foster a sense of family.

Oftentimes I would eat supper with my little people in their mess hall. It was a small thing, but it meant a lot to them.

Although Grant was the commander of all Union armies, he chose to hang his hat with the Army of the Potomac. Meade graciously said he would turn over the command of the army, but Grant wouldn't hear of it. He and the "old snapping turtle," had gotten off on the right foot together, prompting Meade to suggest to his wife in a letter that the newly minted three-star general, "was not an ordinary man."

Grant wasn't a big man in stature, standing 5' 8," and during the war weighing only about 135 pounds. Neither was he a dandy, collecting demerits aplenty for uniform infractions when he was a student at West Point. He was known to have a shot or two of booze, or five or ten. His drinking, probably overblown by his critics, didn't bother Lincoln in the least. Grant was a general who would fight relentlessly until he won. There was no quit in him, and that's what the president had been looking for.

Except for alternating days of rain and snow, and having to carry wood nearly two miles, life in camp was good. Brandy Station would be remembered by many as the most pleasant wintering-over camp of the war. Days were filled with games of football and riotous snowball fights pitting regiments against one another. A measure of genteelness marked the camp due to the great number of officer's wives spending a few months with their husbands. The ladies added a feminine touch to the otherwise mud-drab surroundings, and the men lent a hand by gussying up shanties with evergreen boughs and skillfully weaving intricate arbors and archways throughout the camp.

An even more civilizing element was ushered in by the "Great Revival," which started taking root in the fall of 1863. The religious crusade grew in momentum through the winter and into the summer of 1864. Religious gatherings on Sundays had occurred from the outset of the war with varying degrees of enthusiasm. After the terrible bloodlettings of Chancellorsville, Gettysburg, and Chickamauga many thousands of soldiers, North and South, experienced a spiritual awakening.

Union soldiers by the dozens waded into the frigid water of Hazel River to be baptized, and others answered the call during church services when invited forward to receive the Lord. Evening prayer meetings started being held regularly during the week and enjoyed unprecedented attendance. The Christian Commission, which provided medical services and distributed religious literature and supplies during the war, issued large sheets of canvas to be used for chapel roofs. Soon nearly every brigade had a chapel, some large enough to hold several hundred worshipers.

My first recon team, RT Louisiana, had a history of being inserted into target areas on Sundays.

One sabbath we found ourselves at the Phu Bai launch site waiting for the weather to clear over our target in Laos. Through the barbwire surrounding our isolation area one of my little people noticed a priest getting ready to say mass in a nearby field. Most of the team members, including myself, were Catholic and they asked if they could attend the service. We had time, so we all went over, including the Buddhists.

It was the only mass I attended in Vietnam, which is probably why I remember it so well. The priest had a black, travel kit that held the chalice and other necessary items. I hadn't heard an announcement on a loudspeaker or anything like that, but guys started drifting over, some alone and others in groups of twos and threes.

The priest was a middle-aged guy, wearing green jungle fatigues and a purple and gold stole draped around his neck. He asked if there was a former altar boy who could serve as his attendant, and someone stepped forward. I don't recall receiving communion that day, but I'm sure I did. What I do recollect clearly is that the priest gave us general absolution, because there wasn't time to hear individual confessions. From my first confession onward, I hated everything about that sacrament. I especially detested the creepy confessionals with the dividing curtain that smelled like bread dough and having to answer embarrassing questions.

A dear friend of mine, Ed Jeziorski, jumped into France on D-Day with the 82nd Airborne Division. Prior to the jump he had gone to confession. He told me he gave the priest a pretty good confession but didn't come clean about everything. I probably wouldn't have either, and that's why getting general absolution that morning was wonderful.

Going into Laos in a state of grace relieved me of the fear and tension I'd normally feel. I still hate confession, haven't gone in decades, but I can't deny its psychological impact.

General absolution was commonly given to European soldiers going into battle, but it had never occurred in the United States until July 2, 1863, during the second day of the Battle of Gettysburg. As hell on earth roared nearby, the New York Irish Brigade prepared to descend into it. Sizing up the situation, Father William Corby, climbed onto a small bolder and, to be heard above the thunder of gunfire and explosions, yelled for the soldier's attention. He quickly explained that the Roman Catholic Church had a provision in the sacrament of penance whereby in such a situation he could grant general absolution, absolving them of all their sins. With his raised right hand, he made the sign of the cross and recited the words of absolution. Of the 530 hatless men kneeling before him on the eastern slope of Cemetery Ridge, 17 were killed, 109 wounded and 62 went missing.

During March 1864 a lot of soldiers with the Army of the Potomac were probably praying for a break in the crummy weather. The month had come in like a lion and left the same way. April Fools' Day started out clear and pleasant, but by afternoon it was raining. Around supper time it started to snow and continued through the night. The next day it switched back to rain and didn't let up until well into the night. April 3rd was tolerable but cool. Finally, on April 4th, the men were greeted with morning sunshine, which did wonders for their mood. They soon realized it was no more than a cheap tease when snow started falling at noon, changing to sleet and then to rain.

A peek out a shanty door the next morning revealed falling snow. It was too much for some soldiers who said the hell with it and went back to bed. Spring started getting the upper hand by the second week of April, and there was evidence that a new season of campaigning would soon be under way. Jake and the others sent away their surplus baggage and sharpened their shooting skills at the firing range.

Before joining the Army of the Potomac, Grant had to tie up loose ends at his former command in the Western Theater. He arrived back in Washington on March 23rd, and three days later established his headquarters at Culpeper Court House. The troops had been expecting his arrival, having been alerted weeks previously to be ready at a moment's notice to be reviewed by him.

On April 18th, after weeks of anticipation, Grant reviewed VI Corps. It was a brief affair that gave the men most of the afternoon to kick the leather ball around. Target practice was being held nearly every day and according to Westbrook was sorely needed. On April 28, after coming in from target practice, the men were cleaning their rifles. A sergeant placed a percussion cap on the nipple of his rifle's caplock mechanism to blow dirt out the barrel when fired. He forgot the weapon was loaded with a charge of gunpowder and a bullet. When he fired the rifle, the errant bullet struck a soldier in a nearby tent resulting in the loss of his arm.

I'm not blameless when it comes to unwittingly discharging a firearm. While at CCN I had a Thompson submachine gun. I never took it on a mission because it was too heavy and only fired fully automatic, and I mostly fired single shots to conserve ammo. But to my eye it's one of the coolest looking weapons ever made, and I liked to take it with me when I left camp.

One afternoon I was returning from the PX, riding shotgun in a deuce-and-a-half truck. When I jumped down from the truck, I was holding the Thompson in my right hand with my finger on the trigger. The gun fires from an open-bolt position, and when I hit the ground, the impact was enough to jar the bolt backward enough that when it came forward it started firing.

Billy Brown was walking toward the truck to welcome us back, when the first two bullets hit the ground right in front of him. The recoil made the barrel climb, and I put the next three rounds through a nearby hootch. One of the slugs passed just above a guy taking a nap, and another killed his reel-to-reel tape recorder. The Tommy gun fires about a dozen rounds a second, and it spit out five rounds before I got it under control. In that split second it did a lot of damage. But for the grace of God, it could have been tragic. All Brownie said was, "Geez Dave, you almost shot me."

I had been extremely fortunate, but others were not so lucky.

Captain Travis Beck was an outstanding Special Forces soldier who never got a chance to reach his full combat potential, because of a careless accident. He was at our Quang Tri launch site with his team waiting to get inserted into Laos. One of his indig was fiddling with a pen-flare gun when it fired, sending a .50 caliber flare projectile into the back of Travis' right thigh. The flare ignited, causing excruciating pain and terrible tissue and nerve damage. The surgeon who removed the shell casing did so from behind a wall of sandbags. Travis had to identify what it was. Magnesium drained from the open wound for two months. He didn't lose his leg, but permanent nerve damage ended his promising military career and sentenced him to a life of pain.

Then there was the indig who stupidly put the electrically detonated blasting cap in a claymore mine, connected the attached wire to the detonator, and packed it in his rucksack. After climbing into the back of a truck with several others, he sat down and leaned back against the metal side of the truck bed. His weight pushed in the firing lever of the detonator. He died never feeling a thing, but it was a different story for the others who were seriously wounded.

Close calls, and some would call them miracles, occur as well. The day after returning from a mission I was cleaning my web gear. When I removed a grenade from the canteen cover, I carried them in, I saw a deep groove along its side. Another grenade in the pouch had a dent in its side. A spent AK-47 bullet in the bottom of the pouch explained what happened. Right after diving into the extraction helicopter I had turned in a crouch to return fire and ended up on my butt. I think that's when the bullet struck, knocking me down.

I gingerly carried the grenades down to the beach and set them off. I kept the bullet for a souvenir but lost it somewhere along the line. If that wasn't a miracle, it certainly classified as a close call. I have no doubt that Eldon and I were saved by a miracle on April 1, 1969, on the helipad at CCN. We were there with my team, RT Louisiana, waiting for the helicopter that would ferry us north to a launch site for a mission.

Eldon and I had become best friends in Training Group, and after becoming One-Zeros we wanted to run a mission together. Dick

Meadows was Recon Company commander at the time, and he gave his OK. Eldon and I agreed we would be equals, but because it was my team, I'd have the final say. Jerry Plank was assistant team leader. Our friend, Mike Morehouse, wasn't going on the mission, but he was there to see us off. There were also five Seabees waiting for a ride north, and an assortment of others making a total of 26 people.

Our rucksacks and webgear were lined up in a row on the perforated steel plating, and my little people were sitting on top of a revetment bordering the helipad. Eldon and I had been talking next to the three-quarter-ton truck that brought us to the pad. For whatever reason I playfully put him in a headlock and started walking him away from the truck. I jostled him along like that for 10 or 15 steps. We had our backs to the truck when a tremendous explosion bent us double. Pieces of metal whizzed by so close that I felt rather than heard them passing.

Turning around, I saw smoke, bodies, and wreckage. What immediately drew my attention was a small black hole near my feet that was growing larger by the second. Just as I thought I was going to fall into it, the hood of the truck slammed to the ground not five feet away. That jolted me from my state of wonderment, and with weapon in hand I ran over to the revetment. I thought someone had thrown a satchel charge into the crowd of people, and if I had seen anyone running away, I would have killed them. But when I looked up and down the road next to the helipad all I saw was my indig laying in the sand covered with blood.

None of my little people were killed, but they were all seriously wounded. The explosion brought an end to RT Louisiana, which was one of the best teams at CCN. All the Seabees were killed, and everybody except for Eldon and myself were wounded. What caused the explosion was the truck running over one of the rucksacks. The weight of the truck set off a M-14 "toe popper" mine, causing a sympathetic explosion of two claymore mines, two pounds of C-4 explosives and several hand grenades. Mike was hit in the chest by claymore pellets. When I got to him, he had a bemused what-the-hell-just-happened look on his face. The lenses of his glasses were broken, and his shirt had been blown open revealing a dozen or more small purple marks where the pellets had entered. At the hospital I watched a surgeon pulling sections of Mike's intestines up out of his open belly and holding them up to an overhead light as he looked for perforations.

Because of his wounds, Mike spent the majority of the rest of his life in Veteran hospitals. He died on August 14, 2004, and in 2009 his name was added to the Vietnam Veterans Memorial in Washington D.C. Since its dedication on November 10, 1982, more than 375 names have been added to the wall. Some of the names were added due to clerical errors, but many, like Mike, died as a direct result of their wounds.

War inflicts unavoidable pain in countless ways, making unnecessary harassment by higher-ups all the more infuriating. On May 2, 1864, an inspecting officer with the 49th PV pulled two new shirts out of John N. Patterson's knapsack and threw them on the ground. The enlisted man had received the shirts from home and seeing them treated like trash made his blood boil. After the officer said he was only allowed to carry two shirts, the irate soldier picked them up and said, "I will carry what I damned please." As punishment for the insubordination the officer ordered him to pull three extra days of picket duty. The following morning when the pickets were about to leave camp, Patterson was pulled from the ranks. The officer had decided picket duty wasn't a harsh enough punishment and ordered the offending soldier to carry 60 pounds of rocks in his knapsack for four hours. Patterson dutifully complied, and when the regiment left camp the next morning, there were four shirts in his pack.

During the winter months new recruits arrived almost daily at Brandy Station, replenishing loses due to battle and illness. By the time the Army of the Potomac embarked on the Overland Campaign on May 4, 1864, it numbered more than 100,000 men. Grant was eager to lock horns with Lee, but on ground and circumstances of his choosing. His plan was to use a forbidding 70-square-mile swathe of land called the Wilderness to conceal the army's movements south.

On the far side of the wasteland the terrain was relatively open and favorable for maneuvering troops. It was there that Grant wanted to strike Lee's right flank and hammer his forces with artillery. Lee, outnumbered more than two to one, knew fighting the enemy in the forested area would tip the odds in his favor. The heavy brush and trees wouldn't allow the Yankees to attack in large numbers or make much use of their superior artillery.

The sparsely settled Wilderness was well named. Traversed by few roads it consisted mainly of second-growth pines, scrub oaks, thickets, and underbrush. The tangled maze was about 12 miles wide and six miles long, with frowning ravines and shadowy hollows. Parts of it had been fought over the previous year during the battles of Chancellorsville and Mine Run.

To get to the forest the Federals had to cross the Rapidan River, which had proven time and again to be a risky proposition. River crossings during military operations are inherently dangerous because they channelize troops and equipment and makes it easy for the enemy to pinpoint opposing forces. The river was particularly worrisome for Grant, because of the huge Union supply train consisting of about 4,000 wagons. To his great relief, the Army of the Potomac moved rapidly, crossing the river at Germanna Ford and about four miles farther east at Ely's Ford.

The 49th PV crossed at Germanna Ford and when it halted at 5 p.m., the men made camp two miles south of the river. It had been a particularly pleasant day, made all the more so by songbirds and the profusion of spring wildflowers along the march. But in the gloom of approaching night unsettling sights awaited Federal troops moving into the areas where fierce fighting had occurred months before. Skulls and skeletal remains, partially clothed in shreds of rotting uniforms, rested on dead leaves and in washed out graves. In this charnel of the unclaimed, even the rustling passage of a breeze sounded an ominous tone. It was a terrible night, and for many it would be their last.

Billy Brown, along with two other friends, laid for decades on the ground where they died during a mission in Laos. More than 40 years passed before a farmer happened upon them and reported his findings. The Joint POW/MIA Accounting Command was notified, and after the remains were positively identified, they were returned to the U.S. and buried with full military honors. As of March 2020, 1,587

U.S. personnel were still missing and unaccounted for as a result of the Vietnam War. Each year at the Special Operations Association reunion an in-depth update on ongoing recovery efforts is presented.

For years after the end of the Civil War recovery teams scoured the countryside in an effort to locate and properly bury the fallen. Major battlefields such as the Wilderness were addressed within a few months of the cessation of hostilities. But countless skirmishes and unnamed clashes also left unburied bodies where they fell. Those not discovered by chance were eventually tucked away by Mother Nature.

Some Union veterans later recalled having a feeling before the start of the Overland Campaign that what laid ahead was going to be fighting of a different sort. This was the seventh time the Army of the Potomac had set its sights on capturing Richmond, but unlike the other six generals who had tried and failed, Grant had gone on record saying, "Whatever happens, there will be no turning back." He was determined to whittle the Rebels down, cut by cut, like the sticks he shaved to nubs with his pen knife. Lee was just as unyielding when it came to protecting the capital of the Confederacy. His plan was to bleed the Union white before they got there. With no give in either man, bloodbaths were inevitable.

Sunrise on May 5, 1864, was especially welcomed by those who bedded down among the bones. The 49th PV got an early start that clear, spring day and was on the march when they ran headlong into the enemy. Lee was funneling everything he had up two parallel roads less than three miles apart that cut through the wooded labyrinth. As planned, he caught the Federals in a place of his choosing.

The Wilderness, with its dangling vines, diffused light, and thorny thickets, was as near jungle like as any terrain Jake had fought in. Initially they drove the Rebels, "like a lot of sheep." Then, as they moved deeper into the woods, the entanglements had the effect Lee hoped for. Formations lost cohesiveness and fragmented into squad-sized bands, as gun smoke and thunderous volleys of musketry left only the senses of taste and touch unaffected.

Some men continued to press the attack, while others stalled, uncertain what to do. The regiment was rapidly turning into a disjointed rabble that could be destroyed piecemeal by the Rebels who were fighting on familiar ground. Such times call for someone to bring order from chaos, and slap starch into faltering backbones. This task fell to Lt. Col. Thomas M. Hulings, a 29-year-old father of two and former district attorney for Mifflen County, Pennsylvania.

A few days after the fall of Fort Sumter, Hulings joined the army, and on October 24, 1861, was assigned to the 49 PV at Camp Griffin, Virginia. He led the regiment at Gettysburg, but on this sunny morning in May it was in greater danger. Ignoring the lash of twig and branch he spurred his horse forward until he reached his most advanced fighters who were trading shots with the enemy. With arm gestures and shouts he rode along the line ordering his men to fall back and regroup. How he was able to shoo them rearward without being shot from the saddle was likely seen as an act of providence.

About the time the jumble of soldiers was reformed into something resembling a military unit, the 119th Pennsylvania Volunteers came barreling up to join the fray. Mistaking the 49th PV for the enemy they opened fire on them. After many heated comments, and a few return shots, the friendly fire ceased. There were plenty of Rebels to exchange fire with, and as the day wore on the fighting grew in ferocity. The two armies bludgeoned one another like human battering rams, losing a foot then gaining a yard. Rebel yells heralded a charge, while Yankee cheers announced a repulse or subsequent advance. The vicious, close-quarter slugfest would rise to a hammering crescendo, then fall-off to a patter of gunfire before escalating again.

For me, and probably for Jake as well, pauses between assaults were worse than nose-to-nose combat. Deafened by gunfire and explosions, silence sounds like a stream rushing through your head. Throes of fear pulse in the gut, beat for beat with the heart. Sometimes you forget to breathe, or you catch yourself holding your breath. When the attack comes it's a relief, because then there's no time for fear.

One of the great advantages I had was being able to reload quickly. I could eject an empty magazine from my CAR-15 and replace it almost instantaneously. And I could fire 18 times before I had to reload. I never filled a magazine to its capacity of 20 rounds, because if you did chances were fair to good that it wouldn't feed properly. Jake had to go through nine steps to load his rifle with a single bullet. Even under the best conditions it would take him 10 to 15 seconds to do this. During a firefight your hands are probably sweaty and shaking, and if you're halfway through the loading process and have to duck or hit the ground it would be easy to forget what step you were on.

I have an idea of what Jake had to deal with, because of making the mistake of bringing on a mission as my primary weapon a 12-gauge Remington Model 870 pump shotgun. I had heard from an old-timer that a shotgun loaded with double-aught buckshot was ideal for close combat like you generally have in the jungle. With eight or nine good-sized ball bearings in each shell, it delivers a sledgehammer blow at close range and makes it hard to miss a target. I crammed as many shells as I could into canteen covers on my web belt and away, I went.

When we made contact with some NVA, we were in elephant grass about four feet high.

Several of them sprang up in my area of responsibility and I opened up. The shotgun had a feature that if you held the trigger back it would fire as fast as you could slide the pump forward. It held eight shells, including one in the chamber, and those first blasts knocked down everything in front of me. Then I had to reload.

Grabbing magazines from canteen pouches was easy, but chambering shotgun shells was another story. My hands were shaking, something I hadn't noticed before, and I was only able to fumble a few shells into the shotgun before I had to fire. When I left that position there was a pile of shells on the ground, many of them not having been fired.

The first day of the Battle of the Wilderness was probably the most sustained fighting Jake had experienced, and certainly the most chaotic. Overhead leaf cover dappled the ground in a mosaic of light and shadow, and wherever there was fighting, there were clouds of gun smoke. Fortunately, I went to war in the era of smokeless gunpowder and didn't have to deal with the blinding effect of black powder.

Throughout the day the two sides battered each other, each taking ground and losing it. Like prize fighters exchanging haymakers in the middle of the ring they fought toe-to-toe, each in turn absorbing shocking blows before landing their own. Broadsides of musketry decimated ranks of men and shredded thickets. Spindly trees and brush offered little cover, and many of the ravines were so deep and steep-sided that they were useless as fighting positions. Casualties rose into the hundreds and then thousands.

Among the corpses were the badly wounded who couldn't move on their own. Walking wounded, and those fortunate enough to be carried out of the fighting, went to a gathering point a mile or two in the rear. James C. McCord with Company B, 49th PV, was heading in that direction while using his hands to keep his entrails from spilling out of a yawning laceration a musket ball had opened across his belly. He obviously needed serious medical attention, and probably got it within a reasonable time frame.

The Union's medical system had greatly improved since the start of the war, and although it was hard pressed to handle casualties in the numbers being generated during the Battle of the Wilderness, it did far better than it had previously. About 60 doctors, and some 2,300 ambulance attendants, had crossed the Rapidan River in 600 ambulance wagons on May 4.

Surgeons, nurses, and Christian aid workers administered to the wounded in several field hospitals near the fighting. At these frontline facilities the wounded could only expect quickly applied dressings, a shot or two of whisky and perhaps an opium pill to ease the pain. A large evacuation hospital had been established at Fredericksburg for seriously wounded men. Still, the stunning number of casualties resulted in some men suffering for days before being properly treated. In Vietnam, thanks to the helicopter, a wounded man would often be in a hospital within an hour of being injured. And there certainly weren't the kind of appalling conditions found in care stations and hospitals during the Civil War that so horrified civilians and soldiers alike.

The first day of battle in the Wilderness was slowed by darkness but continued in sporadic bursts of violence throughout the night. Heavy fighting resumed the morning of the second day, with the 49th

PV advancing about 220 yards. By then Lt. Gen. James Longstreet's First Corps had arrived to bolster the hard-pressed Rebels, and at noon the order was given to dig in and build breastworks.

Longstreet's men had saved the day, but his own troops came close to killing him when they mistook his mounted party for the enemy and opened fire. Four men, including Longstreet, were hit by the volley of friendly fire, two of whom died instantly, and another a few hours later. The bullet that hit the general passed through the base of his neck and ended its path in his right shoulder. He survived but was out of action for months.

The wounding of Longstreet slowed the action and gave the Union additional time to work on fortifying their positions. Just before dark the Rebels launched a strong attack and a section of the Union line manned by inexperienced troops gave way. The situation looked grim for a while, but veteran Union troops didn't panic, and with the help of darkness and reinforcements managed to halt the attack and regain lost ground. An often-quoted exchange between Grant and a flustered officer at the height of the crisis shows that he wasn't intimidated by Lee, man nor myth.

"This is a crisis that cannot be looked upon too seriously," the rattled officer told Grant. "I know Lee's methods well by past experience. He will throw his whole army between us and the Rapidan and cut us off completely from our communications."

Grant had stomached as much as he could of the fawning tributes some of his officers had been mouthing about the man he was bent on defeating. He had, "Known Lee personally, and knew he was mortal." He respected his antagonist's abilities, but he wasn't afraid of him. He rose from the stump he was sitting on to address the officer. Some accounts say he took the cigar he had been chomping on out of his mouth before he spoke.

"Oh, I am heartily tired of hearing about what Lee is going to do," Grant said. "Some of you always seem to think he is suddenly going to turn a double somersault and land in our rear and on both our flanks at the same time. Go back to your command and try to think what we are going to do ourselves, instead of what Lee is going to do."

The fighting had been horrific, covering acres of shattered pines, scrub oaks and tinder-dry thickets with dead and wounded. As daylight faded on the second day, it got worse. Fires started by exploding shells and gunfire had plagued both sides during the fighting, but now a sudden wind whipped flames into a roaring inferno. Injured men were prepared to shoot themselves if the fires reached them. One sergeant couldn't stand the screams of a wounded man being burned alive and shot him.

I spent a long night with a friend after he shot a Huey door gunner who was hopelessly pinned beneath a skid of his burning helicopter. He told me he made the decision to do it when he saw the sole of the man's boot starting to melt as the flames rushed toward him. I don't think you could ever completely get over something like that, but in my mind, he did the right thing.

An estimated 200 men were burned alive during the fighting in the Wilderness. The fires became the defining component of the battle, and surly haunted many men to their graves. As hard-nosed as Grant was, he had a heart and wasn't inert to suffering and carnage of this magnitude. He later wrote, "After the battle you begin to think about what has happened and the costs and consequences." After this battle, the worst Grant had thus far experienced, he retired to the privacy of his tent and wept. He broke down, but his resolve and spirit were still very much intact. When he emerged from his tent a short time later his chief of staff, Brig. Gen. John Rawlins, found him conferring with his staff, "in a state of perfect composure."

On the morning of the third day of battle, reconnaissance informed Grant that the Rebels were positioned behind strong defenses. Lee was hoping the Union commander would attack, but Grant wasn't going for it. The two sides sparred off and on during daylight hours, but it was clear the battle was ending. The Union had taken a pounding, losing according to official records 17,666 men either dead, wounded, captured, or missing. The Confederates had fared much better, losing about 11,000. The grim truth, however, was that the Union could quickly make good on their loses, but the same wasn't true for the Rebels.

The reality of the numbers was hardly a balm for the dejected soldiers in blue. The buoyant spirit that had them almost dancing across the Rapidan just a few days before was gone. The man they had put so much hope in had marched them straight into a murderous morass of misery and death. The army's flanks had been pummeled badly, and their leaders had blindly thrashed about in thickets and entanglements like drunks caught up in riverbank vines. Most everyone expected that the army would again turn tail and cross back over the accursed river.

Initially, it appeared that sad scenario was playing out as cannons were hauled out of their positions and units started marching. But Grant, true to his word, was not taking a step backward. His strategy was to circumvent the formidable breastworks by skirting Lee's right flank and getting between his forces and Richmond. Shielded by darkness, the movement got under way in the early evening of May 7. When the disheartened Yankees realized they were moving south, not north, the mood changed from despair to jubilation.

This marked the first time the Army of the Potomac wasn't retreating after a defeat. They had been sponged with the bitterest of gall during the Peninsula Campaign when McClellan ordered withdrawals after they won victories. Yet during nearly three years of war and shattering setbacks they had remained a proud force, never losing faith in themselves. Finally, a man worthy of their loyalty and trust had arrived to lead them to victory.

When Grant and his staff officers were noticed riding forward with the advancing columns the men began to cheer. The joyous outburst was so loud that their commander ordered the exuberant soldiers to shush, least they alert the Rebs to their movement. The men obeyed, but their hearts were brimming with happiness. If the high water mark for the Confederacy was the first and second day at Gettysburg, for many Federals this was their shining moment of the war.

Although Grant's insistence on pressing the attack met with enthusiastic approval, it ensured much more bloodshed ahead. During the Battle of the Wilderness the 49th PV had three men killed, 42 wounded and three taken prisoner. Just down the Brock Road, less than a dozen miles away, was Spotsylvania Courthouse. As the Pennsylvanians marched through the night toward the crossroad hamlet their hearts were light, their steps sure. They were headed south.

Chapter Twelve

Since the unfortunate railroad accident outside Baltimore on September 21, 1861, the 49th PV had been blessed with good fortune. The gods of war had watched over the regiment, holding them in reserve here, letting them be plain lucky there. But winning streaks end, and the outfit's luck started to thin at Rappahannock Station. By the time they reached Spotsylvania Courthouse it had completely played out. Their beloved corps commander, Maj. Gen. John Sedgwick's well of fortuity had also gone dry.

After two days of exhaustive marching and fighting, the morning of May 9, found Jake and the regiment supporting a division heavily engaged with the Rebels. By midmorning Sedgwick was near the front line directing the placement of a battery of artillery and the strengthening of entrenchments. A staff officer had warned him earlier not to venture into this area near Brock Road, because of deadly fire by Confederate sharpshooters. But when the popular general discovered infantry overlapping the cannons, he found it necessary to unravel the glitch himself.

The reshuffling of the soldiers drew the attention of Rebel

marksmen who started peppering the area from high ground 800 to 1,000 yards away. Some of the bullets made a whistling sound as they passed, causing several soldiers to flinch or find comfort on the ground. As Sedgwick straightened out the line, he good-naturedly scolded his men for ducking and dodging the sniper fire. His chief of staff, Lt. Col. Martin McMahon, provided the following account in a letter as to what happen.

"As the bullets whistled by, some of the men dodged," McMahon wrote. "The general said laughingly, 'What! What! Men, dodging this way for single bullets! What will you do when they open fire along the whole line? I am ashamed of you. They couldn't hit an elephant at this distance.' A few seconds later, a man who had been separated from his regiment passed directly in front of the general, and at the same moment a sharpshooters bullet passed with a long shrill whistle very close, and the soldier, who was then just in front of the general, dodged to the ground.

"The general touched him gently with his foot and said, 'Why, my man, I am ashamed of you, dodging that way,' and repeated the remark, 'They couldn't hit an elephant at this distance.' The man rose and saluted, and said good-naturedly, 'General, I dodged a shell once, and if I hadn't, it would have taken my head off. I believe in dodging.' The general laughed and replied, 'All right, my man; go to your place.'"

Truth was, the Rebel sharpshooters could have blown a small watermelon to bits at that range. Most of them were firing accurate Enfield rifles, but the best shots among them were sporting Whitworth rifles, imported from England. Widely accepted as the first sniper rifle, the single-shot muzzleloader could be fitted with a 4-power telescopic sight. Its' innovative hexagonal bullets made that distinctive whistling sound that McMahon referred to.

Sedgwick wasn't vainglorious and was simply trying to steady his troops as any good commander would. He had been wounded during the Peninsula Campaign, and then hit three times by bullets during the Battle of Antietam. While recuperating he said, "If I am ever hit again, I hope it will settle me at once. I want no more wounds." Sadly, the VI Corps commander who was affectionately referred to by his man as

"Pap," or more commonly, "Uncle John," got his wish.

From the far hill the Rebel sharpshooter had missed the general twice, but each shot from his Whitworth helped him to zero in on his target. The third round hit Sedgwick beneath his left eye, creating a small hole less than an inch in size. As a ribbon of blood spurted from the wound a smudge of a smile came to the general's lips. McMahon tried to break his commander's fall, but they both went to the ground. Medical aid was there in a moment, but there was nothing to be done but wash the blood from the general's face.

News that the beloved West Pointer was dead so shocked Jake and the others in the regiment that minutes passed before anyone spoke. Upon receiving word of his friend's passing, Meade wept. Grant couldn't believe it, and twice asked, "Is he really dead?" Even Lee, who was an old friend of Sedgwick, mourned the loss. Confederate cavalry legend, J.E.B. Stuart, another long-time friend of the general, told one of his officers that he would have shared a blanket and last crust of bread with the revered leader from Cornwall Hollow, Connecticut.

Sedgwick's body was brought to Meade's headquarters and placed outdoors on a catafalque of evergreen boughs. Throughout the day he laid in state as soldiers from lowly privates to star-spangled officers paid their respects and wept. The smile, as though appreciative of the farcical irony of his dying words, never left his lips.

For Grant, losing Uncle John was the equivalent of losing an entire division. But the greater the loss the more imperative it is to fill the void, and Meade acted as soon as he got word of Sedgwick's death. He honored the slain commander's wish that Brig. Gen. Horatio G. Wright fill his boots if necessary. The ascension of Wright to the command of VI Corps was favorably received by the grieving men. With the job came another star, as well as a learning curve that headed straight up. Sedgwick's fellow Connecticuter was faced with the task of leading the VI Corps through the third bloodiest battle of the war.

For the 49th PV there was no bloodier day then May 10, 1864. The day opened with exchanges of musketry and artillery that rattled and boomed in continuous waves hour after hour. Soon after first light Jake's Company D, along with Company G, moved onto the skirmish line and started exchanging fire with Rebel pickets. In spite of men dropping dead and wounded, and aided by artillery, they managed to slowly push the Graycoats back through a wooded area that opened onto a large field.

With scant cover in the exposed area, the Southerners fell back about 200 yards to their defenses. Union troops once again marveled at the Confederate's ability to throw up stout defenses at eye-rubbing speed. At Spotsylvania Courthouse, they built a fear-inspiring cat's cradle of log and dirt breastworks fronted by bristling abatis. Union troops dubbed the salient the Mule Shoe because of it bulging shape.

About 3 p.m. Company D and G were pulled back from the line and given a breather. Some of the men dug graves for two of their fallen, as the others waited for further developments. What was developing at higher headquarters was a plan similar to the one used at Rappahannock Station when a relatively small Union force surprised and overran the strongly defended Confederate fortress. Union engineer, Lt. Ranald S. Mackenzie, had broached the plan after recognizing similarities of terrain between Rappahannock Station and the Mule Shoe Salient.

Earlier that day Mackenzie had been reconnoitering the area west of the salient. He had been following a path that led through the woods the Rebels had been driven from. When he reached the edge of the wood line, he saw that it opened onto a field, across which stood the bristling western wall of the Mule Shoe, about 200 yards away. The relatively short distance between the cover of the woods and the Rebel position, induced him to inform Brig. Gen. David Russell about his findings.

Russell had taken over command of VI Corps' First Division the previous day when Wright took Sedgwick's place. He thought the information warranted a look, and when he espied the salient, he realized what had excited the lieutenant. As strong as the Confederate defenses were, he reasoned they could be overpowered by the type of swift, aggressive assault that had worked so well at Rappahannock Station. Col. Emory Upton, a VI Corps' brigade commander, had played an important role in the successful storming of that bastion, and he was picked to lead this effort.

As a plan started being cobbled together, Upton provided important input into how it might best succeed. What he saw work so dramatically at Rappahannock Station was shoulder-to-shoulder veteran regiments rushing forward without stopping to fire until reaching the objective. Without men who would unflinchingly face blistering fire without stopping, the attack was doomed. To this end, 12 hand-picked regiments were chosen for the audacious charge.

When McMahon showed Upton the list of the chosen, the blue-eyed colonel exclaimed, "Mac, these are the best men in the army." The regiments had seen hard fighting and were far from their full strength of 1,000 men each. According to Westbrook's tally the 49th PV had 474 men take part in the assault. The total number of Union men engaged ranges from 4,500 to 5,000.

Although the exact number of attackers varies, the configuration of the regiments is clearly documented. The phalanx was three regiments across and four deep. A farm path arrowing across the field was the guideline to the objective. The four regiments on the far-right file were to hold to the right side of the lane and the remaining eight to the left. The 49th PV was on the right side following the lead regiment on the front rank, the 121st New York. Upton brought all the regiment commanders to the fringe of the woods to show them the terrain to be covered and give them their final instructions.

The front three regiments from right to left were the 12ist New York, 96th Pennsylvania and the 5th Maine. In the second line in the same order were the 49th PV, 6th Maine and 5th Wisconsin.

Following them were the 43rd New York, 77th New York and 119 Pennsylvania. In the last line were the 2nd Vermont, 5th Vermont and 6th Vermont. The men in the three lead regiments were to fully ready their rifles for firing, but all the others were to only load the powder and bullet and not cap the weapon. Upton's reasoning was to make it clear that it was critical that the assaulters got across the field as quickly as possible and not stop to shoot, or even help a wounded comrade. They were all instructed to fix bayonets.

There was a strong emphasis on bayonet training when I was in basic training in 1963. We spent hours on drill fields kicking up dust as we practiced long thrusts, parries, slashes, and butt strokes. The instructors would yell, "What's the spirit of the bayonet fighter?" We answered, "To kill." Since those days the Army has discontinued and restarted bayonet training for various reasons. One reason for discontinuing it was that the M-16 can't withstand repeated plunging impacts like the M-1 or M-14 could.

I'll let others argue the pros and cons of the bayonet and will offer only this in support of it. Having seen charging NVA with their AK-47 bayonets locked in the working position, I can attest to its psychological effect. All you see is that triangular spike coming at you, and it's a fearsome sight.

With bayonets fixed, the men in the front three regiments were to hold their fire until they reached the salient, then open up. Once they boiled over the top of the defenses, the New Yorkers and the 96th Pennsylvania were to turn right and attack four well protected cannons about 100 yards away. The 5th Maine was to turn left and fire on the troops in that quadrant. The second row was to fire straight ahead after the lead regiments broke to the right and left. The third rank was ordered to halt behind the second row of troops and await further directions. The last row was to advance to the tree line where they were to get into a prone position and be ready to be sent where needed.

Upton further instructed the officers to continually shout, "Forward, forward," until the men were inside the Rebel defenses. There wasn't to be any cheering, either, better to use one's breath during the sprint across the field. The attack was to be supported by infantrymen under the command of Brig. Gen. Gershom Mott. The exact number is not known, but probably consisted of between 1,200 and 1,500 soldiers. This force would come in on the left flank of Upton's men and strike the Mule Shoe square on its protruding nose.

Additionally, Maj. Gen. Gouverneur K. Warren, commander of V Corps, was to attack an already bloodied Laurel Hill to the right of the 12 assaulting regiments. This push would be assisted by elements of II Corps. Tragically, the plan became completely undone, because of vague orders, lack of coordination and desperately poor communications.

The assault was scheduled to kick off at 5 p.m., but when Warren thought he saw an earlier opportunity he got permission from Grant and Meade to attack around 3:45 p.m. The effort, just like every other in that sector, was repulsed. Jumping the gun had thrown off the timetable and the 12- regiment assault was postponed for an hour. Mott wasn't told of the delay, and he sent his men forward at 5 p.m., as originally planned.

Rebel pickets in the southern edge of the woods through which Mott's troops were advancing fired a volley or two before skedaddling back to their defenses. Alerted to the approaching Federals the Confederates readied cannons and rifles as they watched the advancing ranks start across the field 600-yards away. When the Yankees were within cannister range, about 400-yards, nearly two dozen Rebel cannons boomed, sending a hailstorm of marble-size projectiles tearing through the Bluecoat's front ranks. It took only a few more broadsides to stop the attackers cold, and those who could hightail back to the woods did so. They were done for the day.

As the gremlins of war gleefully mangled the plan into an olio of disaster, the doomed regiments quietly moved into place. There wouldn't have been any birdsong, as I had heard during my visit to those woods. And in that timeless wait among the pines, each man went into that most private of places where one must go alone.

Once, as I waited by an airstrip for weather to clear over the target area, I picked up a paperback to pass the time. I kept my nose in that book for the better part of an hour before getting word to take my team out to the choppers. I hadn't read one sentence.

"We are laying low, and not a word is spoken above a whisper in our ranks," Westbrook wrote. "We see the duty we are expected to perform, and orders are quietly passed along the line in a whisper."

At 5 p.m. the earth beneath the men began to shiver as half a dozen Union cannons began firing on the intimidating fieldworks encircled by what appeared at a distance to resemble a crown of thorns. When the artillerymen learned the jump off time for the assault had been postponed an hour, they continued to fire at an irregular rate so as not to alert the Rebels to the impending attack. At ten minutes to six, about the time Jake's family was sitting down for supper, additional

Union batteries opened up on the impact point the 12 regiments were focused on.

Around 6 p.m. the bombardment started to abate like trailing thunder of a departing storm. It had been a clear, warm day but the farm boys noted a hint of impending rain in the now hazy air. It was an hour before sunset, another before dark. A quarter after the hour, perhaps a little longer, the awaited moment arrived.

Upton, the lone officer on horseback, held a tight rein with one hand and with the other waved a handkerchief overhead and gave the order to charge. "Up we go, and no rebel army could have stopped us," Westbrook recalled.

The order not to yell was forgotten as the men sprang forward and started racing death across the slight, upward pitch of the featureless fairway. Their throaty, primal battle cry, so different from the Rebel yell, rose to a roar. The salient began sparkling with red and yellow flashes of gunfire coming from narrow firing ports below protective overhead logs. This was the most strongly defended point in the Mule Shoe, and men began dropping at an ever-increasing rate as they neared the outer defenses.

Breath came in ragged gasps, and every jolt from running feet meant another yard gained. Death's arbitrary finger tapped here and there, felling men like discarded chits on a counting house floor. Exceptionally heavy fire to the left of the lead regiments caused the men to bend to the right as though hit by gale force winds. The formation bent but didn't slow. Within a minute or so blue-clad soldiers were dodging and breaking down rows of sharpened sticks intended to slow or impale. Then they were busting through the abatis entanglement like enraged beasts clawing toward their tormentors.

In 1908 British historian, C. F. Atkinson, called the charge across open ground, "One of the classic infantry attacks of military history." Just as at Rappahannock Station, the Federals wouldn't be denied their prize. Mindless of suffered cuts and bruises they clamored over blood-greased logs, stomping the edge of their boots into fresh dug dirt to win another foot upward. The first to summit the head logs and counterscarp were killed or wounded, but those following kept pushing forward in a relentless torrent.

Union troops topping the breastworks descended into a maelstrom of mayhem. Upton later reported that at this critical juncture the Rebels, "Absolutely refused to yield the ground." The Federals were just as hard jawed in their determination to push the Southerners off their perch. When a corporal with the 49th was shot in the arm he was told to head back to the rear. "No, damned if I do," he cursed, and continued to fight. With no time to reload weapons, men swung muskets like clubs and resorted to fists, swords, and bayonets.

Westbrook saw one of his lieutenants strike a Rebel in the head with his saber, knock another down with his fist. He then almost got run through with a bayonet, before being saved by a fellow Yank who uses his bayonet to dispatch the third attacker. Grip-and-tear fighting of this magnitude has limits and according to the 49th's diarist, "In less than ten minutes we have their works, artillery and about 1,000 prisoners."

As frenzied as the fighting was, disciplined Union soldiers didn't lose their heads. When a large group of Confederates with empty muskets were cornered, only a few were shot and the others were allowed to head back across the field as prisoners. This act of chivalry nearly proved costly when a Rebel officer heading to the rear as a prisoner ordered his men to pick up guns littering the ground and fire into the backs of their captors. A Pennsylvanian quelled that treachery by killing the officer on the spot.

When Confederate cannoneers were driven back from their piece, a young boy refused to yield and remained at his post. Because of his grit he wasn't shot but sent back as a prisoner. Even amidst such a swirling tempest of savagery, a moment of levity occurred. It made me think of Gunther Wald and myself getting the giggles in North Vietnam as night fell, even though we wouldn't have bet a dime on the probability of a future.

Westbrook and about 25 other men from the regiment had fought their way to the Rebels' third line of defenses. They and others with the 6th Maine cut to the right to take out three cannons, 60 yards away, that had been firing cannister rounds into their ranks.

"We knock them right and left and take the guns from under the noses of the rebels, for they are massed not over twenty paces in our front," Westbrook wrote. "They are so surprised that they forgot to fire on us but let us turn one of the pieces and fire the load into their ranks. We, at a glance, see it is impossible for us to stay here. Captain Wombacker comes up and says, 'Who has a rat-tail file or nail to spike these pieces?'

"One of Company B says, 'This is a hell of a place to ask for a file.'

"The writer had hold of one of the wheels, and although scared like thunder, he was so amused at the remark that he looked up into the captain's face and laughed."

By this time Confederate reinforcements were streaming into the salient. Upton rode back to send forward the Vermont regiments, only to discover they had already charged forward on their own. Although the Bluecoats were loath to relinquish what they had given so much to gain, without support there was no sane recourse but to fall back. With darkness came an end to the fighting and a hesitant, bitter withdrawal. Survivors sobbed like children for having given so much for so little.

The 49th PV had been decimated, suffering the most casualties of any of the 12 attacking regiments. Of the 474 men in the regiment who went forward, 216 were killed or wounded. Jake laid among the fallen, his war at an end. With his left hip shattered by a Minie ball, he'd have had to marshal all his will to hold mastery against the storming dark and onrush of helplessness. He'd have crawled, if only for a yard or two, to assure himself that he could. He would have had to staunch the flow of blood, probably at first with the press of a hand, and then a heavy cloth. At some point he would have also had to find a place inside the pain where consciousness is endurable.

About 1,000 Union soldiers were killed or wounded during the courageous twilight charge that broke the Confederate line but came a cropper. Some of the wounded languished on the field for days before receiving medical assistance. Jake would have had to be carried by stretcher to a field hospital or ambulance wagon. Many ambulances were still in use transporting wounded from the Battle of the Wilderness. At least Jake was somewhat in the forefront of an even greater exodus of wounded who would flood the arterial roads, rails and waterways weaving northward to Washington in the coming days.

These human scapulars of suffering and devotion were jolted and jarred mile after torturous mile. Voices shrieked for a merciful bullet, as again and again in faint whispers and groans, "Water, please, water." A day, then two passes, and cushioning straw becomes damp and befouled. Wounds crust, and the hot sting of infection joins the throb of ceaseless, crowning pain. Only the blest comforter of unconsciousness ends the agony for a time.

Today, it would take an ambulance less than an hour to transport a patient from Spotsylvania Courthouse to a hospital in Washington DC. At best, Jake was in transit for days. By that point in the war there were as many as 85 hospitals in the capital. Jake was stretchered into the 1,300-bed Carver Army Hospital, and in all likelihood was wearing the uniform he had on when he was wounded. A bath and clean clothes would have restored his dignity, but the prognosis for recovery was bleak.

Volume II of, "The Medical and Surgical History of the War of the Rebellion," covers wounds and injuries of the hip. The section opens with the following sentence. "In the important class of injuries of the joints, those of the hip joint are preeminently hazardous to life, obscure in diagnosis, and difficult in treatment." In case after case the patient does well for a short time and then declines as infections worsen. Tonics, opiates, and stimulants are administered, but little can be done to curb the poison from strengthening in the festering wound.

For more than a month Jake fought to live, each passing hour a tribute to his will and strength. Then at four in the morning, June 18, 1864, his spirit stepped away from all to come, and he was gone. What he left behind in a material sense wouldn't fill a cigar box. A wallet, pocketknife; pen and holder and four dollars and eighty-five cents. Of true worth is the inextinguishable legacy of his noble sacrifice.

Jake's body was, "taken by friends," from the hospital and brought home. Near the steepled, log church his grave was dug and left with summer sweat and perhaps a tear. After the burial shovel had done its work, a morning came when his pine, flag-draped casket was unlimbered in the churchyard.

The chapel's white, double doors still swing open on hinges black as a mourner's veil. The pallbearers would have likely sidestepped their burden through the narrow passageway into the funereal gloom of the nave. Perhaps the tap of crutches was heard on the hardwood floor as Jake's brothers entered the church. The father's nearly blind eyes might have seen the 35-star flag on his son's coffin much the same as his wife and daughters with their vision blurred by tears.

A mass was said, and earnest words tendered, perhaps to fall like bricks in a ruin on those torn asunder by this soldier's death. There was comfort, though, in his coming home to rest. And in the trees that shade his grave, the birds still sing their hushed refrain of remembrance.

About the Author

Dave A. Maurer's first book, *The Dying Place*, was published by Dell Publishing in 1986. It was later published by Real War Stories. Maurer worked for 30 years as the senior feature story writer for *The Daily Progress* newspaper in Charlottesville, Virginia, until his retirement in 2017. He is 76.

Other Titles from Fireship Press

Cartledge Creek

by Sam McGee

Born of contradiction, battered by bloody conflict, a young soldier desperately tries to find his way back home.

Jim, the youngest of Alfred's soldier sons, follows a Civil War path that takes him through some of the war's bloodiest conflicts, and into the North's deadliest prisons.

He daily risks his life for a cause of which he is uncertain, his real cause being to one day get back home.

"***Cartledge Creek*** is a fine piece of fiction. My highest praise for a story is 'a good tale, well told.' And that fits this book precisely."—**Robert Inman**, Author of *The Governor's Lady, Home Fires Burning, Old Dogs and Children,* and *Dairy Queen Days*

See You on the High Ground

The Jared Monti Story

by Len Sandler

Deliberately exposing himself to machine gun and rocket-propelled grenade fire, Jared Monti sacrificed himself attempting not once but three times to rescue one of his squad members from the "kill zone" after his patrol came under attack by insurgents on a mountain in Afghanistan.

The actions we honor today were not a passing moment of courage. They were the culmination of a life of character and commitment, said Barack Obama as he posthumously presented Jared with the first Medal of Honor of his presidency on September 17, 2009. Jared died a heroic death but, more importantly, lived a heroic life. This is the story of that life.

CPSIA information can be obtained
at www.ICGtesting.com
Printed in the USA
LVHW112035261022
731642LV00003B/30

9 781611 794021